Copyright © 2025 by John B. Martin

All rights reserved.

ISBN (Paperback): 978-1-7643001-0-0
ISBN (eBook): 978-1-7643001-1-7

No portion of this book may be reproduced in any form without written permission from the publisher or author, except as permitted by U.S. copyright law.

This publication is designed to provide accurate and authoritative information in regard to the subject matter covered. It is sold with the understanding that neither the author nor the publisher is engaged in rendering legal, investment, accounting or other professional services. While the publisher and author have used their best efforts in preparing this book, they make no representations or warranties with respect to the accuracy or completeness of the contents of this book and specifically disclaim any implied warranties of merchantability or fitness for a particular purpose. No warranty may be created or extended by sales representatives or written sales materials. The advice and strategies contained herein may not be suitable for your situation. You should consult with a professional when appropriate. Neither the publisher nor the author shall be liable for any loss of profit or any other commercial damages, including but not limited to special, incidental, consequential, personal, or other damages.

Cover design features stock images from:
by Aditya / Stock.Adobe.com

1st edition 2025

*This book is dedicated to my Lord and Saviour, Jesus the Christ.
May you find new aspects in Him.*

Index

Preface 1

Introduction 2

Forward 10

In The Beginning 14

Matthew Chapter 1 21

Matthew Chapter 2 27

Matthew Chapter 3 34

Matthew Chapter 4 42

Matthew Chapter 5 63

Matthew Chapter 6 70

Matthew Chapter 7 74

Matthew Chapter 8 77

Matthew Chapter 9 88

Matthew Chapter 10 98

Matthew Chapter 11 107

Matthew Chapter 12 114

Matthew Chapter 13 124

Matthew Chapter 12 136

Matthew Chapter 15 149

Matthew Chapter 16 156

Matthew Chapter 17 162

Matthew Chapter 18 169

Matthew Chapter 19 174

Matthew Chapter 20 188

Matthew Chapter 21	214
Matthew Chapter 22	227
Matthew Chapter 23	235
Matthew Chapter 24	239
Matthew Chapter 25	250
Matthew Chapter 26	253
Matthew Chapter 27	283
Matthew Chapter 28	303
Acts Chapter 1	316
Acts Chapter 7	318
Appendix	325
Basic Rules on Bible interpretation	331
About the Author	334
A personal note from the Author	335

PREFACE

Isa 42:1 Behold my servant, whom I uphold; mine elect, in whom my soul delighteth; I have put my spirit upon him: he shall bring forth judgment to the Gentiles.

Isa 42:2 He shall not cry, nor lift up, nor cause his voice to be heard in the street.

Isa 42:3 A bruised reed shall he not break, and the smoking flax shall he not quench: he shall bring forth judgment unto truth.

Isa 42:4 He shall not fail nor be discouraged, till he have set judgment in the earth: and the isles shall wait for his law.

Isa 42:5 Thus saith God the LORD, he that created the heavens, and stretched them out; he that spread forth the earth, and that which cometh out of it; he that giveth breath unto the people upon it, and spirit to them that walk therein:

Isa 42:6 I the LORD have called thee in righteousness, and will hold thine hand, and will keep thee, and give thee for a covenant of the people, for a light of the Gentiles;

Isa 42:7 To open the blind eyes, to bring out the prisoners from the prison, and them that sit in darkness out of the prison house.

Isa 42:8 I am the LORD (YHWH): that is my name: and my glory will I not give to another, neither my praise to graven images, (statues).

Isa 42:9 Behold, the former things are come to pass, and new things do I declare: before they spring forth, I tell you of them.

Introduction

In my reading of the Bible, it is my desire to always find Jesus in scripture, just like Peter told Jesus, He was the Christ, Jesus then told Peter he was blessed because it was the Father that has revealed it to him. If you find Jesus in scripture then God has allowed you to see His Son. John T.B. says we receive nothing unless the Lord gives it. The word says in;

2Co 3:5 Not that we are sufficient of ourselves to think anything as of ourselves; but our sufficiency is of God; 6 for the letter killeth, but the spirit giveth life.

Every word that Jesus spoke was God's word (Rhema. Matt 4:4, Luke 4:4.) We are all able minsters sent from God, predestined in Christ, born of the Holy Spirit, for the edifying of ourselves and also the saints, to be conformed to the image of His son. The Bible is all about Jesus all the promises and hopes are for Jesus and we can't do anything without Him, it is Jesus in us not us. Yes, we do it but are motivated by God in us.

2Ti 3:16 All scripture is given by inspiration of God, and is profitable for doctrine, for reproof, for correction, for instruction in righteousness: 17 That the man of God may be perfect (Mature), throughly furnished (fitted out) unto all good works.

Being Strong in the Lord and the Power of His might; is to know His word, character, and will; Love is being kind, Agape, charitable, to your fellow humans, enemies or not. The reason I have set out to rearrange the Gospels is because my heart hurt for the people that were saying Gods word contradicts itself, it doesn't. In the 4 gospels we have 4 accounts of Jesus our Messiah, but ONE Message; Although Jesus preached throughout the land, Jesus may have repeated himself many times, thus I believe why the frustration shewing warts and all in Mat 17:17 and Luke 9:41. As you will see Matthew concentrates on the teachings in Galilee and Luke repeats the teachings from throughout Judea, same message different place preached.

Jesus had one message (Mat 4:17, Mark 1:15) and that was to Repent and to get ready for the Kingdom of God, His work was the cross. Jesus walked the land teaching, showing the true nature and character of a Loving Father from a place of obedience showing that relationship is better than sacrifice and the Law, but fulfils the Law. Jesus preached the same message over 3.5 years in Judah and Galilee. In studying the Gospels, I feel the writers have tried not to repeat the words of Jesus, but have gathered the content as not to repeat themselves, so as to get as much information expressed as possible as short as possible. Matthew does an in-depth dive into the beatitudes and Luke writes where Jesus preached the same but in different locations near and in Jerusalem just after visiting Mary's house in Bethany, gathering the required information. Luke interviewed everyone he could find and put the facts together, documenting what he learned.

This work is to enable the study of the gospels to a greater comparative level with less effort. A teacher once told me a good mathematician is a lazy one. The Gospels are 4 different accounts written from memories and testimonies. 4 different views, 4 different personalities. 4 different perspectives from different cultures, hearts, minds and times, but all inspired by God. I sometimes wonder what a gospel written by Judas would have shown in his personality, the crimes and thoughts about Jesus. The name Judah means praise, (satan was a heavenly worship leader with his words being music to the ears, just ask Eve), Judas would have meant almost the same as praise, derived from Judah. Just shows sometimes we don't live up to our name, after all, Jesus did call him a devil.

The names of places and people follow Gods meanings and purposes; If you want to know and expand what God is saying to us, for example, look at the meanings of the names and places: Jacob and Israel; check out their meanings in the Strongs concordance and use the meanings in place of the names. It will open up a whole new world. I have gone through my personal bible and put some of the meanings of the names of the books next to the titles. Did you know that the name Jonah means dove, the same Hebrew word "Dove" Noah sent out a dove and it brought an olive branch back, a representation of the Holy Spirit. The only sign Jesus said that generation would get was the sign of Jonah. Everything Jonah went through is a representation of Jesus, even asleep in the bottom of the boat during a storm but not Jonah`s stubbornness and negativity, it is all there so that we can be shown the path Jesus walked. Ps 119:105.

This reorganising of the Gospels is done using the book of Matthew as the backdrop and mostly the timeline, being the first mention of the four gospels and a part eyewitness. Two gospels I have arranged to line up to Matthew's timeline and things spoken by Jesus, arranged by <u>SUBJECT MATTER not always the timeline</u>. It doesn't take away from Jesus` sermons and miracles but enforces them. There are pivotal points with most lined up, like feeding the 5 thousand and 4 thousand, healing of Peter`s mother, blind Bartimaeus, including the entry into Jerusalem, the colt and many more. But when you see a certain subject like the Lord's Prayer, you have reference points to study with what was said and where Jesus repeated a sermon or teachings.

The facts still remain that they were said and done and do not contradict each other but expand on how things were said and were received by the listener. I.E Debts and Trespasses used in the Lord's Prayer, two separate Greek words used but they still mean offending God on our part and covers a wider area for the pedantic; if only one word would have been used then someone would have made a doctrine about it excluding other points by swapping the usage it broadens the meaning. Same as the Kingdom of God and Kingdom of Heaven can also be interchangeable in some cases, Luke and Paul clarify the Phrase.

Although the timeline may not be exact between the gospels, the things done and said by Jesus can be easily compared; for example: If you wanted to see what Jesus said about salt or marriage, according to subject matter, they are all in one spot starting with Matthew ending with John's account. If an insert from a gospel is missing then the writer didn't mention the event, it doesn't mean it never happened, but adds to the depth of the mystery of Christ; like john not being mentioned in one of the gospels running to the tomb, it doesn't mean he wasn't there just he wasn't mentioned. Hopefully you get a full panorama view of what was said and done where and when.

Johns Gospel is really the trips to and from the feasts letting people know Jesus was a pure Jew and kept all the Laws and God in the Flesh. He misses a lot out of the middle but John scribed the inner circle concourse and personal relationship he had with the Lord. By putting the subject matter together, one can see a subject spoken by the Lord and enables you, the reader, to go and look up the other verses and connections in the bible or concordance, I have referenced the moved verses to Matthew's gospel to be able to find certain verses using Matthew as the main reference for indexing.

<u>My personal take of the Gospel writers according to the Gospel</u>

Matthew; Means Gift of God. Written 50-65 AD

Mattew, a Jew, a tax collector who knows the benefits of gifts and giving, showing this especially through the beatitudes. He was appealing to the Jewish Christians and business people; Matthew seemed to be the storyteller and loved the parables that Jesus taught. As a tax collector he would have had dealing with the establishment and all trade issues and the scuttlebutt of the trade and upper class, but was hated by the lower and middle class. Many times, Jesus mentioned about the Love of money, maybe that was for Judas or to remind Levi, Matthew saw what was going on and John said what everyone was thinking as did Peter.

Matthew was called after the fact that Jesus had already started his ministry and was walking through the country of the Gergesenes and came to his own city in Galilee, Matt 9:1; his own city was Capernaum, as Jesus had been rejected in Nazareth, Judea.

In Mat 9:9, Jesus passed forth from thence, he saw a man, named Matthew, sitting at the receipt of custom: and he saith unto him, Follow me. And he arose, and followed him.

Matthew had a little bit of catchup to do but had heard a lot of rumours and hung out with the best and worse. Matthew being an Ex-Tax Collector would have known the importance of getting things adding up and balanced. Matthew was one forgiven for many digressions, loved much, as Matthews words and feast, portrayed his repentance, nothing was mentioned about Judas, just that he held the money bag and stole from it by John.

Mark means; Warring. (Latin) Dedicated to Mars the god of war.
Written 55-65 A.D.

Mark, having a Roman name, was appealing to the Romans, keeping the Law wasn't his priority. He could have also been John, who`s surname is Mark mentioned in Acts who didn't have a good reputation with Paul the apostle; in saying that, when things got too hard, he ran home, which gives me the impression that he mentioned himself in his own book of Mark in;

Mar 14:52 And he left the linen cloth, and fled from them naked.

In the book of John, John mentioned himself as "the one Jesus loved" also "the one that rested his head on the breast of Jesus". We are not certain but it does seem likely that this is Marks eye witness testimony. Anyhow, this made Mark a part time eye witness but was there for the crucifixion of Jesus, as all but the 12 had left Jesus after He said; "Eat my flesh and drink my Blood" and Mark wasn't named among the 12 and neither was Nathanael. After he mentioned himself, Mark probably ran back home got dressed and came back out to see what was happening, mind you, with the commotion going on no one wouldn't have known what was going on, maybe why the disciple's discourse on the road to Emaus and Peter preaching to the 3000 at Pentecost the word got around.

Jesus knows men's hearts, which includes our hearts and they haven't change since the beginning of time, "curiosity killed the cat" as the saying goes and that can go two ways, for good and bad. Mark definitely had a war on his hands to uphold the Lord in His life and the Romans were against Christianity and the Jews, if you study History. Although Mark ran from the ministry with Paul and Barnabas when it got too hard, his testimony by writing the gospel of Mark tells all as it was, written way after the fact.

Mark`s gospel starts at the baptism of Jesus by John the Baptist. How many of us seem to be like Mark when the going gets tough we fold but are able to contribute in some other way. Someone once said; "If you are not going or giving then you are not helping the cause of Christ." Samson was also like Mark, and came back with a vengeance in the final days of his life. Yes, maybe not a good analogy but God uses the foolish things of this world and the youngest in families; and all things work for good as we are called according to the Lord's purpose. We have Marks letter which means he touched the church, kind of like we have books and sermons from the great men of God. Marks account was found worthy to be saved in Gods eyes and lines up many times with Matthew's encounter, some say copied, who knows? The gospels are all different, filling in the blanks and expanding and subtracting on many situations depending on what they remembered.

Luke means light giver or bearer of truth. Written 58-65 A.D.

The next is Luke he is writing to the Greeks and Luke being a physician was learned and precise in his formulars even down to the correct person to person genealogy, establishing Mary`s connection to Elizabeth, Zecheriah and John to Aaron and the priesthood and servitude in the house of the Lord, even to the genealogy of Joseph by the younger brothers and law of moses, letting everybody know he was precise in his details. I have put the reference scriptures next to the verses so as to expand on what was the basis and reasoning why the two genealogies are different between Matthew and Luke. Luke would have had to interview many witnesses to get what he wrote. It is very detailed and precise, according to his informants and eye witnesses. Luke went with Paul and sneaks in the first mention of Paul consenting to the death of Stephen being the cloke clerk for the perps in acts 8.

Luk 1:1 Forasmuch as many have taken in hand to set forth in order a declaration of those things which are most surely believed among us, 2 Even as they delivered them unto us, which from the beginning were eyewitnesses, and ministers of the word; 3 It seemed good to me also, having had perfect understanding of all things from the very first, to write unto thee in order, most excellent Theophilus, 4 That thou mightest know the certainty of those things, wherein thou hast been instructed.

Luke travelled with Paul writing everything down and writing the Acts of the Apostles. He certainly lives up to his name. Matthew`s testimony being an eye witness and Jesus' sermons and miracles and subject matter I have used as the backbone for Lukes's gospel and the other two. Jesus would have repeated himself many times in many different places but the miracles don't lie and the scattering of Lukes gospel is for study purposes not in a set timeline.

John means Graced by God.
Written 80-95 A.D.

Lastly, we have John, who was truly graced by God by a close relationship with Jesus, which started out with John the Baptist. John was writing to the Greek Christians and also mentions Greeks in Joh 12:20. He concentrates on the trips to Jerusalem and in the Holy City for the feasts. John never mentions Jesus` forty days in the wilderness but he establishes the divinity of Jesus being one with God before all things.

He picks up the story after Jesus gets back and sees John TB again as John talks in the past tense when he says "he saw and he did" when John TB witnesses about Jesus. Then Jesus starts to choose His followers, two of Johns the Baptists followers, John and Andrew, John 1:35-42. Jesus calls Simon and surnames him Petros or Peter. John 1:42. Then here comes Nathanael. John stuck close after that point and followed Jesus.

John knew the inner workings of John the Baptists calling and how he was told to baptize by a man in the wilderness and how John TB would know how to recognise who the Christ was. I start with John 1:1, because of his reference to the beginning of time. John mainly concentrates about the Feast trips to and from Jerusalem like the Samaritan woman and doesn't go into other details other than what he saw and heard close to Jesus. John refers to himself as one "whom Jesus Loved." He thought of himself special and was to the Lord.

Joh 20:2 Then she runneth, and cometh to Simon Peter, and to the other disciple, whom Jesus loved, and saith unto them; "They have taken away the Lord out of the sepulchre, and we know not where they have laid him."

John was in the inner circle and the one that beat Peter to the tomb and leaned in to see, we have to do the same and that is to lean in looking for Jesus. Everything said and written in the scriptures is there for a reason. John was privy to the most detailed account of things said in private to the disciples, check out John chapters 15, 16 and 17, John was a man of Love and affection and hung out with the girls. John was entrusted to look after Mary, Jesus` mother, and was close enough to Jesus when He was on the cross, to hear Jesus look down and say;

Joh 19:27 Then saith he to the disciple; "Behold thy mother!" And from that hour that disciple took her unto his own home.

Love never leaves you nor forsakes you no matter what situation you are in. John was on the mount of transfiguration and in the room of the girl being raised from the dead, he saw it all and probably listen to the women talk as well. Definitely a true eye witness. Personally, I would tend to study more of Johns recollection of the personal incidents and concourse with Jesus.

I tried, when I first started, to keep John's account up front and the others confirming John's eye witness account but as I dug deeper found that the 4 gospels gave different aspects to the Lord, some agreed and some mentioned things the others didn't. Just because John never documented it all doesn't mean that it was never said or done by Jesus. John doesn't emphasise the preaching in the wilderness but the intimate side of his relationship that we all can have with Jesus. Chapter 15 onwards.

<u>I Emphasise.</u>

I have <u>underlined each corresponding phrases from each gospel, in most subtitles</u> connecting the things said, like blind Bartimaeus when he Cried out and incidences also with the healing of the man with Palsy, (the four friends), to give you an idea of the connection. The chances of people saying the same exact thing in different places, is probable, although not entirely likely, but are possibly. Re-worded by the writers to suit the way they talked. It's like reading a book once you have heard someone speak. Like Hebrews being written by Paul, was it, or wasn't it? Personally, I think we are missing the first page, but the book of Hebrews is far deeper and more poetic that the other letters written by Paul yet there are similarities of phrases by Paul connecting the other books; thus, suggesting it was written by him. Possibly why he tells the Corinthians (paraphrased) I can't give you meat because you are still babies and want milk, but giving the fulness to the Hebrews.

Although this rendition messes with the timeline of two Gospels, Mark and Luke, hopefully you will grasp the connections and how they have been arranged. I have not changed any scriptures, all I have done is shed a light in collecting them, gathering more connectivity between the gospels and showing you that what Jesus did was true and confirmed, but maybe not in that particular timeline of 4 of the accounts.

Php 2:12 Wherefore, my beloved, as ye have always obeyed, not as in my presence only, but now much more in my absence, work out your own salvation with fear and trembling.

Forward.

I wanted to combine the 4 books of the Good News to one story, so as to make it make sense for the ones that don't read a lot and find it all too hard and confusing, flipping between gospels trying to remember what was said and where. Although we are to let the Holy Spirit enlighten the Word to us and all we have to remember is the "Prophetic Phrases" not necessarily the verse numbers. The Holy Spirit will enlighten us with verses and chapter, as Jesus said He will remind you of what Jesus said, there were no verse numbers back then. You will be judged on what the Spirit tells you to do and Your obedience, not what others do or say. Your confidence in Jesus will override your fears and being emotionally controlled by others.

I have found it to be a bigger job than I initially thought, finding that Jesus walked in and out of Judaea and Galilee many times throughout His three and a half years in ministry. The things said and done have pivotal points of reference, I have put some Old Testament reference verses in, that the Lord has shown myself for personal study. Referencing certain verses like Isaiah, Psalms, and Jerimiah as they are referred to in the scriptures and what scriptures Jesus lived through on the cross, just a few examples. As you come across them, I hope you can see the connection. Remember, Jesus kept the Law explicitly and so did His mother and adopted father, Joseph, at all times states Luke.

When Jesus touched and healed a person, they were totally forgiven of their sins and healed, as are we. When we touch the hem of His garment in our hearts, our sins are remised and we can be healed at the same time, if we believe. Walking in wholeness the same as we walk in forgiveness, if we stay in Christ. Jesus has done it all, now all we have to do is receive, you will know when it happens because you will know, that you know, that you know, it drops from your head to your heart.

God gives us what we ask for and believe for and if it's not enough for you then ask for bigger, believe for bigger. If you read my book the "How Do I? book", it explains Faith, according to Heb 11. Faith is hearing God, then doing what God said, because we believe what the Lord said we act on it. God is a Good Father and wants to give us the Best, so when a verse stands out it is the Holy Spirit talking to you, yes, God Himself. The Lord sees us for what we will be when we stay in Him, not what we are or have done or are in our own eyes. It's all about what Jesus has done, by the shedding of His blood through the work of the Cross. We have to repent and acknowledging His sacrifice and in believing that God raised him from the dead, we shall be saved and our adoption back into Gods family begins. I say back because the bible says your name was written in the Lambs book of life before the foundations of the World. Rev 17:8, and that the spirit of man returns to God whom sent it. Ecc 12:7 If you are in Christ then you have been sent from God to do His will and be a little Jesus on this earth and were chosen before time itself for Gods Glory, no I am not saying you are predestined no matter what, we all have choices to make. Salvation is a gift so treat it as such, with thankfulness and respect to the giver. Choose life because you have been given a free will to choose or not. God will not refuse anyone, when we choose to humble ourselves and come to Him.

No exact personal records have been preserved from those times and we have to rely upon the testimonies of the witnesses, fact gathering of Luke and the 3 other faithful true eye witness although Paul was a youngster and probably an eye witness also. For Luke to get the prophesies of the two in the temple, more than likely would have come from Mary, Jesus` mother, I cant see anyone else who would have that type of knowledge, unless she told her children and they passed it on as the scripture says; "Mary kept everything in her heart." Luke 2:51 and if Mary was 17 when Jesus was born then when Jesus died, she would have be 47 years old and maybe lived long enough for

Luke to inteview her, I am sure she was the centre of attention at all the parties.

Please contact me on jbmbuilder1@gmail.com if you wish to give me some feed back.

<u>To see my other works</u>

<u>The How Do I Book. Published by Xlibris.</u>

Bless you all. Enjoy.

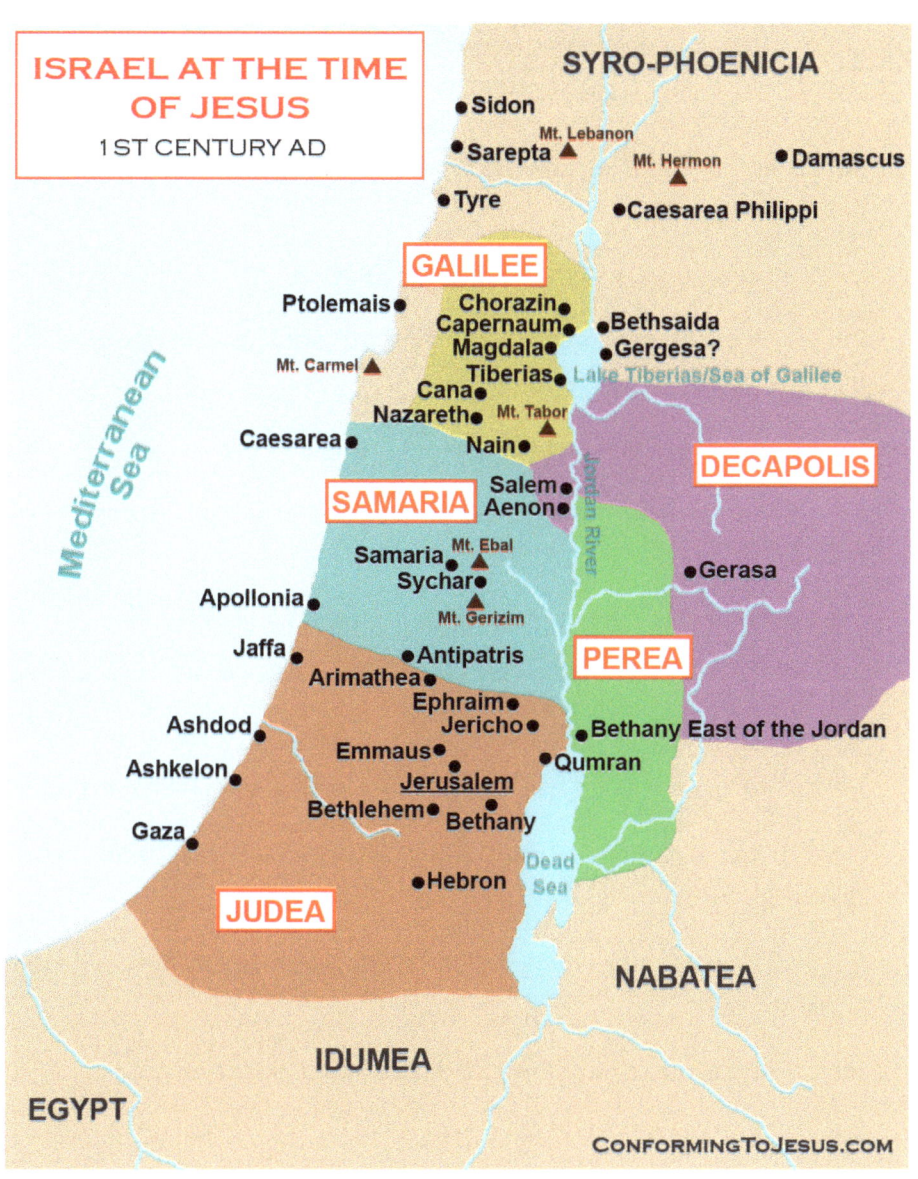

Maps have been used with permission

In The Beginning

The Word Became Flesh

Joh 1:1 In the beginning was the Word, and the Word was with God, and the Word was God.

Joh 1:2 The same was in the beginning with God.

Joh 1:3 All things were made by him; and without him was not anything made that was made.

Joh 1:4 In him was life; and the life was the light of men.

Joh 1:5 And the light shineth in darkness; and the darkness comprehended it not.

Joh 1:6 There was a man sent from God, whose name was John.

Joh 1:7 The same came for a witness, to bear witness of the Light, that all men through him might believe.

Joh 1:8 He was not that Light, but was sent to bear witness of that Light.

Joh 1:9 That was the true Light, which lighteth every man that cometh into the world.

Joh 1:10 He was in the world, and the world was made by him, and the world knew him not.

Joh 1:11 He came unto his own, and his own received him not.

Joh 1:12 But as many as received him, to them, gave he power to become the sons of God, even to them that believe on his name:

Joh 1:13 Which were born, not of blood, nor of the will of the flesh, nor of the will of man, but of God.

Joh 1:14 And the Word was made flesh, and dwelt among us, (and we beheld his glory, the glory as of the only <u>begotten</u> *(G3439 Monogenes, the only genetically born* of the Father), full of grace and truth.

(The word begotten is a very important word, it means "born of". God is His specific Father, Monogenes, Mono means single or one and Genes where we get the word generation. God passed His perfect Genes on to Jesus mixed with Mary`s, a direct descendant of Levi and Adam. We all have to be Born Again into Gods family and are a new creation, born of God not for, or by, but of; Jesus took the pain of being borne on the cross. His pierced side represents the birth of Eve and of the future church so that the born-again experience is not one of pain but of Joy.

Many versions have removed begotten, especially from John 3:16. Take Note. You are born of God which makes you His child, removing the word begotten cancels you out of being Gods children if Jesus was his only son or child. The KJV clearly states that Jesus was the firstborn of <u>many brethren</u>. Rom 8:29. That means you and me, male or female are Gods children. Also, the word for "Son or sons" in the Greek means child. John 1:12. Teknon, G5043)

Luke`s introduction

Luk 1:1 Forasmuch as many have taken in hand to set forth in order a declaration of those things which are most surely believed among us.

Luk 1:2 Even as they delivered them unto us, which from the beginning were eyewitnesses, and ministers of the word;

Luk 1:3 It seemed good to me also, having had perfect understanding of all things from the very first, to write unto thee in order, most excellent Theophilus,

Luk 1:4 That thou mightest know the certainty of those things, wherein thou hast been instructed.

Jerusalem

Country of Judaea

We can say Zacharias a priest and Elizabeth, a daughter of Aaron, (Explains why God didn't kill Aaron for making a golden calf in the wilderness, or Lots daughters as Ruth came from one of them, Moab. God can use you too if you

turn fully to Him wiping out your past. We can see why those stories are important.) Luke 1:5 Mary being Elizabeths cousin would make Mary the same linage, Luke establishes their heritage for the Jews, they possibly lived near Jerusalem because Zacharias ministered as a priest in the temple and was from the eighth course of Abijah (the Hebrew name.) 1chron 24:10. The name Abijah means "Father of Jah" or worshiper of Jah. 8 = new beginnings or resurrection. John was filled with the Holy Spirit from birth, I believe when the presence of Jesus was felt and Elisabeth prophesied. Luke 1:41. The Lord has spoken, who can but prophesy? Amos 3:8.

<u>Birth of John the Baptist promised</u>

Luk 1:5 There was in the days of Herod, the king of Judaea, a certain priest named Zacharias, of the course of Abijah: and his wife was of the daughters of Aaron, and her name was Elisabeth.

Luk 1:6 And they were both righteous before God, walking in all the commandments and ordinances of the Lord blameless.

Luk 1:7 And they had no child, because that Elisabeth was barren, and they both were now well stricken in years.

Luk 1:8 And it came to pass, that while he executed the priest's office before God in the order of his course,

Luk 1:9 According to the custom of the priest's office, his lot was to burn incense when he went into the temple of the Lord.

Luk 1:10 And the whole multitude of the people were praying without at the time of incense.

Luk 1:11 And there appeared unto him an angel of the Lord standing on the right side of the altar of incense.

Luk 1:12 And when Zacharias saw him, he was troubled, and fear fell upon him.

Luk 1:13 But the angel said unto him; "Fear not, Zacharias: for thy prayer is heard; and thy wife Elisabeth shall bear thee a son, and thou shalt call his name John. 14 And thou shalt have joy and gladness; and many shall rejoice at his birth. 15 For he shall be great in the sight of the Lord, and shall drink neither wine nor strong drink; and he shall be filled with the Holy Ghost, even from his mother's womb. 16 And many of the children of Israel shall he turn to the Lord their God. 17 And he shall go before him in the spirit and power of Elias, to turn the hearts of the fathers to the children, and the disobedient to the wisdom of the just; to make ready a people prepared for the Lord."

Luk 1:18 And Zacharias said unto the angel; "Whereby shall I know this? for I am an old man, and my wife well stricken in years."

There are 4 things that destroy Faith, "Pistis; G4102 is Gods truthfulness;" Fear, Doubt, Reason and Anxiety and the traditions of men make Gods word ineffective, Mat 15:6.

Luk 1:19 And the angel answering said unto him; "I am Gabriel, that stand in the presence of God; and am sent to speak unto thee, and to shew thee these glad tidings. 20 And, behold, thou shalt be dumb, and not able to speak, until the day that these things shall be performed, because thou believest not my words, which shall be fulfilled in their season."

Luk 1:21 And the people waited for Zacharias, and marvelled that he tarried so long in the temple.

Luk 1:22 And when he came out, he could not speak unto them: and they perceived that he had seen a vision in the temple: for he beckoned unto them, and remained speechless.

Luk 1:23 And it came to pass, that, as soon as the days of his ministration were accomplished, he departed to his own house.

Luk 1:24 And after those days his wife Elisabeth conceived, and hid herself five months, saying;

Luk 1:25 "Thus hath the Lord dealt with me in the days wherein he looked on me, to take away my reproach among men."

Nazareth

Country of Galilee

Birth of Jesus Promised

Luk 1:26 And in the sixth month the angel Gabriel was sent from God unto a city of Galilee, named Nazareth,

Luk 1:27 To a virgin espoused to a man whose name was Joseph, of the house of David; and the virgin's name was Mary. *(Isaiah 7:14)*

Luk 1:28 And the angel came in unto her, and said; "Hail, thou that art highly favoured, the Lord is with thee: blessed art thou among women."

Luk 1:29 And when she saw him, she was troubled at his saying, and cast in her mind what manner of salutation this should be.

Luk 1:30 And the angel said unto her; "Fear not, Mary: for thou hast found favour with God. 31 And, behold, thou shalt conceive in thy womb, and bring forth a son, and shalt call his name JESUS. 32 He shall be great, and shall be called the Son of the Highest: and the Lord God shall give unto him the throne of his father David: 33 And he shall reign over the house of Jacob for ever; and of his kingdom there shall be no end." *(Daniel 2:44)*

Luk 1:34 Then said Mary unto the angel; "How shall this be, seeing I know not a man?"

Luk 1:35 And the angel answered and said unto her; "The Holy Ghost shall come upon thee, and the power of the Highest shall overshadow thee: therefore, also that holy thing which shall be born of thee shall be called the Son of God. 36 And, behold, thy cousin Elisabeth, she hath also conceived a son in her old age: and this is the sixth month with her, who was called barren. 37 For with God nothing shall be impossible."

Luk 1:38 And Mary said; "Behold the handmaid of the Lord; be it unto me according to thy word." And the angel departed from her.

A town in the hills of Judea. Possible near Jerusalem.

Mary Visits Elizabeth

Luk 1:39 And Mary arose in those days, and went into the hill country with haste, into a city of Juda;

Luk 1:40 And entered into the house of Zacharias, and saluted Elisabeth.

Luk 1:41 And it came to pass, that, when Elisabeth heard the salutation of Mary, the babe leaped in her womb; and Elisabeth was filled with the Holy Ghost: *(Jerimiah 1:5)*

Elizabeth prophesies over Mary

Luk 1:42 And she spoke out with a loud voice, and said; "Blessed art thou among women, and blessed is the fruit of thy womb. 43 And whence is this to me, that the mother of my Lord should come to me? 44 For, lo, as soon as the voice of thy salutation sounded in mine ears, the babe leaped in my womb for joy. 45 And blessed is she that believed: for there shall be a performance of those things which were told her from the Lord."

Mary's Prophetic Song of Praise

Luk 1:46 And Mary said; "My soul doth magnify the Lord, 47 And my spirit hath rejoiced in God my Saviour. 48 For he hath regarded the low estate of his handmaiden: for, behold, from henceforth all generations shall call me blessed. 49 For he that is mighty hath done to me great things; and holy is his name. 50 And his mercy is on them that fear him from generation to generation. 51 He hath shewed strength with his arm; he hath scattered the proud in the imagination of their hearts. 52 He hath put down the mighty from their seats, and exalted them of low degree. 53 He hath filled the hungry with good things; and the rich he hath sent empty away. 54 He hath holpen his servant Israel, in remembrance of his mercy; 55 As he spoke to our fathers, to Abraham, and to his seed for ever."

Nazareth, Galilee

Mary returns to her home (just after the birth of john the Baptist.)

Luk 1:56 And Mary abode with her about three months and returned to her own house.

Meanwhile back in Elizabeths house

The Birth of John the Baptist

Luk 1:57 Now Elisabeth's full time came that she should be delivered; and she brought forth a son.

Luk 1:58 And her neighbours and her cousins heard how the Lord had shewed great mercy upon her; and they rejoiced with her.

Luk 1:59 And it came to pass, that on the eighth day they came to circumcise the child; and they called him Zacharias, after the name of his father.

Luk 1:60 And his mother answered and said; "Not so; but he shall be called John."

Luk 1:61 And they said unto her; "There is none of thy kindred that is called by this name."

Luk 1:62 And they made signs to his father, how he would have him called.

Luk 1:63 And he asked for a writing table, and wrote, saying; "His name is John." And they marvelled all.

Luk 1:64 And his mouth was opened immediately, and his tongue loosed, and he spake, and praised God.

Luk 1:65 And fear came on all that dwelt round about them: and all these sayings were noised abroad throughout all the hill country of Judaea.

Luk 1:66 And all they that heard them laid them up in their hearts, saying; "What manner of child shall this be!" And the hand of the Lord was with him.

Zacharias's Prophecy over John

(The name Zacharia means "Jah remembers" John means "Graced by God")

Luk 1:67 And his father Zacharias was filled with the Holy Ghost, and prophesied, saying;

Luk 1:68 "Blessed be the Lord God of Israel; for he hath visited and redeemed his people, 69 And hath raised up an horn of salvation for us in the house of his servant David; 70 As he spake by the mouth of his holy prophets, which have been since the world began: 71 That we should be saved from our enemies, and from the hand of all that hate us; 72 To perform the mercy promised to our fathers, and to remember his holy covenant; 73 The oath which he sware to our father Abraham, 74 That he would grant unto us, that we being delivered out of the hand of our enemies might serve him without fear, 75 in holiness and righteousness before him, all the days of our life. 76 And thou, child, shalt be called the prophet of the Highest: for thou shalt go before the face of the Lord to prepare his ways; 77 To give knowledge of salvation unto his people by the remission of their sins, 78 Through the tender mercy of our God; whereby the dayspring from on high hath visited us, 79 To give light to them that sit in darkness and in the shadow of death, to guide our feet into the way of peace." *(Isaiah 40.)*

Luk 1:80 And the child grew, and waxed strong in spirit, and was in the deserts till the day of his shewing unto Israel.

The Genealogy of Joseph according to the official Books. (1 chronicles Ch. 9)

(I will intertwine Lukes's genealogy, which is ascending up, in this to compare notes. In Lukes I explain the difference and why and also added scriptural references.)

If too confusing Just read the BLUE

Mat 1:1 The book of the generation of Jesus Christ, the son of David, the son of Abraham.

Mat 1:2 Abraham begat Isaac; and Isaac begat Jacob; and Jacob begat Judas *(Judah)* and his brethren;

(I wonder if Judas was called Judah in Hebrew the Greek word is Ioudas, Jehudah, G2455. A mix of Jehu the crazy one.)

Luk 3:34 Which was *the son* of Jacob, which was *the son* of Isaac, which was *the son* of Abraham, which was *the son* of Thara, which was *the son* of Nachor

Mat 1:3 And Judas begat Phares and Zara of Thamar; and Phares begat Esrom; and Esrom begat Aram;

Luk 3:33 Which was *the son* of Aminadab, which was *the son* of Aram, which was *the son* of Esrom, which was *the son* of Phares, which was *the son* of Juda,

Mat 1:4 And Aram *(Ram)* begat Aminadab; and Aminadab begat Naasson; and Naasson begat Salmon;

Mat 1:5 And Salmon begat Booz *(Boaz)* of Rachab; *(not the prostitute Rahab, different place and time 4 generations previous)* and Booz begat Obed of Ruth; and Obed begat Jesse;

Luk 3:32 Which was *the son* of Jesse, which was *the son* of Obed, which was *the son* of Booz, which was *the son* of Salmon, which was *the son* of Naasson,

Mat 1:6 And Jesse begat David the king; and David the king begat Solomon of her that had been the wife of Urias;

Luk 3:31 Which was *the son* of Melea, which was *the son* of Menan, which was *the son* of Mattatha, which was *the son* of Nathan, which was *the son* of David,

At this point Luke says that Nathan, the younger brother, took Solomons place as Matthew is establishing the Kingly Blood line and records as per the heads of the families, Lukes does the younger brothers.

Mat 1:7 And Solomon begat Roboam; and Roboam begat Abia; and Abia begat Asa;

Mat 1:8 And Asa begat Josaphat; and Josaphat begat Joram; and Joram begat Ozias;

Luk 3:30 Which was *the son* of Simeon, which was *the son* of Juda, which was *the son* of Joseph, which was *the son* of Jonan, which was *the son* of Eliakim,

Mat 1:9 And Ozias begat Joatham; and Joatham begat Achaz; and Achaz begat Ezekias;

Mat 1:10 And Ezekias begat Manasses; and Manasses begat Amon; and Amon begat Josias;

Luk 3:29 Which was *the son* of Jose, which was *the son* of Eliezer, which was *the son* of Jorim, which was *the son* of Matthat, which was *the son* of Levi,

Mat 1:11 And Josias begat Jechonias and his brethren, about the time they were carried away to Babylon:

Luk 3:28 Which was *the son* of Melchi, which was *the son* of Addi, which was *the son* of Cosam, which was *the son* of Elmodam, which was *the son* of Er,

Mat 1:12 And after they were brought to Babylon, Jechonias begat Salathiel; and Salathiel begat Zorobabel;

Here they both confer at the rebuilding of Jerusalem. Zerubbabel in the genealogy. You can find Zerubbabel in Ezra, Neheimiah, Haggai and Zech 4:6-10

Mat 1:13 And Zorobabel begat Abiud; and Abiud begat Eliakim; and Eliakim begat Azor;

Luk 3:27 Which was *the son* of Joanna, which was *the son* of Rhesa, which was *the son* of Zorobabel, which was *the son* of Salathiel, which was *the son* of Neri,

Luk 3:26 Which was *the son* of Maath, which was *the son* of Mattathias, which was *the son* of Semei, which was *the son* of Joseph, which was *the son* of Juda,

Mat 1:14 And Azor begat Sadoc; and Sadoc begat Achim; and Achim begat Eliud;

Luk 3:25 Which was *the son* of Mattathias, which was *the son* of Amos, which was *the son* of Naum, which was *the son* of Esli, which was *the son* of Nagge,

Mat 1:15 And Eliud begat Eleazar; and Eleazar begat Matthan; and Matthan begat Jacob (*and Heli the younger brother*);

Luk 3:24 Which was *the son* of Matthat, which was *the son* of Levi, which was *the son* of Melchi, which was *the son* of Janna, which was *the son* of Joseph,

Mat 1:16 And Jacob begat Joseph the husband of Mary, of whom was born Jesus, who is called Christ.

Luk 3:23 And Jesus himself began to be about thirty years of age, being (as was supposed) the son of Joseph, which was *the son* of Heli,

Mat 1:17 So all the generations from Abraham to David are fourteen generations; and from David until the carrying away into Babylon are fourteen generations; and from the carrying away into Babylon unto Christ are fourteen generations.

Nazareth, Galilee.

Josephs Dream, justifying Mary

Mat 1:18 Now the birth of Jesus Christ was on this wise: When as his mother Mary was espoused to Joseph, before they came together, she was found with child of the Holy Ghost.

Mat 1:19 Then Joseph her husband, being a just man, and not willing to make her a publick example, was minded to put her away privily.

Mat 1:20 But while he thought on these things, behold, the angel of the Lord appeared unto him in a dream, saying; "Joseph, thou son of David, fear not to take unto thee Mary thy wife: for that which is conceived in her is of the Holy Ghost. 21 And she shall bring forth a son, and thou shalt call his name JESUS:" For he shall save his people from their sins.

(Yesha; H3468, Isaiah 62:11 also means salvation and talks about Jesus) *

Jesus is pronounced Yeh-Sous, spelt "Iesous." in Greek. A Commonly used name is Yeshua also meaning salvation, but it has 3 syllables, 2 syllables would make more sense when Jesus` name is translated from the Hebrew into the Greek and then into Latin. (My opinion only, but worth a thought, but it does makes sense and would fit why we know Him as Je-sus.

Mat 1:22 Now all this was done, that it might be fulfilled which was spoken of the Lord by the prophet, saying; *Isaiah 7:14.*

(7: 7+7 for all numbers people, 3 sevens, check out john 6:66)

Mat 1:23 "Behold, a virgin shall be with child, and shall bring forth a son, and they shall call his name Emmanuel, which being interpreted is, God with us." *Joh 3:34.*

Mat 1:24 Then Joseph being raised from sleep did as the angel of the Lord had bidden him, and took unto him his wife:

Mat 1:25 And knew her not till she had brought forth her firstborn son: and he called his name JESUS.

Mary was still a Virgin when Jesus was born

The Decree from Augustus

His rule (31 B.C – A.D 14) Born 63 B.C. Founder of the Roman Empire, AKA Octavianus.

Luk 2:1 And it came to pass in those days, that there went out a decree from Caesar Augustus, that all the world should be taxed.

Luk 2:2 (And this taxing was first made when Cyrenius was governor of Syria.)

Luk 2:3 And all went to be taxed, everyone into his own city.

Nazareth to Bethlehem.

Approx. 70 miles 112 Klms, from Nazareth.

Jesus born in Bethlehem

Mic 5:2, Isa 11:1. Joseph and King David came from Bethlehem and the Tribe of Judah.

Luk 2:4 And Joseph also went up from Galilee, out of the city of Nazareth, into Judaea, unto the city of David, which is called Bethlehem; (because he was of the house and lineage of David:)

Luk 2:5 To be taxed with Mary his espoused wife, being great with child.

Luk 2:6 And so it was, that, while they were there, the days were accomplished that she should be delivered.

Luk 2:7 And she brought forth her firstborn son, and wrapped him in swaddling clothes, and laid him in a manger; because there was no room for them in the inn.

The Fields Surrounding Bethlehem.

Lambing time, early springtime, Northern Hemisphere, in the Country of Judaea; Davids and Josephs tribe of Judah. Rev 5:5, 2 Sam 2:4. The 10th of the first month is when the lamb was chosen for the passover.

The Shepherds and the Angels. *Micah 5:2*

Luk 2:8 And there were in the same country shepherds abiding in the field, keeping watch over their flock by night.

Luk 2:9 And, lo, the angel of the Lord came upon them, and the glory of the Lord shone round about them: and they were sore afraid.

Luk 2:10 And the angel said unto them; "Fear not: for, behold, I bring you good tidings of great joy, which shall be to all people. 11 For unto you is born this day in the city of David a Saviour, which is Christ the Lord. 12 And this shall be a sign unto you; Ye shall find the babe wrapped in swaddling clothes, lying in a manger."

Luke 2:13 And suddenly there was with the angel a multitude of the heavenly host praising God, and saying;

Luk 2:14 "Glory to God in the highest, and on earth peace, good will toward men."

Luk 2:15 And it came to pass, as the angels were gone away from them into heaven, the shepherds said one to another; "Let us now go even unto Bethlehem, and see this thing which is come to pass, which the Lord hath made known unto us."

Luk 2:16 And they came with haste, and found Mary, and Joseph, and the babe lying in a manger.

Luk 2:17 And when they had seen it, they made known abroad the saying which was told them concerning this child.

Luk 2:18 And all they that heard it wondered at those things which were told them by the shepherds.

Luk 2:19 But Mary kept all these things and pondered them in her heart.

Luk 2:20 And the shepherds returned, glorifying and praising God for all the things that they had heard and seen, as it was told unto them.

(Shepards have possibly come and gone before the eighth day.)

Luk 2:21 And when eight days were accomplished for the circumcising of the child, his name was called JESUS, *(Matt 1:20, Isa 62:11)* which was so named of the angel before he was conceived in the womb. *(PS 139:16)*

Herod in Jerusalem.

The Visit of the Wise Men.

They were wise because they asked for directions. 😜 *I personally believe they were Chinese. Do a study of Christ in Chinese history and you will even find their word for Garden even has two trees in it. Job came from the land of consultation and Daniel was the chief of all the Maggi. They were all east of Jerusalem. Chuck Missler also points out that the languages' east of Jerusalem go right to left and the ones west go left to right all pointing back to Jerusalem.*

Mat 2:1 Now when Jesus was born in Bethlehem of Judaea in the days of Herod the king, behold, there came wise men from the east to Jerusalem,

Mat 2:2 Saying; "Where is he that is born King of the Jews? for we have seen his star in the east, and are come to worship him."

Mat 2:3 When Herod the king had heard these things, he was troubled, and all Jerusalem with him.

Mat 2:4 And when he had gathered all the chief priests and scribes of the people together, he demanded of them where Christ should be born.

Mat 2:5 And they said unto him; "In Bethlehem of Judaea: for thus it is written by the prophet, 6 And thou Bethlehem, in the land of Juda, art not the least among the princes of Juda: for out of thee shall come a Governor, that shall rule my people, Israel." *(Micah 5:2)*

Mat 2:7 Then Herod, when he had privily called the wise men, enquired of them diligently what time the star appeared.

Mat 2:8 And he sent them to Bethlehem, and said; "Go and search diligently for the young child; and when ye have found him, bring me word again, that I may come and worship him also."

Wise men directed to Bethlehem

Mat 2:9 When they had heard the king, they departed; and, lo, the star, which they saw in the east, went before them, till it came and stood over where the young child was.

Mat 2:10 When they saw the star, they rejoiced with exceeding great joy.

Mat 2:11 And when they were come into the house, they saw the young child with Mary his mother, and fell down, and worshipped him: and when they had opened their treasures, they presented unto him gifts; gold, and frankincense, and myrrh.

Mat 2:12 And being warned of God in a dream that they should not return to Herod, they departed into their own country another way.

Mary and Joseph travel to Jerusalem. 9klms.

On the 33rd day to sacrifice for the first-born male. Lev Chapter 12. We can safely say the wise men went to Bethlehem sometime before the 32nd day of the birth of Jesus as Joseph and Mary kept the law explicitly and had to be at the temple on the 33rd day for the sacrifice for the First Male Child. Lev 12.

Jesus Presented at the Temple

Luk 2:22 And when the days of her purification according to the law of Moses were accomplished, they brought him to Jerusalem, to present him to the Lord;

Luk 2:23 (As it is written in the law of the Lord, every male that openeth the womb shall be called holy to the Lord;) *(Lev. 12.)*

Luk 2:24 And to offer a sacrifice according to that which is said in the law of the Lord, A pair of turtledoves, or two young pigeons.

Luk 2:25 And, behold, there was a man in Jerusalem, whose name was Simeon; and the same man was just and devout, waiting for the consolation of Israel: and the Holy Ghost was upon him.

Luk 2:26 And it was revealed unto him by the Holy Ghost, that he should not see death, before he had seen the Lord's Christ. *(Ps 27:13, Ps 91:16)*

Luk 2:27 And he came by the Spirit into the temple: and when the parents brought in the child Jesus, to do for him after the custom of the law,

Luk 2:28 Then took he him up in his arms, and blessed God, and said;

Luk 2:29 "Lord, now lettest thou thy servant depart in peace, according to thy word: 30 For mine eyes have seen thy salvation **(Soterion G4992)**, 31 Which thou hast prepared before the face of all people; 32 A light to lighten the Gentiles, and the glory of thy people Israel." **(Isaiah 49:6)**

Luk 2:33 And Joseph and his mother marvelled at those things which were spoken of him.

Luk 2:34 And Simeon blessed them, and said unto Mary his mother; "Behold, this child is set for the fall and rising again of many in Israel; and for a sign which shall be spoken against; 35 (Yea, a sword shall pierce through thy own soul also,) that the thoughts of many hearts may be revealed." *Deut. 8:2, not connected, but a good verse to know why things sometimes happen to us and we can't feel the Lord. Matt 6:21, Matt 12:34, 2 Chron 32:31. These verses are all about Jesus and when God left Jesus on the cross, Jesus still chose to forgive.*

Luk 2:36 And there was one Anna, a prophetess, the daughter of Phanuel, of the tribe of Aser: she was of a great age, and had lived with an husband seven years from her virginity;

Luk 2:37 And she was a widow of about fourscore and four years, which departed not from the temple, but served God with fastings and prayers night and day.

Luk 2:38 And she coming in that instant gave thanks likewise unto the Lord, and spake of him to all them that looked for redemption in Jerusalem.

<u>Back Home to Nazareth 103 klms.</u>

<u>The Return to Nazareth</u>

Luk 2:39 And when they had performed all things according to the law of the Lord, they returned into Galilee, to their own city Nazareth.

We can assume the warning dream came while they were in Nazareth, or on their way from sacrificing at the Temple in Jerusalem. Matt 2:13) at this point no one of importance would have been aware of their whereabouts or the identity of Jesus except the ones that heard the prophesies spoken over him in the Temple in Jerusalem.

<u>The Flight to Egypt</u>

Mat 2:13 And when they were departed, (from Bethlehem, no time limit given and were all cashed up from the wise men and had money to travel and had medicine for Marys recovery from birthing and could have happened in transit after sacrificing at the Temple) behold, the angel of the Lord appeareth to Joseph in a dream, saying; "Arise, and take the young child and his mother, and flee into Egypt, and be thou there until I bring thee word: for Herod will seek the young child to destroy him."

Mat 2:14 When he arose, he took the young child and his mother by night, and departed into Egypt:

Mat 2:15 And was there until the death of Herod: that it might be fulfilled which was spoken of the Lord by the prophet, saying; "Out of Egypt have I called my son." *(Hosea 11.1)*

Herod Kills the Children of Bethlehem

Bethlehem was only about 9 klms from Jerusalem. How long do you think it took Herod to feel tricked? Celebrations were usually a week or two and wise men were wealthy which means they would have had a contingent of men and camels for protection and supplies. In Gen 24:10, 10 camels were used. Naaman had 10 talents of silver and 6000 pieces of Gold carried by camels. 2kings 8:9, Hazael took 40 camels to carry gifts from Damascus. We can only guess how many camels the wise men had for the king of kings.

Mat 2:16 Then Herod, when he saw that he was mocked of the wise men, was exceeding wroth, and sent forth, and slew all the children that were in Bethlehem, and in all the coasts thereof, from two years old and under, according to the time which he had diligently enquired of the wise men. *(A copy of Moses journey. Or was it all prophetic? Deut 9:10, Prov 6:16,17)*

Mat 2:17 Then was fulfilled that which was spoken by Jeremy the prophet, saying;

Mat 2:18 "In Rama was there a voice heard, lamentation, and weeping, and great mourning, Rachel weeping for her children, and would not be comforted, because they are not." *(Jer 31.15)*

The Return to Nazareth, Galilee from Egypt. *Luke 2:41*

Mat 2:19 But when Herod was dead, behold, an angel of the Lord appeareth in a dream to Joseph in Egypt,

Mat 2:20 Saying; "Arise, and take the young child and his mother, and go into the land of Israel: for they are dead which sought the young child's life."

Mat 2:21 And he arose, and took the young child and his mother, and came into the land of Israel.

Mat 2:22 But when he heard that Archelaus did reign in Judaea in the room of his father Herod, he was afraid to go thither: notwithstanding, being warned of God in a dream, he turned aside into the parts of Galilee:

Mat 2:23 And he came and dwelt in a city called Nazareth: that it might be fulfilled which was spoken by the prophets; "He shall be called a Nazarene." *(Judges 13:7. Rules for a vow for the Nazirite; Numbers 6:20)*

Jerusalem, Passover.

Approx. April. 14th day of the first month Nisan. (Exodus 12, and 12 is the number of government)

(Jesus` age is specifically mentioned because at 13 a celebration of Bar Mitzvah celebrating the spiritual maturity of the son, Jesus was far ahead of His time for maturity and was taught of the Lord. Isa 54:13 and look at Samuels encounter with God. 1Sam 2:35, 1Sam 3)

The 12-year-old Jesus in the Temple

Luk 2:40 And the child grew, and waxed strong in spirit, filled with wisdom: and the grace of God was upon him.

Luk 2:41 Now his parents went to Jerusalem every year at the feast of the passover.

This may mean that they not have been in Egypt very long also. They kept the Laws very stringently.

Luk 2:42 And when he was twelve years old, they went up to Jerusalem after the custom of the feast.

Luk 2:43 And when they had fulfilled the days, as they returned, the child Jesus tarried behind in Jerusalem; and Joseph and his mother knew not of it.

Luk 2:44 But they, supposing him to have been in the company, went a day's journey; and they sought him among their kinsfolk and acquaintance.

Luk 2:45 And when they found him not, they turned back again to Jerusalem, seeking him.

Luk 2:46 And it came to pass, that after three days they found him in the temple, sitting in the midst of the doctors, *(Masters, Teachers)* both hearing them, and asking them questions.

Luk 2:47 And all that heard him were astonished at his understanding and answers.

Luk 2:48 And when they saw him, they were amazed: and his mother said unto him; "Son, why hast thou thus dealt with us? behold, thy father and I have sought thee sorrowing."

Luk 2:49 And he said unto them; "How is it that ye sought me? wist ye not that I must be about my Father's business?" *(Matt 23:9)*

(Jesus had supernatural revelation of who He was. I believe as Samuel was called, so was Jesus as the whole bible is about Jesus, and Samuel is a picture of Jesus our meditator.)

Luk 2:50 And they understood not the saying which he spake unto them.

Back to Nazareth

Luk 2:51 And he went down with them, and came to Nazareth, and was subject unto them: but his mother kept all these sayings in her heart.

Luk 2:52 And Jesus increased in wisdom and stature, and in favour with God and man.

The Leadership in Jerusalem

Many years in the future, approx. 18 years

Luk 3:1 Now in the fifteenth year of the reign of Tiberius Caesar, Pontius Pilate being governor of Judaea, and Herod being tetrarch of Galilee, and his brother Philip tetrarch of Ituraea and of the region of Trachonitis, and Lysanias the tetrarch of Abilene,

Luk 3:2 Annas and Caiaphas being the high priests, the word of God came unto John the son of Zacharias in the wilderness. *(Jesus became the word of God, the word of God come to John and the prophets, 1 John 5:7. John 1:14. John 3:34.)*

Judaea, Jordon River

According to John 1:28 He was in Bethabara, and then later in Aenon near to Salim John 3:23.

John the Baptist Prepares the Way

Mat 3:1 In those days came John the Baptist, preaching in the wilderness of Judaea,

Mat 3:2 And saying; "Repent ye: for the kingdom of heaven is at hand."

Mat 3:3 For this is he that was spoken of by the prophet Esaias, saying; "The voice of one crying in the wilderness, prepare ye the way of the Lord, make his paths straight." *(Isaiah 40:3)*

Mat 3:4 And the same John had his raiment of camel's hair, and a leathern girdle about his loins; and his meat was locusts and wild honey.

Mat 3:5 Then went out to him Jerusalem, and all Judaea, and all the region round about Jordan,

Mat 3:6 And were baptized of him in Jordan, confessing their sins.

Mat 3:7 But when he saw many of the Pharisees and Sadducees come to his baptism, he said unto them; "O generation of vipers, who hath warned you to flee from the wrath to come? 8 Bring forth therefore fruits meet for repentance: 9 And think not to say within yourselves; "We have Abraham to our father": For I say unto you, that God is able of these stones to raise up children unto Abraham. *(Eze 36:26)* 10 And now also the axe is laid unto the root of the trees: therefore, every tree which bringeth not forth good fruit is hewn down, and cast into the fire. 11 I indeed baptize you with water unto repentance: but he that cometh after me is mightier than I, whose shoes I am not worthy to bear: he shall baptize you with the Holy Ghost, and with fire: 12 Whose fan is in his hand, and he will thoroughly purge his floor, and gather his wheat into the garner; but he will burn up the chaff with unquenchable fire." (Jer 51:20, Jer 15:7, Isa 10:33, Isa 5:24, Dan 2:35, Mal 4:1, Matt 13:30,42)

John the Baptist Preparing the Way.

Mar 1:1 The beginning of the gospel of Jesus Christ, the Son of God;

Mar 1:2 As it is written in the prophets; "Behold, I send my messenger before thy face, which shall prepare thy way before thee. *(Mal 3:1)*. 3 The voice of one crying in the wilderness, prepare ye the way of the Lord, make his paths straight." *(Isaiah 40:3)*

Mar 1:4 John did baptize in the wilderness and preach the baptism of repentance for the remission of sins.

Mar 1:5 And there went out unto him all the land of Judaea, and they of Jerusalem, and were all baptized of him in the river of Jordan, confessing their sins.

Mar 1:6 And John was clothed with camel's hair, and with a girdle of a skin about his loins; and he did eat locusts and wild honey;

Mar 1:7 And preached, saying; "There cometh one mightier than I after me, the latchet of whose shoes I am not worthy to stoop down and unloose. 8 I indeed have baptized you with water: but he shall baptize you with the Holy Ghost."

John the Baptist preparing the way

Luk 3:3 And he came into all the country about Jordan, preaching the baptism of repentance for the remission of sins;

Luk 3:4 As it is written in the book of the words of Esaias the prophet, saying; "The voice of one crying in the wilderness; Prepare ye the way of the Lord, make his paths straight. 5 Every valley shall be filled, and every mountain and hill shall be brought low; and the crooked shall be made straight, and the rough ways shall be made smooth; **(Isa 40:3)**. 6 And all flesh shall see the salvation of God." **(Psalms 98:3)**

Luk 3:7 Then said he to the multitude that came forth to be baptized of him; "O generation of vipers, who hath warned you to flee from the wrath to come? 8 Bring forth therefore fruits worthy of repentance, and begin not to say within yourselves; We have Abraham to our father: for I say unto you, That

God is able of these stones to raise up children unto Abraham. 9 And now also the axe is laid unto the root of the trees: every tree therefore which bringeth not forth good fruit is hewn down and cast into the fire." (Mal 4:1, Jer 51:20.)

True Repentance is Doing Good.

Luk 3:10 And the people asked him, saying; "What shall we do then?"

Luk 3:11 He answereth and saith unto them; "He that hath two coats, let him impart to him that hath none; and he that hath meat, let him do likewise."

Luk 3:12 Then came also publicans to be baptized, and said unto him; "Master, what shall we do?"

Luk 3:13 And he said unto them; "Exact no more than that which is appointed you."

Luk 3:14 And the soldiers likewise demanded of him, saying; "And what shall we do?" And he said unto them; "Do violence to no man, neither accuse any falsely; and be content with your wages."

Luk 3:15 And as the people were in expectation, and all men mused in their hearts of John, whether he is the Christ, or not;

John the Baptists view on the "Last day" *Zec 12:8, Mat 13:30*

Luk 3:16 John answered, saying unto them all; "I indeed baptize you with water; but one mightier than I cometh, the latchet of whose shoes I am not worthy to unloose: he shall baptize you with the Holy Ghost and with fire: 17 Whose fan is in his hand, and he will throughly purge his floor, and will gather the wheat into his garner; but the chaff he will burn with fire unquenchable." *John was also looking for the returning King of Vengeance to rid the world of Evil. Apparent in Matthew 11, as do many of the Jews and zealots. They overlook the sin sacrifice had to come first.*

Luk 3:18 And many other things in his exhortation preached he unto the people.

Galilee to the Jordon River, Bethabara

Baptism of Jesus

Mat 3:13 Then cometh Jesus from Galilee to Jordan unto John, to be baptized of him.

Mat 3:14 But John forbad him, saying; "I have need to be baptized of thee, and comest thou to me?"

Mat 3:15 And Jesus answering said unto him; "Suffer it to be so now: for thus it becometh us to fulfil all righteousness." Then he suffered him.

Mat 3:16 And Jesus, when he was baptized, went up straightway out of the water: and, lo, the heavens were opened unto him, and he saw the Spirit of God descending like a dove, and lighting upon him:

Mat 3:17 And lo a voice from heaven, saying; "THIS IS MY BELOVED SON, IN WHOM I AM WELL PLEASED." *(Ps 2:7, PS 8:4-6, Ps 110:1. Deut 17:6, Mat 18:16)*

Baptism of Jesus

Mar 1:9 And it came to pass in those days, that Jesus came from Nazareth of Galilee, and was baptized of John in Jordan.

Mar 1:10 And straightway coming up out of the water, he saw the heavens opened, and the Spirit like a dove descending upon him:

Mar 1:11 And there came a voice from heaven, saying; "THOU ART MY BELOVED SON, IN WHOM I AM WELL PLEASED."

Baptism of Jesus

Luk 3:19 But Herod the tetrarch, being reproved by him for Herodias his brother Philip's wife, and for all the evils which Herod had done,

Luk 3:20 Added yet this above all, that he shut up John in prison. *(at a later date after Jesus` baptism see John 3)*

Luk 3:21 Now when all the people were baptized, it came to pass, that Jesus also being baptized, and praying, the heaven was opened,

Luk 3:22 And the Holy Ghost descended in a bodily shape like a dove upon him, and a voice came from heaven, which said; "THOU ART MY BELOVED SON; IN THEE I AM WELL PLEASED."

The Genealogy of Joseph according to the Law of Moses, *Mat 22:23, Mar 12:18, Luke 20:27*

(Tribe of Judah verse 33.)

This is the genealogy is according to the law of Moses. Jesus contended with the Sadducees in Matt 22:24. Deuteronomy 25:5. Luke had done some serious homework. This is not a genealogy of Mary as she was of the tribe of Levi being cousins to Elizabeth. 1 Chron 6 is Levi`s genealogy and Nehemiah 12. People name their children after famous people or relatives, times don't change, some even mistaking Rahab the prostitute to be in the blood line of Joseph; (2 different names and timelines) she is not like Ruth but still referred to as a prostitute in the New Testament. When an older brother dies the younger son takes the widow and bears children in his dead brother's name, so does totally explains why Matthew's genealogy is different to Lukes. Same, same, but different.

<u>Something to study</u>

If you look deep into the book Jonah. Deep calls unto deep, Ps 42:7. Study how God prepared things for His purpose throughout time, for his servants; it will give you an appreciation of where you have come from and how you and your parents have been protected in all your generations. Yes, including that car parking spot at the shops when you asked, it had to be prepared, the same as people that you meet. I am sure that your day of salvation was organized, just like my day was orchestrated for that divine appointment with Jesus. This first section to the rebuilding of Jerusalem would have come from the family or the local synagogue just like the Dept of Birth deaths and marriages we have. Joseph being on the list in Bethlehem was called back to be taxed by Ceaser in the consensus. God made a way when there was no way.

In the old days Names were scrubbed from the genealogies because of social status or being unclean, like they never existed, the lord will do the same if we walk away from Him and don't return, He says "Depart from me I never knew you" to those that use him as a pathway to riches and don't find love, having no compassion, 2Tim 3:2-7, Obed 1:18.

Luk 3:23 And Jesus himself began to be about thirty years of age, being (as was supposed) the son of Joseph, which was the son of Heli;

Luk 3:24 Which was the son of Matthat, which was the son of Levi, which was the son of Melchi, which was the son of Janna, which was the son of Joseph,

Luk 3:25 Which was the son of Mattathias, which was the son of Amos, which was the son of Naum, which was the son of Esli, which was the son of Nagge,

Luk 3:26 Which was the son of Maath, which was the son of Mattathias, which was the son of Semei, which was the son of Joseph, which was the son of Juda,

Luk 3:27 Which was the son of Joanna, which was the son of Rhesa, which was the son of Zorobabel, *Zerubbabel, the end of the captivity and rebuilding of the Temple and Jerusalem, Haggai 1&2*, which was the son of Salathiel, *Shealtiel, Haggai 1:1*, which was the son of Neri,

We are working backwards here; Nehemiah is not related but the Lord used him to purify the Hebrews, re-establishing the priesthood, laws and from interbreeding and destroying the blood line of Joseph and Davids kingly heritage and legacy the Lord had promised. It was all documented, (he mentions the men of Bethlehem, Neh 7:26). When you are doing God's work, <u>He Will Always</u> send His prophets to confirm your path by His word. Mark 16:20, Acts 15:32, Eph1:17, 2Pet 1:19-21

Daniel was a eunuch but kept the records from Jerusalem in order. I believe this because of Psalms 137:1 was not a David Psalms but added at a later date, as was Moses`, and kept safe through all of the Babylonian empire to return to Jerusalem intact and in order, Cyrus was mentioned years before as the lord had prepared an avenue of restoration and protection.

I personally believe that the Daniel was put in charge of all the wise men of Babylon for that exact purpose, for understanding and protection of the sacred scripts pillaged from the Temple and Synagogues (including all the

genealogies), Gods word, and why the Torah still exists. We do know that the Ark of the covenant went to Egypt in 2 Chron 12:9, all was taken, and in Ezra 1:7 the other remade vessels were returned from Babylon that was stolen and had been misused, Dan 5:3, but the ark wasn't amongst them. Yes it does raise some questions about certain treasure hunters.

Luk 3:28 Which was the son of Melchi, which was the son of Addi, which was the son of Cosam, which was the son of Elmodam, which was the son of Er,

Luk 3:29 Which was the son of Jose, which was the son of Eliezer, which was the son of Jorim, which was the son of Matthat, which was the son of Levi,

Luk 3:30 Which was the son of Simeon, which was the son of Juda, which was the son of Joseph, which was the son of Jonan, which was the son of Eliakim,

Luk 3:31 Which was the son of Melea, which was the son of Menan, which was the son of Mattatha, which was the son of Nathan, *9th living son, Solomons older brother from Bathshua, 1Chron3:5, Nathan was possibly named after Davids personal Prophet Nathan,* which was the son of David, *2Chron 2:15 the 7th born,*

Luk 3:32 Which was the son of Jesse *2Chron 2:12,* which was the son of Obed *2 Chron 2:11,* which was the son of Booz, *Boaz 2Chron 2:11*, which was the son of Salmon, *Salma, 2Chron 2:11,* which was the son of Naasson, *Nahshon, 2Chron 2:10,*

Luk 3:33 Which was the son of Aminadab *2Chron 2:10,* which was the son of Aram, *Ram, 2Chron 2:10,* which was the son of Esrom, *Hezron, 2 Chron 2:5,* which was the son of Phares *1Chron 2:4,* which was the son of Juda *1Chor 2:1, (Beginning of the Captivity, notice the name of his Juda` son is Egyptian in origin, you can see the influence.)*

Luk 3:34 Which was the son of Jacob *1Chron 2:1,* which was the son of Isaac *1Chron 1:28,* which was the son of Abraham, *1Chron 1:27,* which was the son of Thara, *Terah 1Chron 1:26,* which was the son of Nachor, *Nahor, 1Chron 1:26,*

Luk 3:35 Which was the son of Saruch, *Serug, 1Chron 1:26,* which was the son of Ragau, *Reu, 1Chron 1:25,* which was the son of Phalec, *Peleg, 1 Chron 1:25,* which was the son of Heber *Ebner, 1Chron 18:1,25*, which was the son of Sala, *Salah, Gen 11:12. Shelah 1Chron 1:18,*

Luk 3:36 Which was the son of Cainan *missing from Gen 11 and 1Chron 1:24*, which was the son of Arphaxad *Gen 11:1*, which was the son of Sem, *Shem, Gen 5:32*, which was the son of Noe *Gen 5:29 Noah*, which was the son of Lamech *Gen 5:26*.

Luk 3:37 Which was the son of Mathusala *Gen 5:21*, which was the son of Enoch *Gen 5:18*, which was the son of Jared *Gen 5:15*, which was the son of Maleleel *Gen 5:12*, which was the son of Cainan *Gen 5:9,*

Luk 3:38 Which was the son of Enos *Gen 5:7*, which was the son of Seth *Gen 5:3*, which was the son of Adam *Gen 5:4*, which was the son of God *Gen 5:1*.

Note this genealogy are of "the Sons of God", Psalms 82:6 explains. They are the ones mated with the daughters of Cain, (not angels, as the angels are in chains Jude 1:6.) Not these particular men mentioned but their brothers, as God kept them pure in blood line. (You will more than likely find that the mark of the beast will be a genetic marker to change our DNA.) Study Nehemiah, especially chapter13 and Gen 6:9. More than likely the children of Cain mated with animals making them non-human and having no place found in heaven for them but became spirits which long for a body again and satan being their father. Have you wondered why devils don't look like humans but reptiles? Two seeds, good and evil. Joh 8:44, Gen 3:15

Notice Cain and satan tried to create his own Genealogy according to Gen 4:18 Mehujael means; Smitten of God and Irad means; City of witness. Using Enoch and Mathusael and Lamech, their names tell a story.

Did you know? If you get the meanings of last 10 names; Adam to Noah, the ancestors prophesied the coming of Jesus, by the God given names they called their children prophesied. The name given you is your character. The Lord will sometimes change names for his purposes. look at Joshuah, Gideon, Abraham, Sarah, Saul and Simon for example, and Last of all is Salvation, Isaiah 62:11. Chuck Missler gives an amazing teaching on the last 10 names before the flood.

Jesus in the Wilderness

Mat 4:1 Then was Jesus led up of the Spirit into the wilderness to be tempted of the devil.

Mat 4:2 And when he had fasted forty days and forty nights, he was afterward an hungred.

Mat 4:3 And when the tempter came to him, he said; "If thou be the Son of God, command that these stones be made bread."

Mat 4:4 But he answered and said; "It is written, Man shall not live by bread alone, but by every word **(RHEMA G4487)** that proceedeth out of the mouth of God." *Deut 8:3*

Mat 4:5 Then the devil taketh him up into the holy city, and setteth him on a pinnacle of the temple,

Mat 4:6 And saith unto him; "If thou be the Son of God, cast thyself down: for it is written, He shall give his angels charge concerning thee: and in their hands they shall bear thee up, lest at any time thou dash thy foot against a stone." *Ps 91:12*

Mat 4:7 Jesus said unto him; "It is written again; Thou shalt not tempt the Lord thy God." *Deut 6:16*

Mat 4:8 Again, the devil taketh him up into an exceeding high mountain, and sheweth him all the kingdoms of the world, and the glory of them;

Mat 4:9 And saith unto him; "All these things will I give thee, if thou wilt fall down and worship me."

Mat 4:10 Then saith Jesus unto him; "Get thee hence, Satan: for it is written; Thou shalt worship the Lord thy God, and him only shalt thou serve." *Exo 34:14.*

Mat 4:11 Then the devil leaveth him, and, behold, angels came and ministered unto him.

Jesus in the Wilderness

Mar 1:12 And immediately the Spirit driveth him into the wilderness.

Mar 1:13 And he was there in the wilderness forty days, tempted of Satan; and was with the wild beasts; and the angels ministered unto him. *Ps 50:10,11, Ps 63:1, Ps 95.8 Eze 4:6. 40 days, 1 day for each year the Israelites spent in the wilderness.*

Jesus in the Wilderness

Luk 4:1 And Jesus being full of the Holy Ghost returned from Jordan, and was led by the Spirit into the wilderness,

Luk 4:2 Being forty days tempted of the devil. And in those days, he did eat nothing: and when they were ended, he afterward hungered.

Luk 4:3 And the devil said unto him; "If thou be the Son of God, command this stone that it be made bread."

Luk 4:4 And Jesus answered him, saying; "It is written; That man shall not live by bread alone, but by every word **(RHEMA G4487)** of God." *Deut 8:3*

Luk 4:5 And the devil, taking him up into an high mountain, shewed unto him all the kingdoms of the world in a moment of time.

Luk 4:6 And the devil said unto him; "All this power will I give thee, and the glory of them: for that is delivered unto me; and to whomsoever I will I give it. 7 If thou therefore wilt worship me, all shall be thine."

Luk 4:8 And Jesus answered and said unto him; "Get thee behind me, Satan: for it is written; Thou shalt worship the Lord thy God, and him only shalt thou serve."

Luk 4:9 And he brought him to Jerusalem, and set him on a pinnacle of the temple, and said unto him; "If thou be the Son of God, cast thyself down from hence: 10 For it is written, He shall give his angels charge over thee, to keep thee: 11 And in their hands they shall bear thee up, lest at any time thou dash thy foot against a stone."

Luk 4:12 And Jesus answering said unto him; "It is said; Thou shalt not tempt the Lord thy God."

Luk 4:13 And when the devil had ended all the temptation, he departed from him for a season.

Luk 4:14 And Jesus returned in the power of the Spirit into Galilee: and there went out a fame of him through all the region round about.

Luk 4:15 And he taught in their synagogues, being glorified of all.

Bethabara.

Possibly where John Baptized Jesus.

At this point John doesn't tell us when Jesus was baptized but starts off when John T.B. sees Jesus strolling toward him. But John articulates in the <u>past tense</u> in his testimony to the people of Jesus and himself, so by the past tense I assume that he had already baptized Jesus and Jesus had gone into the wilderness and has returned; because John states "The next day" in John 1:29 and John 1:35 and then Jesus starts to collect his Disciples, John 1:37, thus this excerpt of John is after the temptation in the wilderness. Possibly a lot of people and Clerics asked JTB who he was many times. Surmising that JTB was 6 months older than Jesus, maybe he was in baptizing 6 months earlier but we don't know how long JTB was ministering, long enough to upset the establishment, but remember when we Ass-u-me we make an Ass out of U and ME. God does use donkeys. Lol.

John The Baptist sees Jesus

Joh 1:15 John bare witness of him, and cried, saying; "This was he of whom I spake: He that cometh after me is preferred before me: for he was before me. 16 And of his fulness have all we received, and grace for grace."

Joh 1:17 For the law was given by Moses, but grace and truth came by Jesus Christ. 18 No man hath seen God at any time; the only begotten Son, which is in the bosom of the Father, he hath declared him.

The Testimony of John the Baptist

Joh 1:19 And this is the record of John, when the Jews sent priests and Levites from Jerusalem to ask him; "Who art thou?"

Joh 1:20 And he confessed, and denied not; but confessed; "I am not the Christ."

Joh 1:21 And they asked him; "What then? Art thou Elias?" And he saith, "I am not." "Art thou that prophet?" And he answered; "No."

Joh 1:22 Then said they unto him; "Who art thou? that we may give an answer to them that sent us. What sayest thou of thyself?"

Joh 1:23 He said; "I am the voice of <u>one crying in the wilderness</u>. Make straight the way of the Lord, as said the prophet Esaias." (Isa 40:3)

Joh 1:24 And they which were sent were of the Pharisees.

Joh 1:25 And they asked him, and said unto him; "Why baptizest thou then, if thou be not that Christ, nor Elias, neither that prophet?"

Joh 1:26 John answered them, saying; "I baptize with water: but there standeth one among you, whom ye know not; 27 He it is, who coming after me is preferred before me, whose shoe's latchet I am not worthy to unloose."

Joh 1:28 These things were done in Bethabara beyond Jordan, where John was baptizing.

Behold, the Lamb of God

Joh 1:29 The next day John seeth Jesus coming unto him, and saith; "Behold the Lamb of God, which taketh away the sin of the world. 30 This is he of whom I said, after me cometh a man which is preferred before me: for he was before me. 31 And I knew him not: but that he should be made manifest to Israel, therefore am I come baptizing with water."

If you insert the Hebrew name and meaning of Israel, H3478, and will shed a new light on that verse. John doesn't mention the baptism of Jesus nor his 40 days in the wilderness, just the meetings of John T.B. and Jesus, testifying who Jesus is.

<u>John bears witness of Jesus. (Foretold by the one that sent him Luke 3:2)</u>

Joh 1:32 And John bare record, saying; "I saw the Spirit descending from heaven like a dove, and it abode upon him. 33 And I knew him not: but he that sent me to baptize with water, the same said unto me; "Upon whom thou shalt see the Spirit descending, and remaining on him, the same is he which baptizeth with the Holy Ghost." 34 <u>And I saw,</u> and bare record that this is the Son of God."

Did you notice the messenger never told JTB that Jesus was the Son of God, only that it is He who will baptize with the Holy Spirit. Why didn't he just say "it is Jesus your cousin?" Prophesy is like that, you will get a scripture about someone and instinctively know things about that person. Prophesy senses what the Holy Spirit is doing in a person's life, not what they are doing wrong. Discernment is another story and has much to do with body language. Luk 6:45, there is a difference between discerning the flesh and discerning the spirit. Discernment is the discerning the difference between what is right and what is almost right.

<u>Two of John TB disciples change teachers</u>

Joh 1:35 Again the next day after John stood, and two of his disciples;

Joh 1:36 And looking upon Jesus as he walked, he saith; "Behold the Lamb of God!"

Joh 1:37 And the two disciples (*of John*) heard him speak, and they followed Jesus.

Joh 1:38 Then Jesus turned, and saw them following, and saith unto them; "What seek ye?" They said unto him; "Rabbi, (which is to say, being interpreted, Master,) where dwellest thou?"

Joh 1:39 He saith unto them; "Come and see." They came and saw where he dwelt, and abode with him that day: for it was about the tenth hour.

Joh 1:40 One of the two which heard John speak, and followed him, was Andrew, Simon Peter's brother.

Jesus Sur-names Simon, (Ps 18:2, Mat 16:17, Mark 3:16)

Joh 1:41 He first findeth his own brother Simon, and saith unto him; "We have found the Messias." Which is, being interpreted, the Christ.

Joh 1:42 And he brought him to Jesus. And when Jesus beheld him, he said; "Thou art Simon the son of Jona: thou shalt be called Cephas (Kephas G2786), which is by interpretation, A stone." (*Petros G4074 where we get the name Peter, means a piece of the larger Rock: See also Matt 16:17 where Peter declares Jesus the Christ.*)

Jesus Travels throughout Galilee:

Philip is of Bethsaida, NE of Capernaum

Jesus Befriends Philip and Nathanael

Joh 1:43 The day following Jesus would go forth into Galilee, and findeth Philip, and saith unto him; "Follow me." (*Notice Jesus doesn't ask when He calls a person. It is the same with our walk.*)

Joh 1:44 Now Philip was of Bethsaida, the city of Andrew and Peter.

Joh 1:45 Philip findeth Nathanael, and saith unto him; "We have found him, of whom Moses in the law, and the prophets, did write, Jesus of Nazareth, the son of Joseph."

Joh 1:46 And Nathanael said unto him; "Can there any good thing come out of Nazareth?" Philip saith unto him; "Come and see."

Joh 1:47 Jesus saw Nathanael coming to him, and saith of him; "Behold an Israelite indeed, in whom is no guile!" *(Psa 32:2)*

Joh 1:48 Nathanael saith unto him; "Whence knowest thou me?" Jesus answered and said unto him; "Before that Philip called thee, when thou wast under the fig tree, I saw thee." *(Psa 139:2)*

Joh 1:49 Nathanael answered and saith unto him; "Rabbi, thou art the Son of God; thou art the King of Israel."

Joh 1:50 Jesus answered and said unto him; "Because I said unto thee, I saw thee under the fig tree, believest thou? Thou shalt see greater things than these." 51 And he saith unto him; "Verily, verily, I say unto you, Hereafter ye shall see heaven open, and the angels of God ascending and descending upon the Son of man." *(Nathanael is also with the disciples after the resurrection John 21:2.)*

Cana, Galilee

The Wedding

Joh 2:1 And the third day there was a marriage in Cana of Galilee; and the mother of Jesus was there:

Joh 2:2 And both Jesus was called, and his disciples, to the marriage.

Joh 2:3 And when they wanted wine, the mother of Jesus saith unto him; "They have no wine.

Joh 2:4 Jesus saith unto her; "Woman, what have I to do with thee? mine hour is not yet come."

Joh 2:5 His mother saith unto the servants; "Whatsoever he saith unto you, do it."

Mary`s last recorded words. His mother knew Jesus like no other at that point in time. By Mary`s confidence in Jesus, I have an opinion that Jesus had supplied other necessities for the family in past times of need, Mary knew what Jesus was capable of. Mary just didn't offer an opinion she threw Jesus under the bus, Mary knew something others didn't, although they were never recorded but Jesus` response says it all. This is his first publicly recorded miracle. John 2:11.

Joh 2:6 And there were set there six waterpots of stone, after the manner of the purifying of the Jews, containing two or three firkins apiece. (*Firkin equals approx. 35ltrs or approx. 9 gallons.*)

Joh 2:7 Jesus saith unto them; "Fill the waterpots with water." And they filled them up to the brim.

Joh 2:8 And he saith unto them; "Draw out now, and bear unto the governor of the feast." And they bare it.

Joh 2:9 When the ruler of the feast had tasted the water that was made wine, and knew not whence it was: (but the servants which drew the water knew;) the governor of the feast called the bridegroom,

Joh 2:10 And saith unto him; "Every man at the beginning doth set forth good wine; and when men have well drunk, then that which is worse: but thou hast kept the good wine until now."

Cana to Capernaum, Galilee

40klms apart. Cana is higher than Capernaum which is on the shores of the sea of Galilee

The beginning of Miracles according to John

Joh 2:11 This beginning of miracles did Jesus in Cana of Galilee and manifested forth his glory; and his disciples *(G3101. Pupils)* believed on him.

Joh 2:12 After this he went down to Capernaum, he, and his mother, and his brethren, and his disciples: and they continued there not many days.

(*But lived there, Matt 4:13, off and on, after being rejected in Nazareth. Matt 9:1.*)

Jesus goes to the Passover in Jerusalem.

The First Time in His ministry.

Jesus heads for Jerusalem around March, April. His first passover in ministry. Jesus makes a Scourge. A whip of many braids, made from small ropes and John the Baptist was still free. John 3:24.

Joh 2:13 And the Jews' passover was at hand, and Jesus went up to Jerusalem,

Joh 2:14 And found in the temple those that sold oxen and sheep and doves, and the changers of money sitting:

Joh 2:15 And when he had made a scourge of small cords, he drove them all out of the temple, and the sheep, and the oxen; and poured out the changers' money, and overthrew the tables;

Joh 2:16 And said unto them that sold doves; "Take these things hence; make not my Father's house an house of merchandise."

Joh 2:17 And his disciples remembered that it was written; "The zeal of thine house hath eaten me up." *(PSALMS 69:9)*

Joh 2:18 Then answered the Jews and said unto him; "What sign shewest thou unto us, seeing that thou doest these things? "

<u>Jesus Prophesies His Death the first time.</u> *(Hos. 6:2, 1 Cor 6:19.)*

Joh 2:19 Jesus answered and said unto them; "Destroy this temple, and in three days I will raise it up."

Joh 2:20 Then said the Jews; "Forty and six years was this temple in building, and wilt thou rear it up in three days? "

Joh 2:21 But he spake of the temple of his body.

Joh 2:22 When therefore he was risen from the dead, his disciples remembered that he had said this unto them; and they believed the scripture, and the word which Jesus had said.

<u>Jesus Knew the heart of man</u> *(Jer 17:9, Isa 64:6)*

Joh 2:23 Now when he was in Jerusalem at the passover, in the feast day, many believed in his name, when they saw the miracles which he did.

John 2:23 says he did miracles in Jerusalem. (multiple) but in John 4:54 tells of the Second miracle Jesus did. A contradiction, Or was it a major miracle? I am on the side of a 2nd notable miracle in Cana.

Joh 2:24 But Jesus did not commit himself unto them, because he knew all men,

Joh 2:25 And needed not that any should testify of man: for he knew what was in man.

Nicodemus. You Must Be Born Again.

The beginning of the underground church in Jerusalem amongst the Pharisees

Joh 3:1 There was a man of the Pharisees, named Nicodemus, a ruler of the Jews:

Joh 3:2 The same came to Jesus by night, and said unto him; "Rabbi, we know that thou art a teacher come from God: for no man can do these miracles that thou doest, except God be with him."

Joh 3:3 Jesus answered and said unto him; "Verily, verily, I say unto thee, except a man be born again, he cannot see the kingdom of God."

Joh 3:4 Nicodemus saith unto him; "How can a man be born when he is old? Can he enter the second time into his mother's womb, and be born?"

Joh 3:5 Jesus answered; "Verily, verily, I say unto thee, except a man be born of water and of the Spirit, he cannot enter into the kingdom of God. 6 That which is born of the flesh is flesh; and that which is born of the Spirit is spirit. 7 Marvel not that I said unto thee, Ye must be born again. 8 The wind bloweth where it listeth, and thou hearest the sound thereof, but canst not tell whence it cometh, and whither it goeth: so is every one that is born of the Spirit."

Joh 3:9 Nicodemus answered and said unto him; "How can these things be?"

Joh 3:10 Jesus answered and said unto him; "Art thou a master of Israel, and knowest not these things? 11 Verily, verily, I say unto thee; We speak that we do know, and testify that we have seen; and ye receive not our witness. 12 If I have told you earthly things, and ye believe not, how shall ye believe, if I tell you of heavenly things? 13 And no man hath ascended up to heaven, but he that came down from heaven, even the Son of man which is in heaven. 14 And as Moses lifted up the serpent in the wilderness, even so must the Son of man be lifted up: 15 That whosoever believeth in him should not perish, but have eternal life. 16 For God so loved the world, that he gave his only begotten Son, that whosoever believeth in him should not perish, but have everlasting life. 17 For God sent not his Son into the world to condemn the world; but that the world through him might be saved. 18 He that believeth on him is not condemned: but he that believeth not is condemned already, because he hath not believed in the name of the only begotten Son of God. 19 And this is the condemnation, that light is come into the world, and men loved darkness rather than light, because their deeds were evil. 20 For everyone that doeth evil hateth the light, neither cometh to the light, lest his deeds should be reproved. 21 But he that doeth truth cometh to the light, that his deeds may be made manifest, that they are wrought in God."

From Jerusalem back to JTB in Aenon near to Salim, Travelling Judaea

John the Baptist Exalts Christ

Joh 3:22 After these things came Jesus <u>and his disciples</u> into the land of Judaea; and there he tarried with them and baptized. *(Jesus himself didn't. Joh 4:2)*

(Note; anyone that wanted to learn From Jesus was a disciple and Jesus sets 12 aside in Mat 10:3, Mar 3:18, Luk 6:13. Did you know? 12 tribes, twelve loaves of Bread, Lev 24:5-9, twelve judges, twelve officers set by Solomon, 1Kings 4:7 and 144,000, 12x12 men sealed in Revelation.

Joh 3:23 And John also was baptizing in Aenon near to Salim, because there was much water there: and they came, and were baptized.

Joh 3:24 For John was not yet cast into prison. *(Matt 4:12)*

Joh 3:25 Then there arose a question between some of John's disciples and the Jews about purifying.

Joh 3:26 And they came unto John, and said unto him; "Rabbi, he that was with thee beyond Jordan, to whom thou barest witness, behold, the same baptizeth, and all men come to him."

God is the Giver of All Things. *Mal 4:5*

Joh 3:27 John answered and said; "A man can receive nothing, except it be given him from heaven. 28 Ye yourselves bear me witness, that I said, I am not the Christ, but that I am sent before him. 29 He that hath the bride is the bridegroom: but the friend of the bridegroom, which standeth and heareth him, rejoiceth greatly because of the bridegroom's voice: This my joy therefore is fulfilled. 30 He must increase, but I must decrease. 31 He that cometh from above is above all: he that is of the earth is earthly, and speaketh of the earth: he that cometh from heaven is above all. 32 And what he hath seen and heard, that he testifieth; and no man receiveth his testimony. 33 He that hath received his testimony hath set to his seal that God is true. 34 <u>For he whom God hath sent speaketh the words of God:</u> for God giveth not the Spirit by measure unto him. 35 The Father loveth the Son, and hath given all things into his hand. 36 He that believeth on the Son hath everlasting life: and he that believeth not the Son shall not see life; but the wrath of God abideth on him."

<u>Heading back to Galilee after the Passover through Sychar, Samaria.</u>

<u>Jesus and the Woman at Jacobs well.</u>

Joh 4:1 When therefore the Lord knew how the Pharisees had heard that Jesus made and baptized more disciples than John,

Joh 4:2 (Though Jesus himself baptized not, but his disciples,)

Joh 4:3 He left Judaea, and departed again into Galilee.

Joh 4:4 And he must needs go through Samaria.

Joh 4:5 Then cometh he to a city of Samaria, which is called Sychar, near to the parcel of ground that Jacob gave to his son Joseph. *(Gen 33:18)*

Joh 4:6 Now Jacob's well was there. Jesus therefore, being wearied with his journey, sat thus on the well: and it was about the sixth hour. *(12 o`clock)*

Joh 4:7 There cometh a woman of Samaria to draw water: Jesus saith unto her; "Give me to drink."

Joh 4:8 (For his disciples were gone away unto the city to buy meat.) *(Food.)*

Joh 4:9 Then saith the woman of Samaria unto him; "How is it that thou, being a Jew, askest drink of me, which am a woman of Samaria? for the Jews have no dealings with the Samaritans."

Joh 4:10 Jesus answered and said unto her; "If thou knewest the gift of God, and who it is that saith to thee; Give me to drink; thou wouldest have asked of him, and he would have given thee living water."

Joh 4:11 The woman saith unto him; "Sir, thou hast nothing to draw with, and the well is deep: from whence then hast thou that living water? 12 Art thou greater than our father Jacob, which gave us the well, and drank thereof himself, and his children, and his cattle?"

Joh 4:13 Jesus answered and said unto her; "Whosoever drinketh of this water shall thirst again: 14 But whosoever drinketh of the water that I shall give him shall never thirst; but the water that I shall give him shall be in him a well of water springing up into everlasting life."

Joh 4:15 The woman saith unto him; "Sir, give me this water, that I thirst not, neither come hither to draw."

Joh 4:16 Jesus saith unto her; "Go, call thy husband, and come hither."

Joh 4:17 The woman answered and said; "I have no husband." Jesus said unto her; "Thou hast well said, I have no husband: 18 For thou hast had five husbands; and he whom thou now hast is not thy husband: in that saidst thou truly."

Joh 4:19 The woman saith unto him; "Sir, I perceive that thou art a prophet. 20 Our fathers worshipped in this mountain; and ye say, that in Jerusalem is the place where men ought to worship."

Joh 4:21 Jesus saith unto her; "Woman, believe me, the hour cometh, when ye shall neither in this mountain, nor yet at Jerusalem, worship the Father. 22 Ye worship ye know not what: we know what we worship: for salvation is of the Jews. 23 But the hour cometh, and now is, when the true worshippers shall worship the Father in spirit and in truth: for the Father seeketh such to worship him. 24 **God** *is* **a Spirit**: and they that worship him must worship *Him* in spirit and in truth."

Zec 14:9, Mal 2:10, Deut 6:4, John 20:17, Acts 2:22, 1John 5:7, 1Tim 2;5. When we worship, we have to worship with all our mind and imagination, if your mind is wandering you haven't come into the presence of God. When your mind and heart is truly set on God and your mind is still, then you have reached "Spirit and Truth." (Many false religions try to counterfeit this; David calls it the secret place.) The Lord requires nothing Less. Heb 4:16, Ps 104:4,

Isa 29:13. Many perish thinking they have heard God but are only going through the motions. Heb 11 says Faith is hearing God then acting, the same as salvation, we heard the call, then we acted but it doesn't stop there; the world of faith grows and grows as we act on what we have heard, just like a mustard seed turns into a tree. When a truth is revealed, obedience opens the door for more truth to come.

Strangely enough, the word spirit in the KJV NT shows up 385 times. 5 = the Holy Spirit and Grace. 7 is the number of God, completeness. 385 divided by 5 = 77 God, missing the third 7, Jesus, for completion and Godhead, Godhead appears 3 times in the NT. Bible, Acts17:29, Rom 1:20, Col 2:9.

Joh 4:25 The woman saith unto him; "I know that Messias cometh, which is called Christ: when he is come, he will tell us all things."

Joh 4:26 Jesus saith unto her; "I that speak unto thee am he."

Joh 4:27 And upon this came his disciples, and marvelled that he talked with the woman: yet no man said; What seekest thou? or, why talkest thou with her?

Joh 4:28 The woman then left her waterpot, and went her way into the city, and saith to the men; 29 "Come, see a man, which told me all things that ever I did: is not this the Christ?"

Joh 4:30 Then they went out of the city, and came unto him.

Joh 4:31 In the mean while his disciples prayed him, saying; "Master, eat."

Joh 4:32 But he said unto them; "I have meat *(food)* to eat that ye know not of."

Joh 4:33 Therefore said the disciples one to another; "Hath any man brought him ought to eat?"

<u>The Harvest is Ready. Mat 9:35, Luk 10:1, Joel 3:12-14, Amos 9:13.</u>

Joh 4:34 Jesus saith unto them; "My meat *(food)* is to do the will of him that sent me, and to finish his work. 35 Say not ye; There are yet four months, and then cometh harvest? behold, I say unto you, lift up your eyes, and look on

the fields; for they are white already to harvest.36 And he that reapeth receiveth wages, and gathereth fruit unto life eternal: that both he that soweth and he that reapeth may rejoice together. 37 And herein is that saying true, One soweth, and another reapeth. 38 I sent you to reap that whereon ye bestowed no labour: other men laboured, and ye are entered into their labours." *(Jer 17:10)*

Samaritan woman Evangelises Sychar, *Titus 2:3-5*

Joh 4:39 And many of the Samaritans of that city believed on him for the saying of the woman, which testified; "He told me all that ever I did."

Joh 4:40 So when the Samaritans were come unto him, they besought him that he would tarry with them: and he abode there two days.

Joh 4:41 And many more believed because of his own word.

Joh 4:42 And said unto the woman; "Now we believe, not because of thy saying: for we have heard him ourselves, and know that this is indeed the Christ, the Saviour of the world."

Jesus Leaves Nazareth, Galilee and lives in Capernaum, Galilee

Jer 23:5 The Word Nazareth means branch and Watchtower. We know Jesus was called a Nazarene, Mat2:23. Rule #1; reminds me of Hab 2:1 when he stands his watch and waits to be reproved by the Lord. The Lords message was one of rebuke and comfort. The Branch from God, Jer 33:15.

John in Prison

Mat 4:12 Now when Jesus had heard that John was cast into prison, he departed into Galilee;

Mat 4:13 And leaving Nazareth, he came and dwelt in Capernaum, which is upon the seacoast, in the borders of Zabulon and Nephthalim:

Mat 4:14 That it might be fulfilled which was spoken by Esaias the prophet, saying;

Mat 4:15 "The land of Zabulon, and the land of Nephthalim, by the way of the sea, beyond Jordan, Galilee of the Gentiles; 16 The people which sat in darkness saw great light; and to them which sat in the region and shadow of death light is sprung up." *(Isaiah 9:1)*

Mat 4:17 From that time Jesus began to preach, and to say; "Repent: for the kingdom of heaven is at hand."

John in Prison

Mar 1:14 Now after that John was put in prison, Jesus came into Galilee, preaching the gospel of the kingdom of God,

Mar 1:15 And saying; "The time is fulfilled, and the kingdom of God is at hand: repent ye, and believe the gospel."

Jesus Rejected at Nazareth. *(Expanded by Luke)*

Luk 4:16 And he came to Nazareth, where he had been brought up: and, as his custom was, he went into the synagogue on the sabbath day and stood up for to read.

Luk 4:17 And there was delivered unto him the book of the prophet Esaias. And when he had opened the book, he found the place where it was written;

Luk 4:18 "The Spirit of the Lord is upon me, because he hath anointed me to preach the gospel to the poor; he hath sent me to heal the broken hearted, to preach deliverance to the captives, and recovering of sight to the blind, to set at liberty them that are bruised, 19 To preach the acceptable year of the Lord." *(Isaiah 61:1-)*

Luk 4:20 And he closed the book, and he gave it again to the minister, and sat down. And the eyes of all them that were in the synagogue were fastened on him.

Luk 4:21 And he began to say unto them; "This day is this scripture fulfilled in your ears."

Luk 4:22 And all bare him witness and wondered at the gracious words which proceeded out of his mouth. And they said; "Is not this Joseph's son?"

Luk 4:23 And he said unto them; "Ye will surely say unto me this proverb, Physician, heal thyself: whatsoever we have heard done in Capernaum, do also here in thy country."

A Prophet is not Accepted in His Own Country. *Mat 13:53*

Luk 4:24 And he said; "Verily I say unto you; <u>No prophet is accepted in his own country</u>. 25 But I tell you of a truth, many widows were in Israel in the days of Elias, when the heaven was shut up three years and six months, when great famine was throughout all the land; 26 But unto none of them was Elias sent, save unto Sarepta, a city of Sidon, unto a woman that was a widow. 27 And many lepers were in Israel in the time of Eliseus the prophet; and none of them was cleansed, saving Naaman the Syrian."

Luk 4:28 And all they in the synagogue, when they heard these things, were filled with wrath,

Luk 4:29 And rose up, and thrust him out of the city, and led him unto the brow of the hill whereon their city was built, that they might cast him down headlong.

Luk 4:30 But he passing through the midst of them went his way,

A Prophet has no Honour in His Own Country. *Mat 13:53*

Joh 4:43 Now after two days he departed thence, and went into Galilee.

Joh 4:44 For Jesus himself testified, that <u>a prophet hath no honour in his own country</u>.

Joh 4:45 Then when he was come into Galilee, the Galilaeans received him, having seen all the things that he did at Jerusalem at the feast: for they also went unto the feast.

Jesus travels to Cana from Sychor

Jesus has come back from Jerusalem gone through Samaria to Nazareth then to Cana and then on to Capernaum. Cana is approx 26 klms from Capernaum or 16.5 miles. Matthew says He preached the Beatitudes

after Jesus was in Capernaum then came back out, Capernaum was their home base. All a matter of timing.

Jesus Heals a Nobleman's Son

Joh 4:46 So Jesus came again into Cana of Galilee, where he made the water wine. And there was a certain nobleman, whose son was sick at Capernaum.

Joh 4:47 When he heard that Jesus was come out of Judaea into Galilee, he went unto him, and besought him that he would come down, and heal his son: for he was at the point of death.

Joh 4:48 Then said Jesus unto him; "Except ye see signs and wonders, ye will not believe."

Joh 4:49 The nobleman saith unto him; "Sir, come down ere my child die."

Joh 4:50 Jesus saith unto him; "Go thy way; thy son liveth." And the man believed the word that Jesus had spoken unto him, and he went his way.

Joh 4:51 And as he was now going down, his servants met him, and told him, saying; "Thy son liveth."

Joh 4:52 Then enquired he of them the hour when he began to amend. And they said unto him; "Yesterday at the seventh hour the fever left him."

Joh 4:53 So the father knew that it was at the same hour, in the which Jesus said unto him; "Thy son liveth": and himself believed, and his whole house.

Joh 4:54 This is again the second miracle that Jesus did, when he was come out of Judaea into Galilee.

(Jesus had cast many unclean Spirits out previously in Jerusalem and Judea, probably small healings, John 2:23, but this was notably the second miracle that Jesus did in Cana.)

Capernaum and surrounding Area, Sea of Galilee, North Shore.

Picking up some of the disciples

Fishers of Men

Mat 4:18 And Jesus, walking by the sea of Galilee, saw two brethren, Simon called Peter, and Andrew his brother, casting a net into the sea: for they were fishers.

Mat 4:19 And he saith unto them; "Follow me, and I will make you fishers of men."

Mat 4:20 And they straightway left their nets, and followed him.

Mat 4:21 And going on from thence, he saw other two brethren, James the son of Zebedee, and John his brother, in a ship with Zebedee their father, mending their nets; and he called them.

Mat 4:22 And they immediately left the ship and their father, and followed him.

Fishers of Men

Mar 1:16 Now as he walked by the sea of Galilee, he saw Simon and Andrew his brother casting a net into the sea: for they were fishers.

Mar 1:17 And Jesus said unto them; "Come ye after me, and I will make you to become fishers of men."

Mar 1:18 And straightway they forsook their nets and followed him.

Mar 1:19 And when he had gone a little further thence, he saw James the son of Zebedee, and John his brother, who also were in the ship mending their nets.

Mar 1:20 And straightway he called them: and they left their father Zebedee in the ship with the hired servants, and went after him.

Fishers of Men

Luk 5:1 And it came to pass, that, as the people pressed upon him to hear the word of God, he stood by the lake of Gennesaret,

Luk 5:2 And saw two ships standing by the lake: but the fishermen were gone out of them, and were washing their nets.

Luk 5:3 And he entered into one of the ships, which was Simon's, and prayed him that he would thrust out a little from the land. And he sat down, and taught the people out of the ship.

Luk 5:4 Now when he had left speaking, he said unto Simon; "Launch out into the deep, and let down your nets for a draught."

Luk 5:5 And Simon answering said unto him; "Master, we have toiled all the night, and have taken nothing: nevertheless, at thy word I will let down the net."

Luk 5:6 And when they had this done, they inclosed a great multitude of fishes: and their net brake.

Luk 5:7 And they beckoned unto their partners, which were in the other ship, that they should come and help them. And they came, and filled both the ships, so that they began to sink.

Luk 5:8 When Simon Peter saw it, he fell down at Jesus' knees, saying; "Depart from me; for I am a sinful man, O Lord."

Luk 5:9 For he was astonished, and all that were with him, at the draught of the fishes which they had taken:

Luk 5:10 And so was also James, and John, the sons of Zebedee, which were partners with Simon. And Jesus said unto Simon; "Fear not; from henceforth thou shalt catch men."

Luk 5:11 And when they had brought their ships to land, they forsook all, and followed him.

Preaching Throughout Galilee

Jesus Heals All

Mat 4:23 And Jesus went about all Galilee, teaching in their synagogues, and preaching the gospel of the kingdom, and healing all manner of sickness and all manner of disease among the people.

Mat 4:24 And his fame went throughout all Syria: and they brought unto him all sick people that were taken with divers *(many)* diseases and torments, and those which were possessed with devils, and those which were lunatick, and those that had the palsy; and he healed them.

Mat 4:25 And there followed him great multitudes of people from Galilee, and from Decapolis, and from Jerusalem, and from Judaea, and from beyond Jordan.

Jesus Casts out an unclean spirit

Mar 1:21 And they went into Capernaum; and straightway on the sabbath day he entered into the synagogue and taught.

Mar 1:22 And they were astonished at his doctrine: for he taught them as one that had authority, and not as the scribes.

Mar 1:23 And there was in their synagogue a man with an unclean spirit; and he cried out,

Mar 1:24 Saying; "Let us alone; what have we to do with thee, thou Jesus of Nazareth? art thou come to destroy us? I know thee who thou art, the Holy One of God."

Mar 1:25 And Jesus rebuked him, saying; "Hold thy peace, and come out of him."

Mar 1:26 And when the unclean spirit had torn him, and cried with a loud voice, he came out of him.

Mar 1:27 And they were all amazed, insomuch that they questioned among themselves, saying; "What thing is this? what new doctrine is this? for with authority commandeth he even the unclean spirits, and they do obey him."

Mar 1:28 And immediately his fame spread abroad throughout all the region round about Galilee.

Jesus Casts out and unclean Devil

Luk 4:31 And came down to Capernaum, a city of Galilee, and taught them on the sabbath days.

Luk 4:32 And they were astonished at his doctrine: for his word was with power.

Luk 4:33 And in the synagogue there was a man, which had a spirit of an unclean devil, and cried out with a loud voice,

Luk 4:34 Saying; "Let us alone; what have we to do with thee, thou Jesus of Nazareth? art thou come to destroy us? I know thee who thou art; the Holy One of God."

Luk 4:35 And Jesus rebuked him, saying; "Hold thy peace, and come out of him." And when the devil had thrown him in the midst, he came out of him and hurt him not.

Luk 4:36 And they were all amazed, and spake among themselves, saying; "What a word is this! for with authority and power he commandeth the unclean spirits, and they come out."

Luk 4:37 And the fame of him went out into every place of the country round about.

Mountains above Capernaum.

Sermon on the Mount. The Beatitudes (Luke 6:20)

Mat 5:1 And seeing the multitudes, he went up into a mountain: and when he was set, his disciples came unto him: 2 And he opened his mouth, and taught them, saying;

Mat 5:3 "Blessed are the poor in spirit: for theirs is the kingdom of heaven."

Mat 5:4 "Blessed are they that mourn: for they shall be comforted."

Mat 5:5 "Blessed are the meek: for they shall inherit the earth." **(Ps 37:11)**

Mat 5:6 "Blessed are they which do hunger and thirst after righteousness: for they shall be filled."

Mat 5:7 "Blessed are the merciful: for they shall obtain mercy." (Ps 18:25, 2Sam 22:26)

Mat 5:8 "Blessed are the pure in heart: for they shall see God." (1Chron 28:9)

Mat 5:9 "Blessed are the peacemakers: for they shall be called the children of God." (Isa 26:3, Isa 57:21)

Mat 5:10 "Blessed are they which are persecuted for righteousness' sake: for theirs is the kingdom of heaven." (*Ps 105:14*)

Mat 5:11 "Blessed are ye, when men shall revile you, and persecute you, and shall say all manner of evil against you falsely, for my sake. 12 Rejoice, and be exceeding glad: for great is your reward in heaven: for so persecuted they the prophets which were before you."

The Beatitudes according to Luke. Preached in Judea

Luk 6:20 And he lifted up his eyes on his disciples, and said; "Blessed be ye poor: for yours is the kingdom of God. 21 Blessed are ye that hunger now: for ye shall be filled. Blessed are ye that weep now: for ye shall laugh. 22 Blessed are ye, when men shall hate you, and when they shall separate you from their company, and shall reproach you, and cast out your name as evil, for the Son of man's sake. 23 Rejoice ye in that day, and leap for joy: for, behold, your reward is great in heaven: for in the like manner did their fathers unto the prophets."

The Rich have their reward

Luk 6:24 "But woe unto you that are rich! for ye have received your consolation. 25 Woe unto you that are full! for ye shall hunger. Woe unto you that laugh now! for ye shall mourn and weep. 26 Woe unto you, when all men shall speak well of you! for so did their fathers to the false prophets."

Worthless Salt

Salt was part of the covenant. Lev 2:13.

Mat 5:13 "Ye are the salt of the earth: but if the salt has lost his savour, wherewith shall it be salted? it is thenceforth good for nothing, but to be cast out, and to be trodden under foot of men.

Worthless Salt.

Mar 9:49 For every one shall be salted with fire, and every sacrifice shall be salted with salt. 50 Salt is good: but if the salt has lost his saltness, wherewith will ye season it? Have salt in yourselves, and have peace one with another.

Worthless Salt.

Luk 14:34 "Salt is good: but if the salt have lost his savour, wherewith shall it be seasoned? 35 It is neither fit for the land, nor yet for the dunghill; but men cast it out. He that hath ears to hear, let him hear."

A lamp under a Basket.

Ps 119:105, Isa 58:8, Mat 17:19, Job 24:15, Prov 22:9, Zec 11:17

Mat 5:14 Ye are the light of the world. A city that is set on a hill cannot be hid. 15 Neither do men light a candle, and put it under a bushel, but on a candlestick; and it giveth light unto all that are in the house. 16 Let your light so shine before men, that they may see your good works, and glorify your Father which is in heaven."

A Lamp Under a Basket.

Mar 4:21 And he said unto them; "Is a candle brought to be put under a bushel, or under a bed? and not to be set on a candlestick? 22 For there is nothing hid, which shall not be manifested; neither was anything kept secret, but that it should come abroad. 23 If any man have ears to hear, let him hear."

Mar 4:24 And he said unto them; "Take heed what ye hear: with what measure ye mete, it shall be measured to you: and unto you that hear shall more be given. 25 For he that hath, to him shall be given: and he that hath not, from him shall be taken even that which he hath."

A Candle Under a Vessel.

Luk 8:16 "No man, when he hath lighted a candle, covereth it with a vessel, or <u>putteth it under a bed</u>; but setteth it on a candlestick, that they which enter in may see the light. 17 <u>For nothing is secret, that shall not be made manifest;</u> neither anything hid, that shall not be known and come abroad. 18 Take heed therefore how ye hear: for whosoever hath, <u>to him shall be given</u>; and whosoever hath not, <u>from him shall be taken</u> even that which he seemeth to have."

Don't hide your Light. Preached in Judea,

Luk 11:33 "No man, when he hath lighted a candle, putteth it in a secret place, neither under a <u>bushel,</u> but on a candlestick, that they which come in may see the light. 34 The light of the body is the eye: therefore, when thine eye is single, thy whole body also is full of light; but when thine eye is evil, thy body also is full of darkness. 35 Take heed therefore that the light which is in thee be not darkness. 36 If thy whole body therefore be full of light, having no part dark, the whole shall be full of light, as when the bright shining of a candle doth give thee light."

The Law Passing

Mat 5:17 "Think not that I am come to destroy the law, or the prophets: I am not come to destroy, but to fulfil. 18 For verily I say unto you, <u>till heaven and earth pass</u>, one jot or one tittle shall in no wise pass from the law, till all be fulfilled. 19 Whoso ever therefore shall break one of these least commandments, and shall teach men so, he shall be called the least in the kingdom of heaven: but whosoever shall do and teach them, the same shall be called great in the kingdom of heaven. 20 For I say unto you, that except your righteousness shall exceed the righteousness of the scribes and Pharisees, ye shall in no case enter into the kingdom of heaven."

The Law Passing (Preached in Judea)

Luk 16:14 And the Pharisees also, who were covetous, heard all these things: and they derided him.

Luk 16:15 And he said unto them; "Ye are they which justify yourselves before men; but God knoweth your hearts: for that which is highly esteemed among men is abomination in the sight of God. 16 The law and the prophets were until John: since that time the kingdom of God is preached, and every man presseth into it. 17 And it is easier <u>for heaven and earth to pass</u>, than one tittle of the law to fail."

<u>Don't come to God if you are angry with your brother without cause.</u>

<u>(Prov 3:30, James 1:8)</u>

Mat 5:21 "Ye have heard that it was said by them of old time; "Thou shalt not kill; and whosoever shall kill shall be in danger of the judgment:" 22 But I say unto you; That whosoever is angry with his brother <u>without a cause</u> shall be in danger of the judgment: and whosoever shall say to his brother, Raca, shall be in danger of the council: but whosoever shall say; Thou fool, shall be in danger of hell fire. 23 Therefore if thou bring thy gift to the altar, and there rememberest that thy brother hath ought against thee; 24 Leave there thy gift before the altar, and go thy way; first be reconciled to thy brother, and then come and offer thy gift."

<u>Pay your Debts be Honest.</u> *Deut 23:21*

Mat 5:25 "Agree with thine adversary quickly, whiles thou art in the way with him; lest at any time the <u>adversary deliver thee to the judge,</u> and the judge deliver thee to the officer, and thou be cast into prison. 26 Verily I say unto thee; Thou shalt by no means come out thence, till thou hast paid the uttermost farthing."

<u>Pay your Debts Be Honest</u>

Luke pens Jesus' teaching in Bethany/Jerusalem. Same, same but Different place. Matt Ch 22. From Luke Ch 10

Luk 12:57 "Yea, and why even of yourselves judge ye not what is right? 58 When thou goest with thine <u>adversary to the magistrate</u>, as thou art in the way, give diligence that thou mayest be delivered from him; lest he hale thee to the judge, and the judge deliver thee to the officer, and the officer cast thee into prison. 59 I tell thee, thou shalt not depart thence, till thou hast paid the very last mite."

Adultery defined. Lev 24:10, Prov 6:32, 2 Pet 2:14

Mat 5:27 "Ye have heard that it was said by them of old time; "Thou shalt not commit adultery:" 28 But I say unto you, that whosoever looketh on a woman to lust after her hath committed adultery with her already in his heart. 29 And if thy right eye offend thee, pluck it out, and cast it from thee: for it is profitable for thee that one of thy members should perish, and not that thy whole body should be cast into hell. 30 And if thy right hand offend thee, cut it off, and cast it from thee: for it is profitable for thee that one of thy members should perish, and not that thy whole body should be cast into hell."

Divorce can be Adultery *Mat 19:1, Deut 24:1-3*

Mat 5:31 "It hath been said; "Whosoever shall put away his wife, let him give her a writing of divorcement:" 32 But I say unto you; That whosoever shall put away his wife, saving for the cause of fornication, causeth her to commit adultery: and whosoever shall marry her that is divorced committeth adultery." *(Jesus` own words)*

Speaking Oaths. *Num 30:2-9*

Mat 5:33 "Again, ye have heard that it hath been said by them of old time. Thou shalt not forswear thyself, but shalt perform unto the Lord thine oaths: 34 But I say unto you, swear not at all; neither by heaven; for it is God's throne: 35 Nor by the earth; for it is his footstool: neither by Jerusalem; for it is the city of the great King. 36 Neither shalt thou swear by thy head, because thou canst not make one hair white or black. 37 But let your communication be, Yea, yea; Nay, nay: for whatsoever is more than these cometh of evil."

Don't Retaliate to your enemy, show kindness be Charitable. *Ex 21:24, Lev 24:20*

Mat 5:38 "Ye have heard that it hath been said, an eye for an eye, and a tooth for a tooth: 39 But I say unto you; That ye resist not evil: but whosoever shall smite thee on thy right cheek, turn to him the other also. 40 And if any man will sue thee at the law, and take away thy coat, let him have thy cloke also.

41 And whosoever shall compel thee to go a mile, go with him twain. 42 Give to him that asketh thee, and from him that would borrow of thee turn not thou away."

Do Good (Agape) to your Enemies

Luk 6:27 "But I say unto you which hear; Love your enemies, do good to them which hate you, 28 Bless them that curse you, and pray for them which despitefully use you. 29 And unto him <u>that smiteth thee on the one cheek offer also the other</u>; and him that taketh away thy cloke forbid not to take thy coat also. 30 Give to every man that asketh of thee; and of him that taketh away thy goods ask them not again. 31 And as ye would that men should do to you, do ye also to them likewise.

Agape (show kindness/charity) Your Enemies, like God. Mat 5:45

Mat 5:43 "Ye have heard that it hath been said, thou shalt love thy neighbour, and hate thine enemy. 44 But I say unto you, <u>love your enemies</u>, bless them that curse you, <u>do good</u> to them that hate you, and pray for them which despitefully use you, and persecute you; 45 That ye may be the children of your Father which is in heaven: for he maketh his sun to rise on the evil and on the good, and sendeth rain on the just and on the unjust. 46 For if ye love them which love you, what reward have ye? do not even the publicans the same? 47 And if ye salute your brethren only, what do ye more than others? do not even the publicans so? 48 Be ye therefore perfect, even as your Father which is in heaven is perfect."

Be Merciful as the Father is merciful

Luk 6:32 For if ye love them which love you, what thank have ye? for sinners also love those that love them. 33 And if ye do good to them which do good to you, what thank have ye? for sinners also do even the same. 34 And if ye lend to them of whom ye hope to receive, what thank have ye? for sinners also lend to sinners, to receive as much again. 35 <u>But love ye your enemies, and do good</u>, and lend, hoping for nothing again; and your reward shall be great, and ye shall be the children of the Highest: for he is kind unto the unthankful and to the evil. 36 Be ye therefore merciful, as your Father also is merciful."

Give in Secret

Mat 6:1 "Take heed that ye do not your alms *(compassion toward the poor)* before men, to be seen of them: otherwise ye have no reward of your Father which is in heaven. 2 Therefore when thou doest thine alms, do not sound a trumpet before thee, as the hypocrites do in the synagogues and in the streets, that they may have glory of men. Verily I say unto you; They have their reward. 3 But when thou doest alms, let not thy left hand know what thy right hand doeth: 4 That thine alms may be in secret: and thy Father which seeth in secret himself shall reward thee openly."

Pray in Secret

Mat 6:5 "And when thou prayest, thou shalt not be as the hypocrites are: for they love to pray standing in the synagogues and in the corners of the streets, that they may be seen of men. Verily I say unto you, they have their reward. 6 But thou, when thou prayest, enter into thy closet, and when thou hast shut thy door, pray to thy Father which is in secret; and thy Father which seeth in secret shall reward thee openly. 7 But when ye pray, use not vain repetitions, as the heathen do: for they think that they shall be heard for their much speaking. 8 Be not ye therefore like unto them: for your Father knoweth what things ye have need of, before ye ask him."

The Lord's Prayer.

1Chron 4:10. Jabez`s prayer is similar, he was born in hurt and named "to Grieve".

Mat 6:9 "After this manner therefore pray ye: Our Father which art in heaven; Hallowed be thy name. 10 Thy kingdom come. Thy will be done in earth, as it is in heaven. 11 Give us this day our daily bread. 12 And forgive us our debts *(G3783 Opheilema, something owed)*, as we forgive our debtors. 13 And lead us not into temptation, but deliver us from evil: For thine is the kingdom, and the power, and the glory, for ever. Amen."

Mat 6:14 "For if ye forgive men their trespasses, your heavenly Father will also forgive you: 15 But if ye forgive not men their trespasses, neither will your Father forgive your trespasses." *(G3900 Paraptoma; falls)*

The Lord's Prayer. (Also Taught in Judea)

Luk 11:1 Jesus repeats the beatitudes and this sermon in Mary`s town of Bethany and as he gets closer to Jerusalem. I believe that many different people and disciples would have asked Him the same questions many times, in many different places throughout the Lord's time preaching.

Luk 11:1 And it came to pass, that, as he was praying in a certain place, when he ceased, one of his disciples said unto him; "Lord, teach us to pray, as John also taught his disciples."

Luk 11:2 And he said unto them; "When ye pray, say, Our Father which art in heaven; Hallowed be thy name. Thy kingdom come; Thy will be done, as in heaven, so in earth. 3 Give us day by day our daily bread. 4 And forgive us our sins *(G266 Hamartia, offences)*; for we also forgive every one that is indebted to us. And lead us not into temptation; but deliver us from evil."

Luk 11:5 And he said unto them; "Which of you shall have a friend, and shall go unto him at midnight, and say unto him, Friend, lend me three loaves; 6 For a friend of mine in his journey is come to me, and I have nothing to set before him? 7 And he from within shall answer and say "Trouble me not: the door is now shut, and my children are with me in bed; I cannot rise and give thee. 8 I say unto you;" Though he will not rise and give him, because he is his friend, yet because of his importunity *(annoying persistence)* he will rise and give him as many as he needeth." **Proverbs 3:28,29.**

Fast in Secret (Isaiah 58; Zec 7)

Mat 6:16 "Moreover when ye fast, be not, as the hypocrites, of a sad countenance: for they disfigure their faces, that they may appear unto men to fast. Verily I say unto you, they have their reward. 17 But thou, when thou fastest, anoint thine head, and wash thy face; 18 That thou appear not unto men to fast, but unto thy Father which is in secret: and thy Father, which seeth in secret, shall reward thee openly."

Lay Up Treasures in Heaven. *Deut 15:9,10*

The eyes are the windows to the soul, (Shakespeare). Not in bible but true, a good servant watched the hands and eyes of the king and knew exactly what he wanted. Ps 123:2, Ps 32:8.

Mat 6:19 "Lay not up for yourselves treasures upon earth, where moth and rust doth corrupt, and where thieves break through and steal: 20 But lay up for yourselves treasures in heaven, where neither moth nor rust doth corrupt, and where thieves do not break through nor steal: 21 For where your treasure is, there will your heart be also. 22 The light of the body is the eye: if therefore thine eye be single, thy whole body shall be full of light. 23 But if thine eye be evil, thy whole body shall be full of darkness. If therefore the light that is in thee be darkness, how great is that darkness! 24 No man can serve two masters: for either he will hate the one, and love the other; or else he will hold to the one, and despise the other. Ye cannot serve God and mammon."

Faithful in little. Judea

Luk 16:10 "He that is faithful in that which is least is faithful also in much: and he that is unjust in the least is unjust also in much. 11 If therefore ye have not been faithful in the unrighteous mammon, who will commit to your trust the true riches? 12 And if ye have not been faithful in that which is another man's, who shall give you that which is your own? 13 No servant can serve two masters: for either he will hate the one, and love the other; or else he will hold to the one, and despise the other. Ye cannot serve God and mammon."

Do Not Be Anxious. Pro 3:5,6. Philippians 4:19

(Trust the Lord even to death. Like Elijah, Job and Jesus did. Job 13:15, 1Kings 17:6)

Mat 6:25 "Therefore I say unto you; Take no thought for your life, what ye shall eat, or what ye shall drink; nor yet for your body, what ye shall put on. Is not the life more than meat, and the body than raiment? 26 Behold the fowls of the air: for they sow not, neither do they reap, nor gather into barns; yet your heavenly Father feedeth them. Are ye not much better than they? 27 Which of you by taking thought can add one cubit unto his stature? 28 And why take ye thought for raiment? <u>Consider the lilies</u> of the field, how they grow; they toil not, neither do they spin: 29 And yet I say unto you; That even Solomon in all his glory was not arrayed like one of these. 30 Wherefore, if God so clothe the grass of the field, which today is, and tomorrow is cast into the oven, shall he not much more clothe you, O ye of little faith? 31 Therefore take no thought, saying; What shall we eat? or, what shall we drink? Or; Wherewithal shall we be clothed? 32 (For after all these things do the Gentiles seek:) <u>for your heavenly Father knoweth that ye have need of all these things</u>."

Do Not Be Anxious. Judea

Luk 12:22 And he said unto his disciples; "Therefore I say unto you, take no thought for your life, what ye shall eat; neither for the body, what ye shall put on. 23 The life is more than meat, and the body is more than raiment. 24 Consider the ravens: for they neither sow nor reap; which neither have storehouse nor barn; and God feedeth them: how much more are ye better than the fowls? 25 And which of you with taking thought can add to his stature one cubit? 26 If ye then be not able to do that thing which is least, why take ye thought for the rest? 27 <u>Consider the lilies</u> how they grow: they toil not, they spin not; and yet I say unto you, that Solomon in all his glory was not arrayed like one of these. 28 If then God so clothe the grass, which is to day in the field, and tomorrow is cast into the oven; how much more will he clothe you, O ye of little faith? 29 And seek not ye what ye shall eat, or what ye shall drink, neither be ye of doubtful mind. 30 For all these things do the nations of the world seek after: <u>and your Father knoweth that ye have need of these things</u>."

Seek First the Kingdom of God Luk 17:20, Rom 14:17

Mat 6:33 "<u>But seek ye first the kingdom of God,</u> and his righteousness; and all these things shall be added unto you. 34 Take therefore no thought for the morrow: for the morrow shall take thought for the things of itself. Sufficient unto the day is the evil thereof."

Seek First the Kingdom of God. Luk 17:20, Rom 14:17. Judea

Luk 12:31 <u>But rather seek ye the kingdom of God;</u> and all these things shall be added unto you. 32 Fear not, little flock; for it is your Father's good pleasure to give you the kingdom. 33 Sell that ye have, and give alms; provide yourselves bags which wax not old, a treasure in the heavens that faileth not, where no thief approacheth, neither moth corrupteth. 34 For where your treasure is, there will your heart be also."

The Mote

Mat 7:1 "Judge not, that ye be not judged. 2 For with what judgment ye judge, ye shall be judged: and with what measure ye mete, it shall be measured to you again. 3 And why beholdest thou the mote that is in thy brother's eye, but considerest not the beam that is in thine own eye? 4 Or how wilt thou say to thy brother, let me pull out the mote out of thine eye; and, behold, a beam is in thine own eye? 5 Thou hypocrite, first cast out the beam out of thine own eye; and then shalt thou see clearly to cast out the mote out of thy brother's eye. 6 Give not that which is holy unto the dogs, neither cast ye your pearls before swine, lest they trample them under their feet, and turn again and rend you."

The Mote

Luk 6:37 "Judge not, and ye shall not be judged: condemn not, and ye shall not be condemned: forgive, and ye shall be forgiven: 38 Give, and it shall be given unto you; good measure, pressed down, and shaken together, and running over, shall men give into your bosom. For with the same measure that ye mete withal it shall be measured to you again."

Luk 6:39 And he spake a parable unto them; "Can the blind lead the blind? shall they not both fall into the ditch? 40 The disciple is not above his master: but every one that is perfect shall be as his master. 41 And why beholdest thou the mote that is in thy brother's eye, but perceivest not the beam that is in thine own eye? 42 Either how canst thou say to thy brother, Brother, let me pull out the mote that is in thine eye, when thou thyself beholdest not the beam that is in thine own eye? Thou hypocrite, cast out first the beam out of thine own eye, and then shalt thou see clearly to pull out the mote that is in thy brother's eye."

Ask, It Will Be Given Luk 11:9

Mat 7:7 "Ask, and it shall be given you; seek, and ye shall find; knock, and it shall be opened unto you: 8 For everyone that asketh receiveth; and he that seeketh findeth; and to him that knocketh it shall be opened. 9 Or what man is there of you, whom if his son ask bread, will he give him a stone? 10 Or if he ask a fish, will he give him a serpent? 11 If ye then, being evil, know how to give good gifts unto your children, how much more shall your Father which is in heaven give good things to them that ask him?"

Ask and it Will be Given. Judea.

Luk 11:9 "And I say unto you, Ask, and it shall be given you; seek, and ye shall find; knock, and it shall be opened unto you. 10 For every one that asketh receiveth; and he that seeketh findeth; and to him that knocketh it shall be opened. 11 If a son shall ask bread of any of you that is a father, will he give him a stone? or if he ask a fish, will he for a fish give him a serpent? 12 Or if he shall ask an egg, will he offer him a scorpion? 13 If ye then, being evil, know how to give good gifts unto your children: how much more shall your heavenly Father give the Holy Spirit to them that ask him?"

Do to others as you want done to you

Mat 7:12 "Therefore all things whatsoever ye would that men should do to you, do ye even so to them: for this is the law and the prophets. 13 Enter ye in at the strait gate: for wide is the gate, and broad is the way, that leadeth to destruction, and many there be which go in thereat: 14 Because strait is the gate, and narrow is the way, which leadeth unto life, and few there be that find it."

Beware False Prophets. They Act Like Wolves

Mat 7:15 "Beware of false prophets, which come to you in sheep's clothing, but inwardly they are ravening wolves. 16 Ye shall know them by their fruits. Do men gather grapes of thorns, or figs of thistles? 17 Even so every good tree bringeth forth good fruit; but a corrupt tree bringeth forth evil fruit. 18 A good tree cannot bring forth evil fruit, neither can a corrupt tree bring forth good fruit. 19 Every tree that bringeth not forth good fruit is hewn down and cast into the fire. 20 Wherefore by their fruits ye shall know them." *(James 3:10-12)*

Obedience is Proof of Salvation

Mat 7:21 "Not everyone that saith unto me, Lord, Lord, shall enter into the kingdom of heaven; but he that doeth the will of my Father which is in heaven. 22 Many will say to me in that day, Lord, Lord, have we not prophesied in thy name? and in thy name have cast out devils? and in thy name done many wonderful works? 23 And then will I profess unto them, I never knew you: depart from me, ye that work iniquity." *(Ps 6:8)*

Build Your House on the Rock of Jesus. Ps 18:2 Luke 6:46, James 2:20, Heb 11:6.

Mat 7:24 "Therefore whosoever heareth these sayings of mine, and doeth them, I will liken him unto a wise man, which built his house upon a rock: 25 And the rain descended, and the floods came, and the winds blew, and beat upon that house; and it fell not: for it was founded upon a rock. 26 And every one that heareth these sayings of mine, and doeth them not, shall be likened unto a foolish man, which built his house upon the sand: 27 And the rain descended, and the floods came, and the winds blew, and beat upon that house; and it fell: and great was the fall of it."

Mat 7:28 And it came to pass, when Jesus had ended these sayings, the people were astonished at his doctrine:

Mat 7:29 For he taught them as one having authority, and not as the scribes.

Build Your House on the Rock, *Ps 18:2*

Luk 6:46 "And why call ye me, Lord, Lord, and do not the things which I say? 47 Whosoever cometh to me, and heareth my sayings, and doeth them, I will shew you to whom he is like: 48 He is like a man which built an house, and digged deep, and laid the foundation on a rock: and when the flood arose, the stream beat vehemently upon that house, and could not shake it: for it was founded upon a rock. 49 But he that heareth, and doeth not, is like a man that without a foundation built an house upon the earth; against which the stream did beat vehemently, and immediately it fell; and the ruin of that house was great."

Jesus Cleanses a Leper

Mat 8:1 When he was come down from the mountain, great multitudes followed him.

Mat 8:2 And, behold, there came a leper and worshipped him, saying; "Lord, if thou wilt, thou canst make me clean."

Mat 8:3 And Jesus put forth his hand, and touched him, saying; "I will; be thou clean." And immediately his leprosy was cleansed.

Mat 8:4 And Jesus saith unto him; "See thou tell no man; but go thy way, shew thyself to the priest, and offer the gift that Moses commanded, for a testimony unto them."

Jesus Cleanses a Leper

Mar 1:40 And there came a leper to him, beseeching him, and kneeling down to him, and saying unto him; "If thou wilt, thou canst make me clean."

Mar 1:41 And Jesus, moved with compassion, put forth his hand, and touched him, and saith unto him; "I will; be thou clean."

Mar 1:42 And as soon as he had spoken, immediately the leprosy departed from him, and he was cleansed.

Mar 1:43 And he straitly charged him, and forthwith sent him away;

Mar 1:44 And saith unto him; "See thou say nothing to any man: but go thy way, shew thyself to the priest, and offer for thy cleansing those things which Moses commanded, for a testimony unto them."

Mar 1:45 But he went out, and began to publish *(proclaim)* it much, and to blaze abroad the matter, insomuch that Jesus could no more openly enter into the city, but was without in desert places: and they came to him from every quarter.

Jesus Cleanses a Leper

Luk 5:12 And it came to pass, when he was in a certain city, behold a man full of leprosy: who seeing Jesus fell on his face, and besought him, saying; Lord, if thou wilt, thou canst make me clean.

Luk 5:13 And he put forth his hand, and touched him, saying; "<u>I will: be thou clean</u>." And immediately the leprosy departed from him.

Luk 5:14 And he charged him to tell no man: but go, and shew thyself to the priest, and offer for thy cleansing, according as Moses commanded, for a testimony unto them.

Luk 5:15 But so much the more went there a fame abroad of him: and great multitudes came together to hear, and to be healed by him of their infirmities.

Luk 5:16 And he withdrew himself into the wilderness and prayed.

Back to Capernaum

The Great Faith of a Centurion

Mat 8:5 And when Jesus was entered into Capernaum, there came unto him a centurion, beseeching him,

Mat 8:6 And saying; "Lord, my servant lieth at home sick of the palsy, grievously tormented."

Mat 8:7 And Jesus saith unto him; "I will come and heal him."

Mat 8:8 The centurion answered and said; "Lord, I am not worthy that thou shouldest come under my roof: but speak the word only, and my servant shall be healed. 9 For I am a man under authority, having soldiers under me: and I say to this man, Go, and he goeth; and to another, Come, and he cometh; and to my servant, Do this, and he doeth it."

Mat 8:10 When Jesus heard it, he marvelled, and said to them that followed; "<u>Verily I say unto you, I have not found so great faith, no, not in Israel.</u> 11 And I say unto you; That many shall come from the east and west, and shall sit down with Abraham, and Isaac, and Jacob, in the kingdom of heaven. 12 But the children of the kingdom shall be cast out into outer darkness: there shall be weeping and gnashing of teeth."

Mat 8:13 And Jesus said unto the centurion; "Go thy way; and as thou hast believed, so be it done unto thee. And his servant was healed in the selfsame hour."

The Great Faith of a Centurion

Luk 7:1 Now when he had ended all his sayings in the audience of the people, he entered into Capernaum.

Luk 7:2 And a certain centurion's servant, who was dear unto him, was sick, and ready to die.

Luk 7:3 And when he heard of Jesus, he sent unto him the elders of the Jews, beseeching him that he would come and heal his servant.

Luk 7:4 And when they came to Jesus, they besought him instantly, saying; "That he was worthy for whom he should do this: 5 For he loveth our nation, and he hath built us a synagogue."

Luk 7:6 Then Jesus went with them. And when he was now not far from the house, the centurion sent friends to him, saying unto him; "Lord, trouble not thyself: for I am not worthy that thou shouldest enter under my roof: 7 Wherefore neither thought I myself worthy to come unto thee: but say in a word, and my servant shall be healed. 8 For I also am a man set under authority, having under me soldiers, and I say unto one, Go, and he goeth; and to another, Come, and he cometh; and to my servant, Do this, and he doeth it."

Luk 7:9 When Jesus heard these things, he marvelled at him, and turned him about, and said unto the people that followed him; "I say unto you, I have not found so great faith, no, not in Israel."

Luk 7:10 And they that were sent, returning to the house, found the servant whole that had been sick.

City Called Nain

40 klms southwest of Capernaum

Jesus Raises a Widow's Son

Luk 7:11 And it came to pass the day after, that he went into a city called Nain; and many of his disciples went with him, and much people.

Luk 7:12 Now when he came nigh to the gate of the city, behold, there was a dead man carried out, the only son of his mother, and she was a widow: and much people of the city was with her.

Luk 7:13 And when the Lord saw her, he had compassion on her, and said unto her; "Weep not."

Luk 7:14 And he came and touched the bier: and they that bare him stood still. And he said; "Young man, I say unto thee, Arise."

Luk 7:15 And he that was dead sat up and began to speak. And he delivered him to his mother.

Luk 7:16 And there came a fear on all: and they glorified God, saying; "That a great prophet is risen up among us;" and; "That God hath visited his people." *(Isa 9:6, Mat 1:23 Isa 7:14)*

Luk 7:17 And this rumour of him went forth throughout all Judaea, and throughout all the region round about.

Back to Capernaum

Jesus Heals Peter`s Mother in-law

Mat 8:14 And when Jesus was come into Peter's house, he saw his wife's mother laid, and sick of a fever.

Mat 8:15 And he touched her hand, and the fever left her: and she arose, and ministered unto them.

Mat 8:16 When the even was come, they brought unto him many that were possessed with devils: and he cast out the spirits with his word, and healed all that were sick:

Mat 8:17 That it might be fulfilled which was spoken by Esaias the prophet, saying; "Himself took our infirmities, and bare our sicknesses." (Isaiah 53)

Jesus Heals Peter`s mother in-law.

Mar 1:29 And forthwith, when they were come out of the synagogue, they entered into the house of Simon and Andrew, with James and John.

Mar 1:30 But Simon's wife's mother lay sick of a fever, and anon they tell him of her.

Mar 1:31 And he came and took her by the hand, and lifted her up; and immediately the fever left her, and she ministered unto them.

Jesus heals Peters Mother-in-Law

Luk 4:38 And he arose out of the synagogue, and entered into Simon's house. And Simon's wife's mother was taken with a great fever; and they besought him for her.

Luk 4:39 And he stood over her, and rebuked the fever; and it left her: and immediately she arose and ministered unto them.

Jesus Ministers to Many

Mar 1:32 And at even, when the sun did set, they brought unto him all that were diseased, and them that were possessed with devils.

Mar 1:33 And all the city was gathered together at the door.

Mar 1:34 And he healed many that were sick of divers diseases and cast out many devils; and suffered not the devils to speak, because they knew him.

Jesus rises early to pray

Mar 1:35 And in the morning, rising up a great while before day, he went out, and departed into a solitary place, and there prayed.

Mar 1:36 And Simon and they that were with him followed after him.

Mar 1:37 And when they had found him, they said unto him, "All men seek for thee."

Mar 1:38 And he said unto them, "Let us go into the next towns, that I may preach there also: for therefore came I forth."

Mar 1:39 And he preached in their synagogues throughout all Galilee and cast out devils.

Jesus says Follow

Mat 8:18 Now when Jesus saw great multitudes about him, he gave commandment to depart unto the other side.

Mat 8:19 And a certain scribe came, and said unto him; "Master, I will follow thee whithersoever thou goest."

Mat 8:20 And Jesus saith unto him; "The foxes have holes, and the birds of the air have nests; but the Son of man hath not where to lay his head."

Mat 8:21 And another of his disciples said unto him; "Lord, suffer me first to go and bury my father."

Mat 8:22 But Jesus said unto him; "Follow me; and let the dead bury their dead."

Jesus says Follow

Luk 9:57 And it came to pass, that, as they went in the way, a certain man said unto him; "Lord, I will follow thee whithersoever thou goest."

Luk 9:58 And Jesus said unto him; "Foxes have holes, and birds of the air have nests; but the Son of man hath not where to lay his head."

Luk 9:59 And he said unto another; "Follow me." But he said; "Lord, suffer me first to go and bury my father."

Luk 9:60 Jesus said unto him; "Let the dead bury their dead: but go thou and preach the kingdom of God."

Luk 9:61 And another also said; "Lord, I will follow thee; but let me first go bid them farewell, which are at home at my house."

Luk 9:62 And Jesus said unto him; "No man, having put his hand to the plough, and looking back, is fit for the kingdom of God."

Heading Across the Sea of Galilee to Gergesenes.

Jesus Calms a Storm (Psa 107:27-29 Psa 89:9)

Mat 8:23 And when he was entered into a ship, his disciples followed him.

Mat 8:24 And, behold, there arose a great tempest in the sea, insomuch that the ship was covered with the waves: but he was asleep.

Mat 8:25 And his disciples came to him, and awoke him, saying; "Lord, save us: we perish."

Mat 8:26 And he saith unto them; "Why are ye fearful, O ye of little faith?" Then he arose, and rebuked the winds and the sea; and there was a great calm.

Mat 8:27 But the men marvelled, saying; "What manner of man is this, that even the winds and the sea obey him!"

Jesus Calms a Storm (Psa 107:27-29, Psa 89:9)

Mar 4:35 And the same day, when the even was come, he saith unto them; "Let us pass over unto the other side."

Mar 4:36 And when they had sent away the multitude, they took him even as he was in the ship. And there were also with him other little ships.

Mar 4:37 And there arose a great storm of wind, and the waves beat into the ship, so that it was now full.

Mar 4:38 And he was in the hinder part of the ship, asleep on a pillow: and they awake him, and say unto him; "Master, carest thou not that we perish?"

Mar 4:39 And he arose, and rebuked the wind, and said unto the sea; "Peace, be still." And the wind ceased, and there was a great calm.

Mar 4:40 And he said unto them; "Why are ye so fearful? how is it that ye have no faith?"

Mar 4:41 And they feared exceedingly, and said one to another; "What manner of man is this, that even the wind and the sea obey him?"

Jesus Calms a Storm

Luk 8:22 Now it came to pass on a certain day, that he went into a ship with his disciples: and he said unto them; "Let us go over unto the other side of the lake." And they launched forth.

Luk 8:23 But as they sailed he fell asleep: and there came down a storm of wind on the lake; and they were filled with water, and were in jeopardy.

Luk 8:24 And they came to him, and awoke him, saying; "Master, master, we perish." Then he arose, and rebuked the wind and the raging of the water: and they ceased, and there was a calm.

Luk 8:25 And he said unto them; "Where is your faith?" And they being afraid wondered, saying one to another, "What manner of man is this! for he commandeth even the winds and water, and they obey him."

Country of Gergesenes SW end of the Sea of Galilee

Jesus casts out Legion to Pigs, the man preaches in Decapolis

This happened before Matthew was called, Matt 9:9, and was not an eye witness, possibly why he states 2 men, common to Mathew's gospel, although John wrote Jesus did so many works so many that there wouldn't be enough books in the world. John 21:25. Facts are, it still happened, whether 1 or 2 it doesn't matter and is not a contradiction.

Mat 8:28 And when he was come to the other side into the country of the Gergesenes, there met him two possessed with devils, coming out of the tombs, exceeding fierce, so that no man might pass by that way.

Mat 8:29 And, behold, they cried out, saying; "What have we to do with thee, Jesus, thou Son of God? art thou come hither to torment us before the time?"

Mat 8:30 And there was a good way off from them an herd of many swine feeding.

Mat 8:31 So the devils besought him, saying; "If thou cast us out, suffer us to go away into the herd of swine."

Mat 8:32 And he said unto them; "Go." And when they were come out, they went into the herd of swine: and, behold, the whole herd of swine ran violently down a steep place into the sea, and perished in the waters.

Mat 8:33 And they that kept them fled, and went their ways into the city, and told everything, and what was befallen to the possessed of the devils.

Mat 8:34 And, behold, the whole city came out to meet Jesus: and when they saw him, they besought him that he would depart out of their coasts.

<u>Jesus casts out Legion to Pigs, the man preaches in Decapolis</u>

Mar 5:1 And they came over unto the other side of the sea, into the country of the Gadarenes.

Mar 5:2 And when he was come out of the ship, immediately there met him <u>out of the tombs</u> a man with an unclean spirit,

Mar 5:3 Who had his dwelling among the tombs; and no man could bind him, no, not with chains:

Mar 5:4 Because that he had been often bound with fetters and chains, and the chains had been plucked asunder by him, and the fetters broken in pieces: neither could any man tame him.

Mar 5:5 And always, night and day, he was in the mountains, and in the tombs, crying, and cutting himself with stones.

Mar 5:6 But when he saw Jesus afar off, he ran and worshipped him,

Mar 5:7 And cried with a loud voice, and said; "<u>What have I to do with thee</u>, Jesus, thou Son of the Most-High God? I adjure thee by God, that thou torment me not."

Mar 5:8 For he said unto him; "Come out of the man, thou unclean spirit."

Mar 5:9 And he asked him; "What is thy name?" And he answered, saying; "My name is Legion: for we are many."

Mar 5:10 And he besought him much that he would not send them away out of the country.

Mar 5:11 Now there was there nigh unto the mountains a <u>great herd of swine feeding</u>.

Mar 5:12 And all the devils besought him, saying; "Send us into the swine, that we may enter into them."

Mar 5:13 And forthwith Jesus gave them leave. And the unclean spirits went out and entered into the swine: and the herd ran violently down a steep place into the sea, (they were about two thousand;) and were choked in the sea.

Mar 5:14 And they that fed the swine fled, and told it in the city, and in the country. And they went out to see what it was that was done.

Mar 5:15 And they come to Jesus, and see him that was possessed with the devil, and had the legion, sitting, and clothed, and in his right mind: and they were afraid.

Mar 5:16 And they that saw it told them how it befell to him that was possessed with the devil, and also concerning the swine.

Mar 5:17 And they began to pray him to depart out of their coasts.

Mar 5:18 And when he was come into the ship, he that had been possessed with the devil prayed him that he might be with him.

Mar 5:19 Howbeit Jesus suffered him not, but saith unto him; "Go home to thy friends, and tell them how great things the Lord hath done for thee, and hath had compassion on thee."

Mar 5:20 And he departed, and began to publish in Decapolis how great things Jesus had done for him: and all men did marvel.

<u>Jesus casts out Legion to Pigs, the man preaches in Decapolis</u>

Luk 8:26 And they arrived at the country of the Gadarenes, which is over against Galilee.

Luk 8:27 And when he went forth to land, there met him out of the city a certain man, which had devils long time, and ware no clothes, neither abode in any house, <u>but in the tombs.</u>

Luk 8:28 When he saw Jesus, he cried out, and fell down before him, and with a loud voice said; "What have I to do with thee, Jesus, thou Son of God most high? I beseech thee, torment me not."

Luk 8:29 (For he had commanded the unclean spirit to come out of the man. For oftentimes it had caught him: and he was kept bound with chains and in fetters; and he brake the bands, and was driven of the devil into the wilderness.)

Luk 8:30 And Jesus asked him, saying; "What is thy name?" And he said; "Legion:" because many devils *(G1140 Daimonion, Daemonic being, comprised of Deity and onion representing many layers.)* were entered into him.

Luk 8:31 And they besought him that he would not command them to go out into the deep.

Luk 8:32 And there was there an herd of many swine feeding on the mountain: and they besought him that he would suffer them to enter into them. And he suffered them.

Luk 8:33 Then went the devils out of the man, and entered into the swine: and the herd ran violently down a steep place into the lake, and were choked.

Luk 8:34 When they that fed them saw what was done, they fled, and went and told it in the city and in the country.

Luk 8:35 Then they went out to see what was done; and came to Jesus, and found the man, out of whom the devils were departed, sitting at the feet of Jesus, clothed, and in his right mind: and they were afraid.

Luk 8:36 They also which saw it told them by what means he that was possessed of the devils was healed.

Luk 8:37 Then the whole multitude of the country of the Gadarenes round about besought him to depart from them; for they were taken with great fear: and he went up into the ship, and returned back again.

Luk 8:38 Now the man out of whom the devils were departed besought him that he might be with him: but Jesus sent him away, saying;

Luk 8:39 "Return to thine own house, and shew how great things God hath done unto thee." And he went his way, and published *(preached)* throughout the whole city how great things Jesus had done unto him.

Back to Capernaum "Jesus in the House"

Jesus Heals a man with Palsy, forgiving his sins.

Mat 9:1 And he entered into a ship, and passed over, and came into his own city.

Mat 9:2 And, behold, they brought to him a man sick of the palsy, lying on a bed: and Jesus seeing their faith said unto the sick of the palsy; "Son, be of good cheer; thy sins be forgiven thee."

Mat 9:3 And, behold, certain of the scribes said within themselves; "This man blasphemeth."

Mat 9:4 And Jesus knowing their thoughts said; "Wherefore think ye evil in your hearts? 5 For whether is easier, to say, thy sins be forgiven thee; or to say, Arise, and walk? 6 But that ye may know that the Son of man hath power on earth to forgive sins," (then saith he to the sick of the palsy;) "Arise, take up thy bed, and go unto thine house."

Mat 9:7 And he arose, and departed to his house.

Mat 9:8 But when the multitudes saw it, they marvelled, and glorified God, which had given such power unto men.

Jesus Heals a man of Palsy, forgiving his sins. "Jesus in the House"

Mar 2:1 And again he entered into Capernaum after some days; and it was noised that he was in the house.

Mar 2:2 And straightway many were gathered together, insomuch that there was no room to receive them, no, not so much as about the door: and he preached the word unto them.

Mar 2:3 And they come unto him, bringing one sick of the palsy, which was borne of four.

Mar 2:4 And when they could not come nigh unto him for the press, they uncovered the roof where he was: and when they had broken it up, they let down the bed wherein the sick of the palsy lay.

Mar 2:5 When Jesus saw their faith, he said unto the sick of the palsy; "Son, thy sins be forgiven thee."

Mar 2:6 But there were certain of the scribes sitting there, and reasoning in their hearts; 7 "Why doth this man thus speak blasphemies? who can forgive sins but God only?"

Mar 2:8 And immediately when Jesus perceived in his spirit that they so reasoned within themselves, he said unto them; "Why reason ye these things in your hearts? 9 Whether is it easier to say to the sick of the palsy; Thy sins be forgiven thee; or to say, Arise, and take up thy bed, and walk? 10 But that ye may know that the Son of man hath power on earth to forgive sins," (he saith to the sick of the palsy;)

Mar 2:11 "I say unto thee, Arise, and take up thy bed, and go thy way into thine house."

Mar 2:12 And immediately he arose, took up the bed, and went forth before them all; insomuch that they were all amazed, and glorified God, saying; "We never saw it on this fashion."

<u>Jesus Heals a man of Palsy, forgiving his sins.</u>

Luk 5:17 And it came to pass on a certain day, as he was teaching, that there were Pharisees and doctors of the law sitting by, which were come out of every town of Galilee, and Judaea, and Jerusalem: and the power of the Lord was present to heal them.

Luk 5:18 And, behold, men brought in a bed a man which was taken with a palsy: and <u>they</u> sought means to bring him in, and to lay him before him.

Luk 5:19 And <u>when they</u> could not find by what way they might bring him in because of the multitude, they went upon the housetop and let him down through the tiling with his couch into the midst before Jesus.

Luk 5:20 And when he saw their faith, he said unto him; "Man, thy sins are forgiven thee."

Luk 5:21 And the scribes and the Pharisees began to reason, saying; "Who is this which speaketh blasphemies? Who can forgive sins, but God alone?"

Luk 5:22 But when Jesus perceived their thoughts, he answering said unto them; "What reason ye in your hearts? 23. Whether is easier, to say; Thy sins be forgiven thee; or to say; Rise up and walk? 24. But that ye may know that the Son of man hath power upon earth to forgive sins", (he said unto the sick of the palsy;) "I say unto thee, Arise, and take up thy couch, and go into thine house."

Luk 5:25 And immediately he rose up before them, and took up that whereon he lay, and departed to his own house, glorifying God.

Luk 5:26 And they were all amazed, and they glorified God, and were filled with fear, saying; "We have seen strange things today."

Seaside of Galilee, Capernaum

Matthew Follows

(Matthew calls himself Matthew by name, but the other Gospels call him Levi reminding us of his old life and Jewish ties)

Mat 9:9 And as Jesus passed forth from thence, he saw a man, named Matthew, sitting at the receipt of custom: and he saith unto him; "Follow me." And he arose, and followed him.

Mat 9:10 And it came to pass, as Jesus sat at meat in the house, behold, many publicans and sinners came and sat down with him and his disciples.

Mat 9:11 And when the Pharisees saw it, they said unto his disciples; "Why eateth your Master with publicans and sinners?"

Mat 9:12 But when Jesus heard that, he said unto them; "They that be whole need not a physician, but they that are sick. 13 But go ye and learn what that meaneth, I will have mercy, and not sacrifice: for I am not come to call the righteous, but sinners to repentance."

Levi AKA Matthew Follows.

Mar 2:13 And he went forth again by the seaside and all the multitude resorted unto him, and he taught them.

Mar 2:14 And as he passed by, he saw Levi the son of Alphaeus sitting at the receipt of custom, and said unto him; "Follow me". And he arose and followed him.

Levi, AKA, Matthew Follows.

Luk 5:27 And after these things he went forth, and saw a publican, named Levi, sitting at the receipt of custom: and he said unto him; "Follow me."

Luk 5:28 And he left all, rose up, and followed him.

Matthew's Feast of Repentance

Mar 2:15 And it came to pass, that, as Jesus sat at meat in his house, many publicans and sinners sat also together with Jesus and his disciples: for there were many, and they followed him.

Mar 2:16 And when the scribes and Pharisees saw him eat with publicans and sinners, they said unto his disciples; "How is it that he eateth and drinketh with publicans and sinners?"

Mar 2:17 When Jesus heard it, he saith unto them, "They that are whole have no need of the physician, but they that are sick: I came not to call the righteous, but sinners to repentance."

Matthew's Feast of Repentance

Luk 5:29 And Levi made him a great feast in his own house: and there was a great company of publicans and of others that sat down with them.

Luk 5:30 But their scribes and Pharisees murmured against his disciples, saying; "Why do ye eat and drink with publicans and sinners?"

Luk 5:31 And Jesus answering said unto them; "They that are whole need not a physician; but they that are sick. 32. I came not to call the righteous, but sinners to repentance."

New Cloth, New Wine

Mat 9:14 Then came to him the disciples of John, saying; "Why do we and the Pharisees fast oft, but thy disciples fast not?"

Mat 9:15 And Jesus said unto them; "Can the children of the bridechamber mourn, as long as the bridegroom is with them? but the days will come, when the bridegroom shall be taken from them, and then shall they fast. 16 No man putteth a piece of new cloth unto an old garment, for that which is put in to fill it up taketh from the garment, and the rent is made worse. 17 Neither do men put new wine into old bottles: else the bottles break, and the wine runneth out, and the bottles perish: but they put new wine into new bottles, and both are preserved."

New Cloth, New Wine

Mar 2:18 And the disciples of John and of the Pharisees used to fast: and they come and say unto him, "Why do the disciples of John and of the Pharisees fast, but thy disciples fast not?"

Mar 2:19 And Jesus said unto them; "Can the children of the bridechamber fast, while the bridegroom is with them? as long as they have the bridegroom with them, they cannot fast. 20 But the days will come, when the bridegroom shall be taken away from them, and then shall they fast in those days. 21 No man also seweth a piece of new cloth on an old garment: else the new piece that filled it up taketh away from the old, and the rent is made worse. 22 And no man putteth new wine into old bottles: else the new wine doth burst the bottles, and the wine is spilled, and the bottles will be marred: but new wine must be put into new bottles."

New Cloth New Wine

Luk 5:33 And they said unto him; "Why do the disciples of John fast often, and make prayers, and likewise the disciples of the Pharisees; but thine eat and drink?"

Luk 5:34 And he said unto them; "Can ye make the children of the bridechamber fast, while the bridegroom is with them? 35 But the days will come, when the bridegroom shall be taken away from them, and then shall they fast in those days."

Luk 5:36 And he spake also a parable unto them; "No man putteth a piece of a new garment upon an old; if otherwise, then both the new maketh a rent, and the piece that was taken out of the new agreeth not with the old. 37 And no man putteth new wine into old bottles; else the new wine will burst the bottles, and be spilled, and the bottles shall perish. 38 But new wine must be put into new bottles; and both are preserved. 39 No man also having drunk old wine straightway desireth new: for he saith; "The old is better.""

Ministering from Capernaum.

Jairus`s daughter Restored to Life and woman with the issue of blood Healed.

Mat 9:18 While he spake these things unto them, behold, there came a certain ruler, and worshipped him, saying; "My daughter is even now dead: but come and lay thy hand upon her, and she shall live."

Mat 9:19 And Jesus arose, and followed him, and so did his disciples.

Mat 9:20 And, behold, a woman, which was diseased with an issue of blood twelve years, came behind him, and touched the hem of his garment:

Mat 9:21 For she said within herself; "If I may but touch his garment, I shall be whole."

Mat 9:22 But Jesus turned him about, and when he saw her, he said; "Daughter, be of good comfort; thy faith hath made thee whole." And the woman was made whole from that hour.

Mat 9:23 And when Jesus came into the ruler's house, and saw the minstrels and the people making a noise,

Mat 9:24 He said unto them; "Give place: for the maid is not dead, but sleepeth." And they laughed him to scorn.

Mat 9:25 But when the people were put forth, he went in, and took her by the hand, and the maid arose.

Mat 9:26 And the fame hereof went abroad into all that land.

Jairus's Daughter and the Woman with Issue of Blood Healed

Mar 5:21 And when Jesus was passed over again by ship unto the other side, much people gathered unto him: and he was nigh unto the sea.

Mar 5:22 And, behold, there cometh one of the rulers of the synagogue, Jairus by name; and when he saw him, he fell at his feet,

Mar 5:23 And besought him greatly, saying; "My little daughter lieth at the point of death: I pray thee, come and lay thy hands on her, that she may be healed; and she shall live."

Mar 5:24 And Jesus went with him; and much people followed him, and thronged him.

Mar 5:25 And a certain woman, which had an issue of blood twelve years,

Mar 5:26 And had suffered many things of many physicians, and had spent all that she had, and was nothing bettered, but rather grew worse,

Mar 5:27 When she had heard of Jesus, came in the press behind, and touched his garment.

Mar 5:28 For she said; "If I may touch but his clothes, I shall be whole."

Mar 5:29 And straightway the fountain of her blood was dried up; and she felt in her body that she was healed of that plague.

Mar 5:30 And Jesus, immediately knowing in himself that virtue had gone out of him, turned him about in the press, and said; "Who touched my clothes?"

Mar 5:31 And his disciples said unto him; "Thou seest the multitude thronging thee, and sayest thou, who touched me?"

Mar 5:32 And he looked round about to see her that had done this thing.

Mar 5:33 But the woman fearing and trembling, knowing what was done in her, came and fell down before him, and told him all the truth.

Mar 5:34 And he said unto her; "Daughter, thy faith hath made thee whole; go in peace, and be whole of thy plague."

Mar 5:35 While he yet spake, there came from the ruler of the synagogue's house certain which said; "Thy daughter is dead: why troublest thou the Master any further?"

Mar 5:36 As soon as Jesus heard the word that was spoken *(Num 30:5)*, he saith unto the ruler of the synagogue; "Be not afraid, only believe."

Mar 5:37 And he suffered no man to follow him, save Peter, and James, and John the brother of James.

Mar 5:38 And he cometh to the house of the ruler of the synagogue, and seeth the tumult, and them that wept and wailed greatly.

Mar 5:39 And when he was come in, he saith unto them; "Why make ye this ado, and weep? the damsel is not dead, but sleepeth."

Mar 5:40 And they laughed him to scorn. But when he had put them all out, he taketh the father and the mother of the damsel, and them that were with him, and entereth in where the damsel was lying.

Mar 5:41 And he took the damsel by the hand, and said unto her; "Talitha cumi;" *(Chaldee/Hebrew not Aramaic.)* which is, being interpreted; "Damsel, I say unto thee, arise."

Mar 5:42 And straightway the damsel arose, and walked; for she was of the age of twelve years. And they were astonished with a great astonishment.

Mar 5:43 And he charged them straitly that no man should know it; and commanded that something should be given her to eat.

Jairus's Daughter and the Woman with Issue of Blood Healed

Luk 8:40 And it came to pass, that, when Jesus was returned, the people gladly received him: for they were all waiting for him.

Luk 8:41 And, behold, there came a man named Jairus, and he was a ruler of the synagogue: and he fell down at Jesus' feet, and besought him that he would come into his house:

Luk 8:42 For he had one only daughter, <u>about twelve years of age</u>, and she lay a dying. But as he went the people thronged him.

Luk 8:43 And a woman having <u>an issue of blood twelve years</u>, which had spent all her living upon physicians, neither could be healed of any,

Luk 8:44 Came behind him and touched the border of his garment: and immediately her issue of blood stanched.

Luk 8:45 And Jesus said; "Who touched me?" When all denied, Peter and they that were with him said; "Master, the multitude throng thee and press thee, and sayest thou, "Who touched me?""

Luk 8:46 And Jesus said; "Somebody hath touched me: for I perceive that virtue is gone out of me."

Luk 8:47 And when the woman saw that she was not hid, she came trembling, and falling down before him, she declared unto him before all the people for what cause she had touched him, and how she was healed immediately.

Luk 8:48 And he said unto her; "Daughter, be of good comfort: thy faith hath made thee whole; go in peace."

Luk 8:49 While he yet spake, there cometh one from the ruler of the synagogue's house, saying to him; "Thy daughter is dead; trouble not the Master."

Luk 8:50 But when Jesus heard it, he answered him; saying; "Fear not: believe only, and she shall be made whole."

Luk 8:51 And when he came into the house, he suffered no man to go in, save Peter, and James, and John, and the father and the mother of the maiden.

Luk 8:52 And all wept, and bewailed her: but he said; "Weep not; she is not dead, but sleepeth."

Luk 8:53 And they laughed him to scorn, knowing that she was dead.

Luk 8:54 And he put them all out, and took her by the hand, and called, saying; "Maid, arise."

Luk 8:55 And her spirit came again, and she arose straightway: and he commanded to give her meat.

Luk 8:56 And her parents were astonished: but he charged them that they should tell no man what was done.

Leaving Capernaum

Jesus Heals Two Blind Men

Mat 9:27 And when Jesus departed thence, two blind men followed him, crying, and saying; "Thou Son of David, have mercy on us."

Mat 9:28 And when he was come into the house, the blind men came to him: and Jesus saith unto them; "Believe ye that I am able to do this?" They said unto him; "Yea, Lord."

Mat 9:29 Then touched he their eyes, saying; "According to your faith be it unto you."

Mat 9:30 And their eyes were opened; and Jesus straitly charged them, saying; "See that no man know it."

Mat 9:31 But they, when they were departed, spread abroad his fame in all that country.

Jesus Delivers a Dumb Man

Mat 9:32 As they went out, behold, they brought to him a dumb man possessed with a devil.

Mat 9:33 And when the devil was cast out, the dumb spake: and the multitudes marvelled, saying, "It was never so seen in Israel."

Mat 9:34 But the Pharisees said, "He casteth out devils through the prince of the devils."

Travelling Galilee

The Harvest is Truly Great, *Joel 3:12-14, Amos 9:13*

Mat 9:35 And Jesus went about all the cities and villages, teaching in their synagogues, and preaching the gospel of the kingdom, and healing every sickness and every disease among the people.

Mat 9:36 But when he saw the multitudes, he was moved with compassion on them, because they fainted, and were scattered abroad, as sheep having no shepherd.

Mat 9:37 Then saith he unto his disciples, "The harvest truly is plenteous, but the labourers are few; 38 Pray ye therefore the Lord of the harvest, that he will send forth labourers into his harvest."

The Harvest is Truly Great, Sends Another 70. *Joel 3:13*

Luk 10:1 After these things the Lord appointed other seventy also, and sent them two and two before his face into every city and place, whither he himself would come.

Luk 10:2 Therefore said he unto them; "The harvest truly is great, but the labourers are few: pray ye therefore the Lord of the harvest, that he would send forth labourers into his harvest.

The Twelve Apostles Named, Ordained and Empowered

(This is a common theme of how you know you have been called; The Holy Spirit will call you personally, salvation (Isa 49:16), will train you by experiences and the Word, (Rom 12:1,2) and once you know who you really are, He will empower you to serve His greater purposes. Acts 1:8, Rom 8:28-30) God uses people that know who they are in Him. I heard my calling in 2000 when I was calling out to Jesus in desperation; it also took me a few years to fully surrender.

Mat 10:1 And when he had called unto him his twelve disciples, he gave them power against unclean spirits, to cast them out, and to heal all manner of sickness and all manner of disease.

Mat 10:2 Now the names of the twelve apostles are these; The first, Simon, who is called Peter, and Andrew his brother; James the son of Zebedee, and John his brother;

Mat 10:3 Philip, and Bartholomew; Thomas, and Matthew the publican; James the son of Alphaeus, and Lebbaeus, whose surname was Thaddaeus;

Mat 10:4 Simon the Canaanite, and Judas Iscariot, who also betrayed him.

(This is what qualified Judas for the unforgivable sin, he was walking with Jesus, seeing and tasting of powers of the world to come. Heb 6:4,5. Many of us, included myself have thought that we have committed this ultimate sin, but in actual fact we have to be in full communion with God and Jesus and then betray him; which we have no way been that close to betray Jesus, satan is another example, full in the presence of God yet choosing the opposite, even Ahab repented. If the Holy Spirit is still convicting you of sin, then your conscience is not seared and you still have been given time to repent. Look at what Peter did and he still got accepted back and also Paul, all the murdering he was complicit to and then ordained an apostle to the gentiles. Repentance and pruning bring forth fruit and the fruit is for others to eat. Luk 18:9-14)

<u>The Twelve Apostles Named, Ordained and Empowered</u>

Look up the mountains of Galilee.

Mar 3:13 And he goeth <u>up into a mountain</u>, and calleth unto him whom he would: and they came unto him.

Mar 3:14 And he ordained twelve, that they should be with him, and that he might send them forth to preach, 15. And to have power to heal sicknesses, and to cast out devils:

Mar 3:16 And Simon he surnamed Peter;

Mar 3:17 And James the son of Zebedee, and John the brother of James; and he surnamed them Boanerges, which is, The sons of thunder:

Mar 3:18 And Andrew, and Philip, and Bartholomew, and Matthew, and Thomas, and James the son of Alphaeus, and Thaddaeus, and Simon the Canaanite,

Mar 3:19 And Judas Iscariot, which also betrayed him: and they went into an house.

<u>The Twelve Apostles Named, Ordained and Empowered</u>

Luk 6:12 And it came to pass in those days, that he <u>went out into a mountain</u> to pray, and continued all night in prayer to God.

Luk 6:13 And when it was day, he called unto him his disciples: and of them he chose twelve, whom also he named apostles;

Luk 6:14 Simon, (whom he also named Peter,) and Andrew his brother, James and John, Philip and Bartholomew,

Luk 6:15 Matthew and Thomas, James the son of Alphaeus, and Simon called Zelotes,

Luk 6:16 And Judas the brother of James, and Judas Iscariot, which also was the traitor.

Jesus Sends the Twelve Apostles and Empowers them

Mat 10:5 These twelve Jesus sent forth, and commanded them, saying; "Go not into the way of the Gentiles, and into any city of the Samaritans enter ye not: 6 But go rather to the lost sheep of the house of Israel. 7 And as ye go, preach, saying; The kingdom of heaven is at hand. 8 Heal the sick, cleanse the lepers, raise the dead, cast out devils: freely ye have received, freely give.

The Workman is worthy of His Food

Mat 10:9 Provide neither gold, nor silver, nor brass in your purses, 10 Nor scrip for your journey, neither two coats, neither shoes, nor yet staves: for the workman is worthy of his meat *(Food). (Luk 10:7)*. 11 And into whatsoever city or town ye shall enter, enquire who in it is worthy; and there abide till ye go thence.

Given Power to hold Cities accountable

Matt 10:12 And when ye come into an house, salute it. 13 And if the house be worthy, let your peace come upon it: but if it be not worthy, let your peace return to you. 14 And whosoever shall not receive you, nor hear your words, when ye depart out of that house or city, shake off the dust of your feet. 15 Verily I say unto you; It shall be more tolerable for the land of Sodom and Gomorrha in the day of judgment, than for that city."

Jesus Sends Out the Twelve Apostles and Empowers them

Mar 6:7 And he called unto him the twelve, and began to send them forth by two and two; and gave them power over unclean spirits;

Mar 6:8 And commanded them that they should <u>take nothing for their journey</u>, save a staff only; no scrip, no bread, no money in their purse:

Mar 6:9 But be shod with sandals; and not put on two coats.

Given Power to hold Cities Accountable

Mar 6:10 And he said unto them, "In what place soever ye enter into an house, there abide till ye depart from that place. 11 And whosoever shall not receive you, nor hear you, when ye depart thence, shake off the dust under your feet for a testimony against them. Verily I say unto you;<u> It shall be more tolerable for Sodom and Gomorrha in the day of judgment, than for that city."</u>

Mar 6:12 And they went out, and preached that men should repent.

Mar 6:13 And they cast out many devils, and anointed with oil many that were sick, and healed them. **(James 5:14-16)**

Jesus Sends Out the Twelve Apostles and Empowers them

Luk 9:1 Then he called his twelve disciples together, and gave them power and authority over all devils, and to cure diseases.

Luk 9:2 And he sent them to preach the kingdom of God, and to heal the sick.

Luk 9:3 And he said unto them; "<u>Take nothing for your journey</u>, neither staves, nor scrip, neither bread, neither money; neither have two coats apiece. 4 And whatsoever house ye enter into, there abide, and thence depart.

Given Power to Hold Cities Accountable

Luk 9:5 And whosoever will not receive you, when ye go out of that city, <u>shake off the very dust from your feet for a testimony against them.</u>

Luk 9:6 And they departed, and went through the towns, preaching the gospel, and healing everywhere.

Sheep Amongst Wolves

Mat 10:16 "Behold, I send you forth as sheep in the midst of wolves: be ye therefore wise as serpents, and harmless as doves. 17 But beware of men: for they will deliver you up to the councils, and they will scourge you in their synagogues; 18 And ye shall be brought before governors and kings for my sake, for a testimony against them and the Gentiles. 19 But when they deliver you up, take no thought how or what ye shall speak: for it shall be given you in that same hour what ye shall speak. 20 For it is not ye that speak, but the Spirit of your Father which speaketh in you."

Lambs Among Wolves

Luk 10:3 "Go your ways: behold, I send you forth as lambs among wolves. 4 Carry neither purse, nor scrip, nor shoes: and salute no man by the way. 5 And into whatsoever house ye enter, first say, Peace be to this house. 6 And if the son of peace be there, your peace shall rest upon it: if not, it shall turn to you again. 7 And in the same house remain, eating and drinking such things as they give: for the labourer is worthy of his hire. Go not from house to house. 8 And into whatsoever city ye enter, and they receive you, eat such things as are set before you: 9 And heal the sick that are therein, and say unto them; The kingdom of God is come nigh unto you."

The 70 Also Given Power to Hold Cities Accountable

Luk 10:10 "But into whatsoever city ye enter, and they receive you not, go your ways out into the streets of the same, and say, 11 Even the very dust of your city, which cleaveth on us, we do wipe off against you: notwithstanding be ye sure of this, that the kingdom of God is come nigh unto you. 12 But I say unto you, that it shall be more tolerable in that day for Sodom, than for that city."

Jesus Heads to Marthas House, Bethany.

This is Before Lazareth being sick. Jesus had one message and that was to Repent and to get ready for the Kingdom of God, showing what the Father is like in miracles and grace, Acts 1:8 Acts 2:22. Jesus preached the same message over 3.5 years in Judah and Galilee, I feel the men in writing the gospels, they have tried not to repeat the words of Jesus, but have gathered the content as not to repeat themselves, so as to get as much information written down as possible. Matthew does an in-depth dive into the beatitudes but Luke writes where Jesus preached the same but in a different place and john says the world wouldn't have enough books if everything was written down. Imagine writing down 3 and a half years of a person's life, it would take 3.5 years to read.

The next couple chapters of Luke are broken up for study purposes back to where Matthew, in His time line, has first mentioned the subject matter. Although in three and a half years of preaching and gathering of disciples, as there were many disciples, until Jesus thinned them out by calling Himself the Passover sacrifice, "drink my blood eat my flesh" and left only the twelve. Jesus would have had to repeated himself many times over the 3.5 years just so that the new converts would also have the basic knowledge of prayer, rebuking the teachers throughout the countries of Judea and Galilee. In my opinion that is why Jesus taught the Lord's prayer at the beginning in Matthew's gospel and also at Bethany in the gospel of Luke.

Lukes Subject matter moved for study purposes, assimilated to Matthew`s timeline.

10:13 Woe to Unrepentant Cities and Capernaum. Mat 11:20

10:17 Jesus Saw Satan Thrown out of Heaven. Mat 11:20 (Seventy Return)

10:21 Jesus Rejoices in the Fathers will. Mat 11:25

10:25 Lawyer Temps Jesus. Mat 22.34

10:30 Parable. The Good Samaritan. Mat 22:34

10:38 Martha complains and Mary Receives her Ministry. Mat 22:34

11:1 The Lord's Prayer. Mat 6:9

11:9 Ask and it will be given. Mat 7:7.

11:14 Jesus accused of Beelzebub. Mat 12:24

11:21 Binding the strong man. Matt 12:29

11:24 Return of the unclean spirit. Mat 12:43

11:27 Sign of Jonah the prophet. Mat 12:38

11:33 Don't hide your light. Mat 5:14

11:37 Pharisees Rebuked. Mat 23.25

11:45 Lawyers rebuked. Mat 23:25

12:1 Beware the Leaven of the Pharisees. Mat 16:5

12:4 Fear God not man. Mat 10:26

12:6 Sparrows and Hairs. Mat 10:29

The next three subsections line up in succession in Luke and are placed after Mat 10:32

12:8 Confess Me. Mat 10:32

12:13 Beware Covetousness. Mat 10:32

12:16 Parable of the Rich Fool. Mat 10:32

12:22 Be Not Anxious. Mat 6:25

12:31 Seek Ye First. Mat 6:33

12:35 Watch for the Hour. Mar 13:32 Luk 21:34, Mat 24:43

12:49 Came to Send Fire. Mat 10:34

12:54 Discerning the times. Mat 10:34

12:57 Pay your Debts. Mat 5:25

Your Enemies will be your Family. *Micah 7:6*

Mat 10:21 "And the brother shall deliver up the brother to death, and the father the child: and the children shall rise up against their parents, and cause them to be put to death. 22 And ye shall be hated of all men for my name's sake: but he that endureth to the end shall be saved. 23 But when they persecute you in this city, flee ye into another: for verily I say unto you, Ye shall not have gone over the cities of Israel, till the Son of man be come. 24 The disciple is not above his master, nor the servant above his lord. 25 It is enough for the disciple that he be as his master, and the servant as his lord. If they have called the master of the house Beelzebub, how much more shall they call them of his household?"

Fear God not man. Prov. 1:7, *Prov 8:13, Prov 9:10.*

Mat 10:26 "Fear them not therefore: for there is nothing covered, that shall not be revealed; and hid, that shall not be known. 27 What I tell you in darkness, that speak ye in light: and what ye hear in the ear, that preach ye upon the housetops. 28 <u>And fear not them which kill the body</u>, but are not able to kill the soul: but rather fear him which is able to destroy both soul and body in hell."

Fear God not Man

Luk 12:4 "And I say unto you my friends; <u>Be not afraid of them that kill the body,</u> and after that have no more that they can do. 5 But I will forewarn you whom ye shall fear: Fear him, which after he hath killed hath power to cast into hell, yea, I say unto you; Fear him.

Sparrows and your Hairs

Mat 10:29 "Are not two sparrows sold for a farthing? and one of them shall not fall on the ground without your Father. 30 But the very <u>hairs of your head are all numbered</u>. 31 Fear ye not therefore, ye are of more value than many sparrows."

Sparrows and your Hairs

Luk 12:6 Are not five sparrows sold for two farthings, and not one of them is forgotten before God? 7 But even the very <u>hairs of your head are all numbered</u>. Fear not therefore: ye are of more value than many sparrows."

Confess Me.

Mat 10:32 "<u>Whosoever therefore shall confess me before men</u>, him will I confess also before my Father which is in heaven. 33 But whosoever shall deny me before men, him will I also deny before my Father which is in heaven."

Confess Me. *Prov 3:6*

Luk 12:8 "Also I say unto you; <u>Whosoever shall confess me before men,</u> him shall the Son of man also confess before the angels of God: 9 But he that denieth me before men shall be denied before the angels of God. 10 And whosoever shall speak a word against the Son of man, it shall be forgiven him: but unto him that blasphemeth against the Holy Ghost it shall not be forgiven. 11 And when they bring you unto the synagogues, and unto magistrates, and powers, take ye no thought how or what thing ye shall answer, or what ye shall say: 12 For the Holy Ghost shall teach you in the same hour what ye ought to say."

Beware Covetousness

Luk 12:13 And one of the company said unto him: "Master, speak to my brother, that he divide the inheritance with me."

Luk 12:14 And he said unto him; "Man, who made me a judge or a divider over you?"

Luk 12:15 And he said unto them; "Take heed, and beware of covetousness: for a man's life consisteth not in the abundance of the things which he possesseth."

The Parable of the Rich Fool. *Deut 8:14-20*

Luk 12:16 And he spake a parable unto them, saying; "The ground of a certain rich man brought forth plentifully: 17 And he thought within himself, saying; "What shall I do, because I have no room where to bestow my fruits?" 18 And he said; "This will I do: I will pull down my barns, and build greater; and there will I bestow all my fruits and my goods. 19 And I will say to my soul, Soul, thou hast much goods laid up for many years; take thine ease, eat, drink, *and* be merry." 20 But God said unto him; "THOU FOOL, THIS NIGHT THY SOUL SHALL BE REQUIRED OF THEE": then whose shall those things be, which thou hast provided? 21 So *is* he that layeth up treasure for himself, and is not rich toward God."

Jesus Came to Send a Sword in Families. *Isa 49:2,3. Jer 23:29*

Mat 10:34 "Think not that I am come to send peace on earth: I came not to send peace, but a sword. 35 For I am come to set a man at variance against his father, and the daughter against her mother, <u>and the daughter in law against her mother-in-law</u>. 36 And a man's foes shall be they of his own household. 37 He that loveth father or mother more than me is not worthy of me: and he that loveth son or daughter more than me is not worthy of me. 38 And he that taketh not his cross, and followeth after me, is not worthy of me. 39 He that findeth his life shall lose it: and he that loseth his life for my sake shall find it.

Jesus Came to Send Fire in Families. Isa 49:2, Jer 5:14, Jer 17:27, Jer 23:29

Luk 12:49 "I am come to send fire on the earth; and what will I, if it be already kindled? 50 But I have a baptism to be baptized with; and how am I straitened till it be accomplished! 51 Suppose ye that I am come to give peace on earth? I tell you, Nay; but rather division: 52 For from henceforth there shall be five in one house divided, three against two, and two against three. 53 The father shall be divided against the son, and the son against the father; the mother against the daughter, <u>and the daughter against the mother</u>; the mother-in-law against her daughter in law, and the daughter in law against her mother-in-law."

Prophets Reward

Mat 10:40 "He that receiveth you receiveth me, and he that receiveth me receiveth him that sent me. 41 He that receiveth a prophet in the name of a prophet shall receive a prophet's reward; and he that receiveth a righteous man in the name of a righteous man shall receive a righteous man's reward. 42 And whosoever shall give to drink unto one of these little ones a cup of cold water only in the name of a disciple, verily I say unto you, he shall in no wise lose his reward."

Mat 11:1 And it came to pass, when Jesus had made an end of commanding his twelve disciples, he departed thence to teach and to preach in their cities.

John in Prison; Jesus reassures Johns Disciples. *Isaiah 35. Acts 1:6*

Mat 11:2 Now when John had heard in the prison the works of Christ, he sent two of his disciples,

Mat 11:3 And said unto him; "Art thou he that should come, or do we look for another?"

Mat 11:4 Jesus answered and said unto them; "Go and shew John again those things which ye do hear and see: 5 The blind receive their sight, and the lame walk, the lepers are cleansed, and the deaf hear, the dead are raised up, and the poor have the gospel preached to them. 6 And blessed is he, whosoever shall not be offended in me."

John in Prison; Jesus reassures Johns Disciples. *Isaiah 35. Acts 1:6*

Luk 7:18 And the disciples of John shewed him of all these things.

Luk 7:19 And John calling unto him two of his disciples sent them to Jesus, saying; "Art thou he that should come? or look we for another? "

Luk 7:20 When the men were come unto him, they said; "John Baptist hath sent us unto thee, saying; "Art thou he that should come? or look we for another?""

Luk 7:21 And in that same hour he cured many of their infirmities and plagues, and of evil spirits; and unto many that were blind he gave sight.

Luk 7:22 Then Jesus answering said unto them; "Go your way, and tell John what things ye have seen and heard; how that the blind see, the lame walk, the lepers are cleansed, the deaf hear, the dead are raised, to the poor the gospel is preached. 23 And blessed is he, whosoever shall not be offended in me."

Jesus bears witness of John T.B. Calling

Mat 11:7 And as they departed, Jesus began to say unto the multitudes concerning John; "What went ye out into the wilderness to see? A reed shaken with the wind? 8 But what went ye out for to see? A man clothed in soft raiment? behold, they that wear soft clothing are in kings' houses. 9 But what went ye out for to see? A prophet? yea, I say unto you, and more than a prophet. 10 For this is he, of whom it is written, "Behold, I send my messenger before thy face, which shall prepare thy way before thee." 11 Verily I say unto you; Among them that are born of women there hath not risen a greater than John the Baptist: notwithstanding he that is least in the kingdom of heaven is greater than he. 12 And from the days of John the Baptist until now the kingdom of heaven suffereth violence, and the violent take it by force. 13 For all the prophets and the law prophesied until John. 14 And if ye will receive it, this is Elias, which was for to come. 15 He that hath ears to hear, let him hear. 16 But whereunto shall I liken this generation? It is like unto children sitting in the markets, and calling unto their fellows, 17 And saying; "We have piped unto you, and ye have not danced; we have mourned unto you, and ye have not lamented." 18 For John came neither eating nor drinking, and they say; "He hath a devil." 19 The Son of man came eating and drinking, and they say; "Behold a man gluttonous, and a winebibber, a friend of publicans and sinners." But wisdom is justified of her children."

Jesus bears witness of John T.B. Calling.

Luk 7:24 And when the messengers of John were departed, he began to speak unto the people concerning John; "What went ye out into the wilderness for to see? A reed shaken with the wind? 25 But what went ye out for to see? A man clothed in soft raiment? Behold, they which are gorgeously apparelled, and live delicately, are in kings' courts. 26 But what went ye out for to see? A prophet? Yea, I say unto you, and much more than a prophet. 27 This is he, of whom it is written, Behold, I send my messenger before thy face, which shall prepare thy way before thee. 28 For I say unto you, among those that are born of women there is not a greater prophet than John the Baptist: but he that is least in the kingdom of God is greater than he."

Luk 7:29 And all the people that heard him, and the publicans, justified God, being baptized with the baptism of John.

Luk 7:30 But the Pharisees and lawyers rejected the counsel of God against themselves, being not baptized of him.

Luk 7:31 And the Lord said; "Whereunto then shall I liken the men of this generation? and to what are they like? 32 They are like unto children sitting in the marketplace, and calling one to another, and saying; "We have piped unto you, and ye have not danced; we have mourned to you, and ye have not wept." 33 For John the Baptist came neither eating bread nor drinking wine; and ye say; "He hath a devil." 34 The Son of man is come eating and drinking; and ye say; "Behold a gluttonous man, and a winebibber, a friend of publicans and sinners!" 35 But wisdom is justified of all her children."

<u>Mary Magedeline Forgiven and anoints Jesus' feet,</u> *Ruth 3:7*

See also Matt 26:7 and Mark 14:3. Mary Magdeline also anointed Jesus' head, but closer to Jesus' burial. John says it was Mary Magdeline anointed Jesus' feet and washed her tears off Jesus' feet with her hair. John 11:2.

Luk 7:36 And one of the Pharisees desired him that he would eat with him. And he went into the Pharisee's house and sat down to meat.

Luk 7:37 And, behold, a woman in the city, which was a sinner, when she knew that Jesus sat at meat in the Pharisee's house, brought an alabaster box of ointment,

Luk 7:38 And stood at his feet behind him weeping, and began to wash his feet with tears, and did wipe them with the hairs of her head, and kissed his feet, and anointed them with the ointment.

Luk 7:39 Now when the Pharisee which had bidden him saw it, he spake within himself, saying; "This man, if he were a prophet, would have known who and what manner of woman this is that toucheth him: for she is a sinner."

Luk 7:40 And Jesus answering said unto him; "Simon, I have somewhat to say unto thee." And he saith; "Master, say on."

Luk 7:41 "There was a certain creditor which had two debtors: the one owed five hundred pence, and the other fifty. 42 And when they had nothing to pay, he frankly forgave them both. Tell me therefore, which of them will love him most?"

Luk 7:43 Simon answered and said; "I suppose that he, to whom he forgave most." And he said unto him; "Thou hast rightly judged."

Luk 7:44 And he turned to the woman, and said unto Simon; "Seest thou this woman? I entered into thine house, thou gavest me no water for my feet: but she hath washed my feet with tears, and wiped them with the hairs of her head. 45 Thou gavest me no kiss: but this woman since the time I came in hath not ceased to kiss my feet. 46 My head with oil thou didst not anoint: but this woman hath anointed my feet with ointment. 47 Wherefore I say unto thee; Her sins, which are many, are forgiven; for she loved much: but to whom little is forgiven, the same loveth little."

Luk 7:48 And he said unto her; "Thy sins are forgiven."

Luk 7:49 And they that sat at meat with him began to say within themselves; "Who is this that forgiveth sins also?"

Luk 7:50 And he said to the woman; "Thy faith hath saved thee; go in peace."

The Women named that supplied Jesus and His Disciples.

Women are to teach Titus 2:3-5.

Luk 8:1 And it came to pass afterward, that he went throughout every city and village, preaching and shewing the glad tidings of the kingdom of God: and the twelve were with him,

Luk 8:2 And certain women, which had been healed of evil spirits and infirmities, Mary called Magdalene, out of whom went seven devils,

Luk 8:3 And Joanna the wife of Chuza Herod's steward, and Susanna, and many others, which ministered unto him of their substance.

Woe to Unrepentant Cities and Capernaum

Mat 11:20 Then began he to upbraid the cities wherein most of his mighty works were done, because they repented not:

Mat 11:21 "Woe unto thee, Chorazin! woe unto thee, Bethsaida! for if the mighty works, which were done in you, had been done in Tyre and Sidon, they would have repented long ago in sackcloth and ashes. 22 But I say unto you; It shall be more tolerable for Tyre and Sidon at the day of judgment, than for you. 23 And thou, Capernaum, which art exalted unto heaven, shalt be brought down to hell: for if the mighty works, which have been done in thee, had been done in Sodom, it would have remained until this day. 24 But I say unto you; That it shall be more tolerable for the land of Sodom in the day of judgment, than for thee."

Woe to Unrepentant Cities and Capernaum

Luk 10:13 "Woe unto thee, Chorazin! Woe unto thee, Bethsaida! For if the mighty works had been done in Tyre and Sidon, which have been done in you, they had a great while ago repented, sitting in sackcloth and ashes. 14 But it shall be more tolerable for Tyre and Sidon at the judgment, than for you. 15 And thou, Capernaum, which art exalted to heaven, shalt be thrust down to hell. 16 He that heareth you heareth me; and he that despiseth you despiseth me; and he that despiseth me despiseth him that sent me."

The Seventy Return

Jesus Saw Satan Thrown out of Heaven

Luk 10:17 And the seventy returned again with joy, saying; "Lord, even the devils are subject unto us through thy name."

Luk 10:18 And he said unto them; "I beheld Satan as lightning fall from heaven. 19 Behold, I give unto you power to tread on serpents and scorpions, and over all the power of the enemy: and nothing shall by any means hurt you. 20 Notwithstanding in this rejoice not, that the spirits are subject unto you; but rather rejoice, because your names are written in heaven."

Take My Yoke Jesus Rejoices in the Father's Will

The Yoke represents obedience and servitude and the Burden represents Love. We Obey the Holy Spirit and minister to others because of Love. People see our love for God by the way we love others. We carry the Love of the Father in us. (1 Sam 15:22, Prov 14:22, Prov 23:7, Joh 1:17, 1 Joh 4:16, Jon 13:35.)

Mat 11:25 At that time Jesus answered and said; "I thank thee, O Father, Lord of heaven and earth, because thou hast hid these things from the wise and prudent, and hast revealed them unto babes. 26 Even so, Father: for so it seemed good in thy sight. 27 All things are delivered unto me of my Father: and no man knoweth the Son, but the Father; neither knoweth any man the Father, save the Son, and he to whomsoever the Son will reveal him. 28 Come unto me, all ye that labour and are heavy laden, and I will give you rest. 29 Take my yoke upon you, and learn of me; for I am meek and lowly in heart: and ye shall find rest unto your souls. 30 For my yoke is easy, and my burden is light."

Jesus Rejoices in the Father's Will

Luk 10:21 In that hour Jesus rejoiced in spirit, and said; "I thank thee, O Father, Lord of heaven and earth, that thou hast hid these things from the wise and prudent, and hast revealed them unto babes: even so, Father; for so it seemed good in thy sight. 22 All things are delivered to me of my Father: and no man knoweth who the Son is, but the Father; and who the Father is, but the Son, and he to whom the Son will reveal him."

Luk 10:23 And he turned him unto his disciples, and said privately; "Blessed are the eyes which see the things that ye see: 24 For I tell you, that many prophets and kings have desired to see those things which ye see, and have not seen them; and to hear those things which ye hear, and have not heard them."

<u>Jesus in the corn field on Sabbath</u>

Corn is usually planted spring and harvested in summer depending on the need for human consumption or for animals. To eat corn means they were ripe but not dried out and hard, an indication of early summer.

Mat 12:1 At that time Jesus went on the <u>sabbath day through the corn</u>; and his disciples were an hungred, and began to pluck the ears of corn, and to eat.

Mat 12:2 But when the Pharisees saw it, they said unto him; "Behold, thy disciples do that which is not lawful to do upon the sabbath day."

Mat 12:3 But he said unto them; "Have ye not read what David did, when he was an hungred, and they that were with him; 4 How he entered into the house of God, and did eat the shewbread, which was not lawful for him to eat, neither for them which were with him, but only for the priests? 5 Or have ye not read in the law, how that on the sabbath days the priests in the temple profane the sabbath, and are blameless? But I say unto you, that in this place is one greater than the temple. 7 But if ye had known what this meaneth; "I will have mercy, and not sacrifice, ye would not have condemned the guiltless." **(Hos 6:6)** 8 For the Son of man is Lord even of the sabbath day."

<u>Jesus in the corn field on Sabbath</u>

Mar 2:23 And it came to pass, that he went through the <u>corn fields on the sabbath day</u>; and his disciples began, as they went, to pluck the ears of corn.

Mar 2:24 And the Pharisees said unto him; "Behold, why do they on the sabbath day that which is not lawful?"

Mar 2:25 And he said unto them; "Have ye never read what David did, when he had need, and was an hungred, he, and they that were with him? 26 How he went into the house of God in the days of Abiathar the high priest, and did eat the shewbread, which is not lawful to eat but for the priests, and gave also to them which were with him?" 27 And he said unto them; "The sabbath was made for man, and not man for the sabbath: 28. Therefore the Son of man is Lord also of the sabbath."

Jesus in corn field on Sabbath

Luk 6:1 And it came to pass on the <u>second sabbath</u> after the first, that he went <u>through the corn fields</u>; and his disciples plucked the ears of corn, and did eat, rubbing them in their hands.

Luk 6:2 And certain of the Pharisees said unto them; "Why do ye that which is not lawful to do on the sabbath days?"

Luk 6:3 And Jesus answering them said; "Have ye not read so much as this, what David did, when himself was an hungred, and they which were with him; 4 How he went into the house of God, and did take and eat the shewbread, and gave also to them that were with him; which it is not lawful to eat but for the priests alone?" 5 And he said unto them; "That the Son of man is Lord also of the sabbath."

A Man with a Withered Hand

Mat 12:9 And when he was departed thence, he went into their synagogue:

Mat 12:10 And, behold, there was a man which had his <u>hand withered</u>. And they asked him, saying; "<u>Is it lawful to heal on the sabbath days</u>?" that they might accuse him.

Mat 12:11 And he said unto them; "What man shall there be among you, that shall have one sheep, and if it fall into a pit on the sabbath day, will he not lay hold on it, and lift it out? 12 How much then is a man better than a sheep? Wherefore it is lawful to do well on the sabbath days."

Mat 12:13 Then saith he to the man; "<u>Stretch forth thine hand.</u>" And he stretched it forth; and it was restored whole, like as the other.

Mat 12:14 Then the Pharisees went out, and held a council against him, how they might destroy him.

A Man with a Withered Hand

Mar 3:1 And he entered again into the synagogue; and there was a man there which had a withered hand.

Mar 3:2 And they watched him, whether he would heal him on the sabbath day; that they might accuse him.

Mar 3:3 And he saith unto the man which had the withered hand; "Stand forth."

Mar 3:4 And he saith unto them; "Is it lawful to do good on the sabbath days, or to do evil? to save life, or to kill?" But they held their peace.

Mar 3:5 And when he had looked round about on them with anger, being grieved for the hardness of their hearts, he saith unto the man; "Stretch forth thine hand." And he stretched it out: and his hand was restored whole as the other.

Mar 3:6 And the Pharisees went forth, and straightway took counsel with the Herodians against him, how they might destroy him.

A Man with a Withered Right Hand

Luk 6:6 And it came to pass also on another sabbath, that he entered into the synagogue and taught: and there was a man whose right hand was withered.

Luk 6:7 And the scribes and Pharisees watched him, whether he would heal on the sabbath day; that they might find an accusation against him.

Luk 6:8 But he knew their thoughts, and said to the man which had the withered hand; "Rise up, and stand forth in the midst." And he arose and stood forth.

Luk 6:9 Then said Jesus unto them; "I will ask you one thing; Is it lawful on the sabbath days to do good, or to do evil? to save life, or to destroy it?"

Luk 6:10 And looking round about upon them all, he said unto the man; "Stretch forth thy hand." And he did so: and his hand was restored whole as the other.

Luk 6:11 And they were filled with madness; and communed one with another what they might do to Jesus.

Jesus Healed Them All

Mat 12:15 But when Jesus knew it, he withdrew himself from thence: and great multitudes followed him, and he healed them all;

Mat 12:16 And charged them that they should not make him known:

Mat 12:17 That it might be fulfilled which was spoken by Esaias the prophet, saying;

Mat 12:18 "Behold my servant, whom I have chosen; my beloved, in whom my soul is well pleased: I will put my spirit upon him, and he shall shew judgment to the Gentiles. 19 He shall not strive, nor cry; neither shall any man hear his voice in the streets. 20 A bruised reed shall he not break, and smoking flax shall he not quench, till he send forth judgment unto victory. 21 And in his name shall the Gentiles trust." **(Isaiah 42)**

Jesus Ministers to a Great Multitude from Judaea

Mar 3:7 But Jesus withdrew himself with his disciples to the sea: and a great multitude from Galilee followed him, and from Judaea,

Mar 3:8 And from Jerusalem, and from Idumaea, and from beyond Jordan; and they about Tyre and Sidon, a great multitude, when they had heard what great things he did, came unto him.

Mar 3:9 And he spake to his disciples, that a small ship should wait on him because of the multitude, lest they should throng him.

Jesus Ministers to a Great Multitude from Judaea

Luk 6:17 And he came down with them, and stood in the plain, and the company of his disciples, and a great multitude of people out of all Judaea and Jerusalem, and from the sea coast of Tyre and Sidon, which came to hear him, and to be healed of their diseases;

Luk 6:18 And they that were vexed with unclean spirits: and they were healed.

Luk 6:19 And the whole multitude sought to touch him: for there went virtue out of him, and healed them all.

Unclean spirits Witness of Jesus

Mar 3:10 For he had healed many; insomuch that they pressed upon him for to touch him, as many as had plagues.

Mar 3:11 And unclean spirits, when they saw him, fell down before him, and cried, saying; "Thou art the Son of God."

Mar 3:12 And he straitly charged them that they should not make him known.

Devils Witness of Jesus

Luk 4:40 Now when the sun was setting, all they that had any sick with divers diseases brought them unto him; and he laid his hands on every one of them, and healed them.

Luk 4:41 And devils also came out of many, crying out, and saying; "Thou art Christ the Son of God." And he rebuking them suffered them not to speak: for they knew that he was Christ.

Luk 4:42 And when it was day, he departed and went into a desert place: and the people sought him, and came unto him, and stayed him, that he should not depart from them.

Luk 4:43 And he said unto them; "I must preach the kingdom of God to other cities also: for therefore am I sent."

Luk 4:44 And he preached in the synagogues of Galilee. *(Matt 4:4, Luk 4:4. 44 authors of the bible)*

Jesus Casts out a Devil

Mat 12:22 Then was brought unto him one possessed with a devil, blind, and dumb: and he healed him, insomuch that the blind and dumb both spake and saw.

Mat 12:23 And all the people were amazed, and said; "Is not this the son of David?"

Jesus accused of using the power of Beelzebub.

Mat 12:24 But when the Pharisees heard it, they said; "This fellow doth not cast out devils, but by Beelzebub the prince of the devils."

Mat 12:25 And Jesus knew their thoughts, and said unto them; "Every kingdom divided against itself is brought to desolation; and every city or house divided against itself shall not stand: 26 And if Satan cast out Satan, he is divided against himself; how shall then his kingdom stand? 27 And if I by Beelzebub cast out devils, by whom do your children cast them out? therefore they shall be your judges. 28 But if I cast out devils by the Spirit of God, then the kingdom of God is come unto you."

Jesus accused of using the power of Beelzebub.

Mar 3:20 And the multitude cometh together again, so that they could not so much as eat bread.

Mar 3:21 And when his friends heard of it, they went out to lay hold on him: for they said; "He is beside himself."

Mar 3:22 And the scribes which came down from Jerusalem said; "He hath Beelzebub, and by the prince of the devils casteth he out devils."

Jesus accused of using the power of Beelzebub.

Luk 11:14 And he was casting out a devil, and it was dumb. And it came to pass, when the devil was gone out, the dumb spake; and the people wondered.

Luk 11:15 But some of them said; "He casteth out devils through Beelzebub the chief of the devils."

Luk 11:16 And others, tempting him, sought of him a sign from heaven.

Luk 11:17 But he, knowing their thoughts, said unto them; "Every kingdom divided against itself is brought to desolation; and a house divided against a house falleth. 18 If Satan also be divided against himself, how shall his kingdom stand? Because ye say that I cast out devils through Beelzebub. 19 And if I by Beelzebub cast out devils, by whom do your sons cast them out?

Therefore, shall they be your judges. 20 But if I with the finger of God cast out devils, no doubt the kingdom of God is come upon you.

Binding The Strong Man and Blasphemy against God. *Joh 4:24*

Mat 12:29 "Or else how can one enter into a strong man's house, and spoil his goods, except he first bind the strong man? and then he will spoil his house. 30 He that is not with me is against me; and he that gathereth not with me scattereth abroad. 31 Wherefore I say unto you; all manner of sin and blasphemy shall be forgiven unto men: but the blasphemy against the Holy Ghost shall not be forgiven unto men. 32 And whosoever speaketh a word against the Son of man, it shall be forgiven him: but whosoever speaketh against the Holy Ghost, it shall not be forgiven him, neither in this world, neither in the world to come."

Binding The Strong Man and Blasphemy against God.

Mar 3:23 And he called them unto him, and said unto them in parables; "How can Satan cast out Satan? 24 And if a kingdom be divided against itself, that kingdom cannot stand. 25 And if a house be divided against itself, that house cannot stand. 26 And if Satan rise up against himself, and be divided, he cannot stand, but hath an end. 27 No man can enter into a strong man's house, and spoil his goods, except he will first bind the strong man; and then he will spoil his house. 28 Verily I say unto you; All sins shall be forgiven unto the sons of men, and blasphemies wherewith soever they shall blaspheme: 29. But he that shall blaspheme against the Holy Ghost hath never forgiveness, but is in danger of eternal damnation:"

Mar 3:30 Because they said; "He hath an unclean spirit."

Binding the Strong Man.

Luk 11:21 When a strong man armed keepeth his palace, his goods are in peace: 22 But when a stronger than he shall come upon him, and overcome him, he taketh from him all his armour wherein he trusted, and divideth his spoils. 23 He that is not with me is against me: and he that gathereth not with me scattereth."

Good Treasures of the Heart, *Luk 6:43*

Mat 12:33 "Either make the tree good, and his fruit good; or else make the tree corrupt, and his fruit corrupt: for the tree is known by his fruit. 34 O generation of vipers, how can ye, being evil, speak good things? for out of the abundance of the heart the mouth speaketh. 35 A good man out of the good treasure of the heart bringeth forth good things: and an evil man out of the evil treasure bringeth forth evil things. 36 But I say unto you; That every idle word that men shall speak, they shall give account thereof in the day of judgment. 37 For by thy words thou shalt be justified, and by thy words thou shalt be condemned."

Good Treasures of the Heart, *Matt 12:33*

Luk 6:43 "For a good tree bringeth not forth corrupt fruit; neither doth a corrupt tree bring forth good fruit. :44 For every tree is known by his own fruit. For of thorns men do not gather figs, nor of a bramble bush gather they grapes. 45 A good man out of the good treasure of his heart bringeth forth that which is good; and an evil man out of the evil treasure of his heart bringeth forth that which is evil: for of the abundance of the heart his mouth speaketh."

The Sign of Jonah the Prophet. Mat 17:22

Do you realise that in Acts when Paul was preaching on Mars Hill, he preached Jesus and the appointed day, could it be also related that the sign of Jonah being a picture of Jesus? Jonah warned of Gods appointed Judgement Day on Ninevah, 3 days in the deep. Acts 17:30-32. Maybe Jonah could also be compared to that angry older brother in the parable of the prodigal Son, a lot of comparisons there? It`s all about Gods mercy and Jesus. Jesus Refines this statement in Matthew 17:22 confirming Hos 6:2. Jesus was in torment until he Submitted to the Father being our Thursday night, His Friday, and crucified that day. Rested on the sabbath, 7th day and raised again on the First day of the week.

Mat 12:38 Then certain of the scribes and of the Pharisees answered, saying; "Master, we would see a sign from thee."

Mat 12:39 But he answered and said unto them; "An evil and adulterous generation seeketh after a sign; and there shall no sign be given to it, but the sign of the prophet Jonas: 40 For as Jonas was three days and three nights in the whale's belly; so shall the Son of man be three days and three nights in the heart of the earth. 41 The men of Nineveh shall rise in judgment with this generation, and shall condemn it: because they repented at the preaching of Jonas; and, behold, a greater than Jonas is here. 42 The queen of the south shall rise up in the judgment with this generation, and shall condemn it: for she came from the uttermost parts of the earth to hear the wisdom of Solomon; and, behold, a greater than Solomon is here."

The Sign of Jonah the Prophet

Luk 11:27 And it came to pass, as he spake these things, a certain woman of the company lifted up her voice, and said unto him; "Blessed is the womb that bare thee, and the paps which thou hast sucked."

Luk 11:28 But he said; "Yea rather, blessed are they that hear the word of God, and keep it."

Luk 11:29 And when the people were gathered thick together, he began to say; "This is an evil generation: they seek a sign; and there shall no sign be given it, but the sign of Jonas the prophet. 30 For as Jonas was a sign unto the Ninevites, so shall also the Son of man be to this generation. 31 The queen of the south shall rise up in the judgment with the men of this generation, and condemn them: for she came from the utmost parts of the earth to hear the wisdom of Solomon; and, behold, a greater than Solomon is here. 32 The men of Nineve shall rise up in the judgment with this generation, and shall condemn it: for they repented at the preaching of Jonas; and, behold, a greater than Jonas is here."

Return of an Unclean Spirit (2 Pet 2:21)

Mat 12:43 "When the unclean spirit is gone out of a man, he walketh through dry places, seeking rest, and findeth none. 44 Then he saith; "I will return into my house from whence I came out;" and when he is come, he findeth it empty, swept, and garnished. 45 Then goeth he, and taketh with himself seven other spirits more wicked than himself, and they enter in and dwell there: and the last state of that man is worse than the first. Even so shall it be also unto this wicked generation."

Return of an Unclean Spirit

Luk 11:24 "When the unclean spirit is gone out of a man, he walketh through dry places, seeking rest; and finding none, he saith, I will return unto my house whence I came out. 25 And when he cometh, he findeth it swept and garnished. 26 Then goeth he, and taketh to him seven other spirits more wicked than himself; and they enter in, and dwell there: and the last state of that man is worse than the first."

Jesus' Mother and Brothers. *PS 69:7,8*

Mat 12:46 While he yet talked to the people, behold, his mother and his brethren stood without, desiring to speak with him.

Mat 12:47 Then one said unto him; "Behold, thy mother and thy brethren stand without, desiring to speak with thee."

Mat 12:48 But he answered and said unto him that told him; "Who is my mother? and who are my brethren?"

Mat 12:49 And he stretched forth his hand toward his disciples, and said; "Behold my mother and my brethren! 50 For whosoever shall do the will of my Father which is in heaven, the same is my brother, and sister, and mother."

Jesus' Mother and Brothers

Mar 3:31 There came then his brethren and his mother, and, standing without, sent unto him, calling him.

Mar 3:32 And the multitude sat about him, and they said unto him; "Behold, thy mother and thy brethren without seek for thee."

Mar 3:33 And he answered them, saying; "Who is my mother, or my brethren?"

Mar 3:34 And he looked round about on them which sat about him, and said; "Behold my mother and my brethren! 35 For whosoever shall do the will of God, the same is my brother, and my sister, and mother."

Jesus' Mother and Brothers

Luk 8:19 Then came to him his mother and his brethren and could not come at him for the press.

Luk 8:20 And it was told him by certain which said; "Thy mother and thy brethren stand without, desiring to see thee."

Luk 8:21 And he answered and said unto them; "My mother and my brethren are these which hear the word of God and do it."

Preaching from a Boat, Capernaum, Sea of Galilee

The Parable of the sower, 4 soils, 4 heart conditions, *Rev 3:15,16, Mat 7:21.*

Mat 13:1 The same day went Jesus out of the house, and sat by the sea side.

Mat 13:2 And great multitudes were gathered together unto him, so that he went into a ship, and sat; and the whole multitude stood on the shore.

Mat 13:3 And he spake many things unto them in parables, saying; "Behold, a sower went forth to sow; 4 And when he sowed, some seeds fell by the way side, and the fowls came and devoured them up: 5 Some fell upon stony places, where they had not much earth: and forthwith they sprung up, because they had no deepness of earth: 6 And when the sun was up, they were scorched; and because they had no root, they withered away. 7 And some fell among thorns; and the thorns sprung up, and choked them: 8 But other fell into good ground, and brought forth fruit, some an hundredfold, some sixtyfold, some thirtyfold. 9 Who hath ears to hear, let him hear."

Why Parables? Eze 20:49

Mat 13:10 And the disciples came, and said unto him; "Why speakest thou unto them in parables?"

Mat 13:11 He answered and said unto them; "Because it is given unto you to know the mysteries of the kingdom of heaven, but to them it is not given. 12 For whosoever hath, to him shall be given, and he shall have more abundance: but whosoever hath not, from him shall be taken away even that he hath. 13 Therefore speak I to them in parables: because they seeing see not; and hearing they hear not, neither do they understand. 14 And in them is fulfilled the prophecy of Esaias, which saith; "By hearing ye shall hear, and shall not understand; and seeing ye shall see, and shall not perceive: **(Isa 6:9,10)** 15 For this people's heart is waxed gross, and their ears are dull of hearing, and their eyes they have closed; lest at any time they should see with their eyes, and hear with their ears, and should understand with their heart, and should be converted, and I should heal them." 16 But blessed are your eyes, for they see: and your ears, for they hear. 17 For verily I say unto you; That many prophets and righteous men have desired to see those things which ye see, and have not seen them; and to hear those things which ye hear, and have not heard them."

The Parable Explained

Mat 13:18 "Hear ye therefore the parable of the sower. 19 When any one heareth the word of the kingdom, and understandeth it not, then cometh the wicked one, and catcheth away that which was sown in his heart. This is he which received seed by the way side. 20 But he that received the seed into stony places, the same is he that heareth the word, and anon with joy receiveth it; 21 Yet hath he not root in himself, but dureth for a while: for when tribulation or persecution ariseth because of the word, by and by he is offended. 22 He also that received seed among the thorns is he that heareth the word; and the care of this world, and the deceitfulness of riches, choke the word, and he becometh unfruitful. 23 But he that received seed into the good ground is he that heareth the word, and understandeth it; which also beareth fruit, and bringeth forth, some an hundredfold, some sixty, some thirty."

The Parable of the sower, 4 soils, 4 heart conditions.

Mar 4:1 And he began again to teach by the sea side: and there was gathered unto him a great multitude, so that he entered into a ship, and sat in the sea; and the whole multitude was by the sea on the land.

Mar 4:2 And he taught them many things by parables, and said unto them in his doctrine;

Mar 4:3 "Hearken; Behold, there went out a sower to sow: 4 And it came to pass, as he sowed, some <u>fell by the wayside</u>, and the fowls of the air came and devoured it up. 5 And some fell on stony ground, where it had not much earth; and immediately it sprang up, because it had no depth of earth: 6 But when the sun was up, it was scorched; and because it had no root, it withered away. 7 And some fell among thorns, and the thorns grew up, and choked it, and it yielded no fruit. 8 And other fell on good ground, and did yield fruit that sprang up and increased; and brought forth, some thirty, and some sixty, and some an hundred."

Mar 4:9 And he said unto them; "<u>He that hath ears to hear, let him hear.</u>"

<u>The parable of the sower and 4 grounds explained</u>

Mar 4:10 And when he was alone, they that were about him with the twelve asked of him the parable.

Mar 4:11 And he said unto them; "Unto you it is given to know the mystery of the kingdom of God: but unto them that are without, all these things are done in parables: 12 That seeing they may see, and not perceive; and hearing they may hear, and not understand; lest at any time they should be converted, and their sins should be forgiven them."

Mar 4:13 And he said unto them; "Know ye not this parable? and how then will ye know all parables? 14 The sower soweth the word. 15 And these are they by the wayside, where the word is sown; but when they have heard, Satan cometh immediately, and taketh away the word that was sown in their hearts. 16 And these are they likewise which are sown on stony ground; who, when they have heard the word, immediately receive it with gladness; 17 And have no root in themselves, and so endure but for a time: afterward, when affliction or persecution ariseth for the word's sake, immediately they are offended. 18 And these are they which are sown among thorns, such as hear the word, 19 And the cares of this world, and the deceitfulness of riches, and the lusts of other things entering in, choke the word, and it becometh unfruitful. 20 And these are they which are sown on good ground, such as hear the word, and receive it, and bring forth fruit, some thirtyfold, some sixty, and some an hundred. "

The Parable of the sower, 4 soils, 4 heart conditions. Rev 3:15,16, Mat 7:21.

Luk 8:4 And when much people were gathered together, and were come to him out of every city, he spake by a parable:

Luk 8:5 "A sower went out to sow his seed: and as he sowed, some fell by the way side; and it was trodden down, and the fowls of the air devoured it. 6 And some fell upon a rock; and as soon as it was sprung up, it withered away, because it lacked moisture. 7 And some fell among thorns; and the thorns sprang up with it, and choked it. 8 And other fell on good ground, and sprang up, and bare fruit an hundredfold." And when he had said these things, he cried; "He that hath ears to hear, let him hear."

Parable of the 4 grounds explained

Luk 8:9 And his disciples asked him, saying; "What might this parable be?"

Luk 8:10 And he said; "Unto you it is given to know the mysteries of the kingdom of God: but to others in parables; that seeing they might not see and hearing they might not understand. 11 Now the parable is this: The seed is the word of God. 12 Those by the wayside are they that hear; then cometh the devil, and taketh away the word out of their hearts, lest they should believe and be saved. 13 They on the rock are they, which, when they hear, receive the word with joy; and these have no root, which for a while believe, and in time of temptation fall away. 14 And that which fell among thorns are they, which, when they have heard, go forth, and are choked with cares and riches and pleasures of this life, and bring no fruit to perfection. 15 But that on the good ground are they, which in an honest and good heart, having heard the word, keep it, and bring forth fruit with patience."

The Parable of the tares and wheat; The Last day, Jesus` Return. *Joh 6:40, John 17:15, Zec 12:10*

Mat 13:24 Another parable put he forth unto them, saying; "The kingdom of heaven is likened unto a man which sowed good seed in his field: 25 But while men slept, his enemy came and sowed tares among the wheat, and went his way. 26 But when the blade was sprung up, and brought forth fruit, then appeared the tares also. 27 So the servants of the householder came and said unto him; "Sir, didst not thou sow good seed in thy field? from whence then hath it tares?" 28 He said unto them; "An enemy hath done this." The servants said unto him; "Wilt thou then that we go and gather them up?" 29 But he said; "Nay; lest while ye gather up the tares, ye root up also the wheat with them. 30 Let both grow together until the harvest: and in the time of harvest I will say to the reapers, gather ye together first the tares, and bind them in bundles to burn them: but gather the wheat into my barn.""

The Kingdom of Heaven is like a Mustard Seed

Mat 13:31 Another parable put he forth unto them, saying; "The kingdom of Heaven is like to a grain of mustard seed, which a man took, and sowed in his field: 32 Which indeed is the least of all seeds: but when it is grown, it is the greatest among herbs, and becometh a tree, so that the birds of the air come and lodge in the branches thereof."

Mat 13:33 Another parable spake he unto them; "The kingdom of heaven is like unto leaven, which a woman took, and hid in three measures of meal, till the whole was leavened." *(Isa 11:9 and Dan 2:35)*

Mat 13:34 All these things spake Jesus unto the multitude in parables; and without a parable spake he not unto them:

Mat 13:35 That it might be fulfilled which was spoken by the prophet, saying; "I will open my mouth in parables; I will utter things which have been kept secret from the foundation of the world." *(Ps 78:2)*

The Kingdom of God is like a Mustard Seed

Mar 4:26 And he said; "So is the kingdom of God, as if a man should cast seed into the ground; 27 And should sleep, and rise night and day, and the seed should spring and grow up, he knoweth not how. 28 For the earth bringeth forth fruit of herself; first the blade, then the ear, after that the full corn in the ear. 29 But when the fruit is brought forth, immediately he putteth in the sickle, because the harvest is come."

Mar 4:30 And he said; "Whereunto shall we liken the kingdom of God? or with what comparison shall we compare it? 31 It is like a grain of mustard seed, which, when it is sown in the earth, is less than all the seeds that be in the earth: 32 But when it is sown, it groweth up, and becometh greater than all herbs, and shooteth out great branches; so that the fowls of the air may lodge under the shadow of it."

Mar 4:33 And with many such parables spake he the word unto them, as they were able to hear it.

Mar 4:34 But without a parable spake he not unto them: and when they were alone, he expounded all things to his disciples.

The Kingdom of God is like a Mustard Seed

Luk 13:18 Then said he; "Unto what is the kingdom of God like? and whereunto shall I resemble it? 19 It is like a grain of mustard seed, which a man took, and cast into his garden; and it grew, and waxed a great tree; and the fowls of the air lodged in the branches of it." 20 And again he said; "Whereunto shall I liken the kingdom of God? 21 It is like leaven, which a woman took and hid in three measures of meal, till the whole was leavened."

Repent or Perish

Luk 13:1 There were present at that season some that told him of the Galilaeans, whose blood Pilate had mingled with their sacrifices.

Luk 13:2 And Jesus answering said unto them, "Suppose ye that these Galilaeans were sinners above all the Galilaeans, because they suffered such things? 3 I tell you, Nay: but, except ye repent, ye shall all likewise perish. 4 Or those eighteen, upon whom the tower in Siloam fell, and slew them, think ye that they were sinners above all men that dwelt in Jerusalem? 5 I tell you, Nay: but, except ye repent, ye shall all likewise perish."

The Parable of the Barren Fig Tree

Luk 13:6 He spake also this parable; "A certain man had a fig tree planted in his vineyard; and he came and sought fruit thereon, and found none. 7 Then said he unto the dresser of his vineyard, Behold, these three years I come seeking fruit on this fig tree, and find none: cut it down; why cumbereth it the ground? 8 And he answering said unto him, Lord, let it alone this year also, till

I shall dig about it, and dung it: 9 And if it bear fruit, well: and if not, then after that thou shalt cut it down."

A Woman with a Spirit of Infirmity. *Ps 145:14*

Luk 13:10 And he was teaching in one of the synagogues on the sabbath.

Luk 13:11 And, behold, there was a woman which had a spirit of infirmity eighteen years, and was bowed together, and could in no wise lift up herself.

Luk 13:12 And when Jesus saw her, he called her to him, and said unto her; "Woman, thou art loosed from thine infirmity."

Luk 13:13 And he laid his hands on her: and immediately she was made straight, and glorified God.

Luk 13:14 And the ruler of the synagogue answered with indignation, because that Jesus had healed on the sabbath day, and said unto the people; "There are six days in which men ought to work: in them therefore come and be healed, and not on the sabbath day."

Luk 13:15 The Lord then answered him, and said; "Thou hypocrite, doth not each one of you on the sabbath loose his ox or his ass from the stall, and lead him away to watering? 16 And ought not this woman, being a daughter of Abraham, whom Satan hath bound, lo, these eighteen years, be loosed from this bond on the sabbath day?"

Luk 13:17 And when he had said these things, all his adversaries were ashamed: and all the people rejoiced for all the glorious things that were done by him.

Faith (Pistis = Gods truthfulness) like a Mustard Seed.

A mustard seed knows what it is and what its purpose is; to die and reproduce. It has all of its potential programmed within its DNA passed down from its parent tree. We have to be born again. If we only knew who we really are in Christ, we would move mountains out of our lives and give shade and a home to the homeless. Solomon in all his glory had a dream and the Lord told him that he had already put wisdom into him. 1Kings 3:12. God has already put within you your destiny and Gifts, it is up to us to hone and use those talents for His Glory. Mat 25.

Luk 17:5 And the apostles said unto the Lord; "Increase our faith."

Luk 17:6 And the Lord said; "If ye had faith as a grain of mustard seed, ye might say unto this sycamine tree, be thou plucked up by the root, and be thou planted in the sea; and it should obey how you. 7 But which of you, having a servant ploughing or feeding cattle, will say unto him by and by, when he is come from the field, Go and sit down to meat? 8 And will not rather say unto him, make ready wherewith I may sup, and gird thyself, and serve me, till I have eaten and drunken; and afterward thou shalt eat and drink? 9 Doth he thank that servant because he did the things that were commanded him? I trow *(think)* not. 10 So likewise ye, when ye shall have done all those things which are commanded you, say, we are unprofitable servants: we have done that which was our duty to do."

Jesus Explains the Final Day as a Harvest

(John 17:15, Mat 24, 1 Cor 15:52 the Last Trump. 1 Thes 4:16 Dead in Christ rise first. 2 Thess 2:3 antichrist revealed first. Mat 24:30, Rev 20:4-6 The first resurrection, includes the tribulation saints. Jude 1:14, 1Thess 3:13 Jesus comes with all His Saints. Dan 2:35 Jesus fills the earth. Mark 13:10 Gospel preached to the whole world first. Zec 14:5 Jesus brings His saints. Fit all the rapture scriptures to fit Jesus` words not the other way around. Jesus doesn't correct Martha when saying the Last Day, John 11:24.)

Mat 13:36 Then Jesus sent the multitude away, and went into the house: and his disciples came unto him, saying; "Declare unto us the parable of the tares of the field."

Mat 13:37 He answered and said unto them; "He that soweth the good seed is the Son of man *(Adam in the Hebrew)*; 38 The field is the world; the good seed *(Wheat)* are the children of the kingdom; but the tares are the children of the wicked one; 39 The enemy that sowed them is the devil; the harvest is the end of the world; and the reapers are the angels. 40 As therefore the tares are gathered and burned in the fire; So shall it be in the end of this world. 41 The Son of man shall send forth his angels, and they shall gather out of his kingdom all things that offend, and them which do iniquity; 42 And shall cast them into a furnace of fire: there shall be wailing and gnashing of teeth. (*Ps 112:10)* 43 Then shall the righteous shine forth as the sun in the kingdom of their Father. Who hath ears to hear, let him hear."

Finding the Kingdom is like Finding a Hidden Treasure

To enter the kingdom of God you have to give up everything, Race, Ethnicity, culture and Colour. I am told many Japanese People hold back from Christianity because they can't worship their relatives anymore and serve Jesus at the same time. Jesus did say you can't have two masters. We cannot bring the culture of a people into the church. Gal 3:28.

Mat 13:44 "Again, the kingdom of heaven is like unto treasure hid in a field; the which when a man hath found, he hideth, and for joy thereof goeth and selleth all that he hath, and buyeth that field."

Mat 13:45 "Again, the kingdom of heaven is like unto a merchant man, seeking goodly pearls: 46 Who, when he had found one pearl of great price, went and sold all that he had, and bought it."

The Judgement Day, evil ones taken and burnt (*Mat 24, Isa 13:9)*

Mat 13:47 "Again, the kingdom of heaven is like unto a net, that was cast into the sea, and gathered of every kind: 48 Which, when it was full, they drew to shore, and sat down, and gathered the good into vessels, but cast the bad away. 49 So shall it be at the end of the world: the angels shall come forth, and sever the wicked from among the just, 50 And shall cast them into the furnace of fire: there shall be wailing and gnashing of teeth."

New and Old Treasures

Mat 13:51 Jesus saith unto them; "Have ye understood all these things?" They say unto him; "Yea, Lord."

Mat 13:52 Then said he unto them; "Therefore every scribe which is instructed unto the kingdom of heaven is like unto a man that is an householder, which bringeth forth out of his treasure things new and old."

Galilee, Nazareth.

No Honour for a Prophet. Joh 4:43, Luk 4:24.

Mat 13:53 And it came to pass, that when Jesus had finished these parables, he departed thence.

Mat 13:54 And when he was come into his own country, he taught them in their synagogue, insomuch that they were astonished, and said; "Whence hath this man this wisdom, and these mighty works? 55 Is not this the carpenter's son? is not his mother called Mary? and his brethren, James, and Joses, and Simon, and Judas? 56 And his sisters, are they not all with us? Whence then hath this man all these things?"

Mat 13:57 And they were offended in him. But Jesus said unto them, "A prophet is not without honour, save in his own country, and in his own house."

Mat 13:58 And he did not many mighty works there because of their unbelief.

No Honour for a Prophet

Mar 6:1 And he went out from thence, and came into his own country; and his disciples follow him.

Mar 6:2 And when the sabbath day was come, he began to teach in the synagogue: and many hearing him were astonished, saying, "From whence hath this man these things? and what wisdom is this which is given unto him, that even such mighty works are wrought by his hands? 3 Is not this the carpenter, the son of Mary, the brother of James, and Joses, and of Juda, and Simon? and are not his sisters here with us?" And they were offended at him.

Mar 6:4 But Jesus said unto them, "A prophet is not without honour, but in his own country, and among his own kin, and in his own house."

Mar 6:5 And he could there do no mighty work, save that he laid his hands upon a few sick folk, and healed them.

Mar 6:6 And he marvelled because of their unbelief. And he went round about the villages, teaching.

Jerusalem Feast.

The Healing at the Pool of Bethesda

Joh 5:1 After this there was a feast of the Jews; and Jesus went up to Jerusalem.

Joh 5:2 Now there is at Jerusalem by the sheep market a pool, which is called in the Hebrew tongue Bethesda, having five porches. *(Because this book was written in Greek John mentions the tongue)*

Joh 5:3 In these lay a great multitude of impotent folk, of blind, halt, withered, waiting for the moving of the water.

Joh 5:4 For an angel went down at a certain season into the pool, and troubled the water: whosoever then first after the troubling of the water stepped in was made whole of whatsoever disease he had.

Joh 5:5 And a certain man was there, which had an infirmity thirty and eight years.

Joh 5:6 When Jesus saw him lie, and knew that he had been now a long time in that case, he saith unto him; "Wilt thou be made whole?"

Joh 5:7 The impotent man answered him; "Sir, I have no man, when the water is troubled, to put me into the pool: but while I am coming, another steppeth down before me."

Joh 5:8 Jesus saith unto him; "Rise, take up thy bed, and walk."

Joh 5:9 And immediately the man was made whole, and took up his bed, and walked: and on the same day was the sabbath.

Joh 5:10 The Jews therefore said unto him that was cured; "It is the sabbath day: it is not lawful for thee to carry thy bed."

Joh 5:11 He answered them; "He that made me whole, the same said unto me; Take up thy bed, and walk."

Joh 5:12 Then asked they him; "What man is that which said unto thee; Take up thy bed, and walk?"

Joh 5:13 And he that was healed wist not who it was: for Jesus had conveyed himself away, a multitude being in that place.

Joh 5:14 Afterward Jesus findeth him in the temple, and said unto him; "Behold, thou art made whole: sin no more, lest a worse thing come unto thee."

Joh 5:15 The man departed, and told the Jews that it was Jesus, which had made him whole.

Joh 5:16 And therefore did the Jews persecute Jesus, and sought to slay him, because he had done these things on the sabbath day.

Joh 5:17 But Jesus answered them; "My Father worketh hitherto, and I work."

Jesus Is Equal with His Father, *Zec 12:8*

Joh 5:18 Therefore the Jews sought the more to kill him, because he not only had broken the sabbath, but said also that God was his Father, making himself equal with God.

Jesus only does what the Father shows Him, *1 Sam 15:22.*

Joh 5:19 Then answered Jesus and said unto them; "Verily, verily, I say unto you, The Son can do nothing of himself, but what he seeth the Father do: for what things soever he doeth, these also doeth the Son likewise. 20 For the Father loveth the Son, and sheweth him all things that himself doeth: and he will shew him greater works than these, that ye may marvel. 21 For as the Father raiseth up the dead, and quickeneth them; even so the Son quickeneth whom he will. 22 For the Father judgeth no man, but hath committed all judgment unto the Son: 23 That all men should honour the Son, even as they honour the Father. He that honoureth not the Son honoureth not the Father which hath sent him. 24 Verily, verily, I say unto you, He that heareth my word, and believeth on him that sent me, hath everlasting life, and shall not come into condemnation; but is passed from death unto life. 25 Verily, verily, I say unto you; The hour is coming, and now is, when the dead shall hear the voice of the Son of God: and they that hear shall live. 26 For as the Father hath life in himself; so hath he given to the Son to have life in himself; 27 And hath given him authority to execute judgment also, because he is the Son of man.

28 Marvel not at this: for the hour is coming, in the which all that are in the graves shall hear his voice, 29 And shall come forth; they that have done good, unto the resurrection of life; and they that have done evil, unto the resurrection of damnation. 30 "I can of mine own self do nothing: as I hear, I judge: and my judgment is just; because I seek not mine own will, but the will of the Father which hath sent me. 31 If I bear witness of myself, my witness is not true. 32 There is another that beareth witness of me; and I know that the witness which he witnesseth of me is true. 33 Ye sent unto John, and he bare witness unto the truth. 34 But I receive not testimony from man: but these things I say, that ye might be saved. 35 He was a burning and a shining light: and ye were willing for a season to rejoice in his light. 36 But I have greater witness than that of John: for the works which the Father hath given me to finish, the same works that I do, bear witness of me, that the Father hath sent me. 37 And the Father himself, which hath sent me, hath borne witness of me. Ye have neither heard his voice at any time, nor seen his shape. 38 And ye have not his word abiding in you: for whom he hath sent, him ye believe not. 39 Search the scriptures; for in them ye think ye have eternal life: and they are they which testify of me. 40 And ye will not come to me, that ye might have life. 41 I receive not honour from men. 42 But I know you, that ye have not the love of God in you. 43 I am come in my Father's name, and ye receive me not: if another shall come in his own name, him ye will receive. 44 How can ye believe, which receive honour one of another, and seek not the honour that cometh from God only? 45 Do not think that I will accuse you to the Father: There is one that accuseth you, even Moses, in whom ye trust. 46 For had ye believed Moses, ye would have believed me: for he wrote of me. 47 But if ye believe not his writings, how shall ye believe my words?"

Herod Is Perplexed, wonders who Jesus is after killing John T.B.

Mat 14:1 At that time Herod the tetrarch heard of the fame of Jesus,

Mat 14:2 And said unto his servants; "This is John the Baptist; he is risen from the dead; and therefore, mighty works do shew forth themselves in him."

Mat 14:3 For Herod had laid hold on John, and bound him, and put him in prison for Herodias' sake, his brother Philip's wife.

Mat 14:4 For John said unto him; "It is not lawful for thee to have her."

Mat 14:5 And when he would have put him to death, he feared the multitude, because they counted him as a prophet.

The Reason and Why John T.B. was Murdered

Mat 14:6 But when Herod's birthday was kept, the daughter of Herodias danced before them, and pleased Herod.

Mat 14:7 Whereupon he promised with an oath to give her whatsoever she would ask.

Mat 14:8 And she, being before instructed of her mother, said; "Give me here John Baptist's head in a charger."

Mat 14:9 And the king was sorry **(G3076 sad)**: nevertheless, for the oath's sake, and them which sat with him at meat, he commanded it to be given her.

Mat 14:10 And he sent, and beheaded John in the prison.

Mat 14:11 And his head was brought in a charger, and given to the damsel: and she brought it to her mother.

Mat 14:12 And his disciples came, and took up the body, and buried it, and went and told Jesus.

Herod Is Perplexed, wonders who Jesus is after killing John T.B.

Mar 6:14 And king Herod heard of him; (for his name was spread abroad:) and he said; "That John the Baptist was risen from the dead, and therefore mighty works do shew forth themselves in him."

Mar 6:15 Others said, that it is Elias. And others said, that it is a prophet, or as one of the prophets.

Mar 6:16 But when Herod heard thereof, he said; "It is John, whom I beheaded: he is risen from the dead."

Mar 6:17 For Herod himself had sent forth and laid hold upon John, and bound him in prison for Herodias' sake, his brother Philip's wife: for he had married her.

Mar 6:18 For John had said unto Herod; "It is not lawful for thee to have thy brother's wife."

Mar 6:19 Therefore Herodias had a quarrel against him, and would have killed him; but she could not:

Mar 6:20 For Herod feared John, knowing that he was a just man and an holy, and observed him; and when he heard him, he did many things, and heard him gladly.

Mar 6:21 And when a convenient day was come, that Herod on his birthday made a supper to his lords, high captains, and chief estates of Galilee;

Mar 6:22 And when the daughter of the said Herodias came in, and danced, and pleased Herod and them that sat with him, the king said unto the damsel; "Ask of me whatsoever thou wilt, and I will give it thee."

Mar 6:23 And he sware unto her; "Whatsoever thou shalt ask of me, I will give it thee, unto the half of my kingdom."

Mar 6:24 And she went forth, and said unto her mother; "What shall I ask?" And she said; "The head of John the Baptist."

Mar 6:25 And she came in straightway with haste unto the king, and asked, saying; "I will that thou give me by and by in a charger the head of John the Baptist."

Mar 6:26 And the king was exceeding sorry; yet for his oath's sake, and for their sakes which sat with him, he would not reject her.

Mar 6:27 And immediately the king sent an executioner, and commanded his head to be brought: and he went and beheaded him in the prison,

Mar 6:28 And brought his head in a charger, and gave it to the damsel: and the damsel gave it to her mother.

Mar 6:29 And when his disciples heard of it, they came and took up his corpse, and laid it in a tomb.

Herod Is Perplexed, wonders who Jesus is after killing JTB

Luk 9:7 Now Herod the tetrarch heard of all that was done by him: and he was perplexed, because that it was said of some, that John was risen from the dead;

Luk 9:8 And of some, that Elias had appeared; and of others, that one of the old prophets was risen again.

Luk 9:9 And Herod said; "John have I beheaded: but who is this, of whom I hear such things?" And he desired to see him."

Desert Place near Bethsaida

The four gospels line up in this pivotal point. He has come back from the feast in Jerusalem, Joh 5:1 and come back out to Bethsaida, gets in a ship to shorten the walk. Luk 9:10. 131 klms from Jerusalem or 81 miles.

Jesus Feeds the Five Thousand

Mat 14:13 When Jesus heard of it, he departed thence by ship into a desert place apart: and when the people had heard thereof, they followed him on foot out of the cities.

Mat 14:14 And Jesus went forth, and saw a great multitude, and was moved with compassion toward them, and he healed their sick.

Mat 14:15 And when it was evening, his disciples came to him, saying, "This is a desert place, and the time is now past; send the multitude away, that they may go into the villages, and buy themselves victuals."

Mat 14:16 But Jesus said unto them, "They need not depart; give ye them to eat."

Mat 14:17 And they say unto him, "We have here but five loaves, and two fishes."

Mat 14:18 He said, "Bring them hither to me."

Mat 14:19 And he commanded the multitude to sit down on the grass, and took the five loaves, and the two fishes, and looking up to heaven, he blessed, and brake, and gave the loaves to his disciples, and the disciples to the multitude.

Mat 14:20 And they did all eat, and were filled: and they took up of the fragments that remained twelve baskets full.

Mat 14:21 And they that had eaten were about five thousand men, beside women and children.

Jesus Feeds the Five Thousand

Mar 6:30 And the apostles gathered themselves together unto Jesus, and told him all things, both what they had done, and what they had taught.

Mar 6:31 And he said unto them, "Come ye yourselves apart into a desert place, and rest a while:" for there were many coming and going, and they had no leisure so much as to eat.

Mar 6:32 And they departed into a desert place by ship privately.

Mar 6:33 And the people saw them departing, and many knew him, and ran afoot thither out of all cities, and outwent them, and came together unto him.

Mar 6:34 And Jesus, when he came out, saw much people, and was moved with compassion toward them, because they were as sheep not having a shepherd: and he began to teach them many things.

Mar 6:35 And when the day was now far spent, his disciples came unto him, and said, "This is a desert place, and now the time is far passed: 36 Send them away, that they may go into the country round about, and into the villages, and buy themselves bread: for they have nothing to eat."

Mar 6:37 He answered and said unto them, "Give ye them to eat." And they say unto him, "Shall we go and buy two hundred penny-worth of bread, and give them to eat?"

Mar 6:38 He saith unto them, "How many loaves have ye? go and see." And when they knew, they say, "Five, and two fishes."

Mar 6:39 And he commanded them to make all sit down by companies upon the green grass.

Mar 6:40 And they sat down in ranks, by hundreds, and by fifties.

Mar 6:41 And when he had taken the five loaves and the two fishes, he looked up to heaven, and blessed, and brake the loaves, and gave them to his disciples to set before them; and the two fishes divided he among them all.

Mar 6:42 And they did all eat, and were filled.

Mar 6:43 And they took up twelve baskets full of the fragments, and of the fishes.

Mar 6:44 And they that did eat of the loaves were about five thousand men.

Jesus Feeds the Five Thousand

Luk 9:10 And the apostles, when they were returned, told him all that they had done. And he took them, and went aside privately into a desert place belonging to the city called Bethsaida.

Luk 9:11 And the people, when they knew it, followed him: and he received them, and spake unto them of the kingdom of God, and healed them that had need of healing.

Luk 9:12 And when the day began to wear away, then came the twelve, and said unto him, "Send the multitude away, that they may go into the towns and country round about, and lodge, and get victuals: for we are here in a desert place."

Luk 9:13 But he said unto them; "Give ye them to eat. And they said, we have no more but five loaves and two fishes; except we should go and buy meat for all this people."

Luk 9:14 For they were about five thousand men. And he said to his disciples; "Make them sit down by fifties in a company."

Luk 9:15 And they did so, and made them all sit down.

Luk 9:16 Then he took the five loaves and the two fishes, and looking up to heaven, he blessed them, and brake, and gave to the disciples to set before the multitude.

Luk 9:17 And they did eat, and were all filled: and there was taken up of fragments that remained to them twelve baskets.

Jesus Feeds the Five Thousand

Joh 6:1 After these things Jesus went over the sea of Galilee, which is the sea of Tiberias.

Joh 6:2 And a great multitude followed him, because they saw his miracles which he did on them that were diseased.

Joh 6:3 And Jesus went up into a mountain, and there he sat with his disciples.

Joh 6:4 And the passover, a feast of the Jews, was nigh.

Joh 6:5 When Jesus then lifted up his eyes, and saw a great company come unto him, he saith unto Philip; "Whence shall we buy bread, that these may eat?"

Joh 6:6 And this he said to prove him: for he himself knew what he would do.

Joh 6:7 Philip answered him; "Two hundred pennyworth of bread is not sufficient for them, that every one of them may take a little."

Joh 6:8 One of his disciples, Andrew, Simon Peter's brother, saith unto him; 9 "There is a lad here, which hath five barley loaves, and two small fishes: but what are they among so many?"

Joh 6:10 And Jesus said, "Make the men sit down. Now there was much grass in the place. So the men sat down, in number about five thousand."

Joh 6:11 And Jesus took the loaves; and when he had given thanks, he distributed to the disciples, and the disciples to them that were set down; and likewise of the fishes as much as they would.

Joh 6:12 When they were filled, he said unto his disciples; "Gather up the fragments that remain, that nothing be lost."

Joh 6:13 Therefore they gathered them together, and filled twelve baskets with the fragments of the five barley loaves, which remained over and above unto them that had eaten.

Joh 6:14 Then those men, when they had seen the miracle that Jesus did, said, "This is of a truth that prophet that should come into the world."

Joh 6:15 When Jesus therefore perceived that they would come and take him by force, to make him a king, he departed again into a mountain himself alone.

<u>To Bethsaida. sailing across the Sea of Galilee.</u>

<u>Jesus Walks on the Water, Job 9:8. The Sea of Galilee is 13 klms, 8 miles wide.</u>

Mat 14:22 And straightway Jesus constrained his disciples to get into a ship, and to go before him unto the other side, while he sent the multitudes away.

Mat 14:23 And when he had sent the multitudes away, he went up into a mountain apart to pray: and when the evening was come, he was there alone.

Mat 14:24 But the ship was now in the midst of the sea, tossed with waves: for the wind was contrary.

Mat 14:25 And in the fourth watch of the night Jesus went unto them, walking on the sea.

Mat 14:26 And when the disciples saw him walking on the sea, they were troubled, saying; "It is a spirit;" and they cried out for fear.

Mat 14:27 But straightway Jesus spake unto them, saying; "Be of good cheer; <u>it is I; be not afraid</u>."

Mat 14:28 And Peter answered him and said; "Lord, if it be thou, bid me come unto thee on the water."

Mat 14:29 And he said; "Come." And when Peter was come down out of the ship, he walked on the water, to go to Jesus.

Mat 14:30 But when he saw the wind boisterous, he was afraid; and beginning to sink, he cried, saying; "Lord, save me."

Mat 14:31 And immediately Jesus stretched forth his hand, and caught him, and said unto him; "O thou of little faith, wherefore didst thou doubt?"

Mat 14:32 And when they were come into the ship, the wind ceased.

Mat 14:33 Then they that were in the ship came and worshipped him, saying; "Of a truth thou art the Son of God."

Jesus Walks on Water (Job 9:8)

Mar 6:45 And straightway he constrained his disciples to get into the ship, and to go to the other side before unto Bethsaida, while he sent away the people.

Mar 6:46 And when he had sent them away, he departed into a mountain to pray.

Mar 6:47 And when even was come, the ship was in the midst of the sea, and he alone on the land.

Mar 6:48 And he saw them toiling in rowing; for the wind was contrary unto them: and about the fourth watch of the night, he cometh unto them, walking upon the sea, and would have passed by them.

Mar 6:49 But when they saw him walking upon the sea, they supposed it had been a spirit, and cried out:

Mar 6:50 For they all saw him, and were troubled. And immediately he talked with them, and saith unto them; "Be of good cheer: it is I; be not afraid."

Mar 6:51 And he went up unto them into the ship; and the wind ceased: and they were sore amazed in themselves beyond measure, and wondered.

Mar 6:52 For they considered not the miracle of the loaves: for their heart was hardened.

Jesus Walks on Water (Job 9:8)

Joh 6:16 And when even was now come, his disciples went down unto the sea,

Joh 6:17 And entered into a ship, and went over the sea toward Capernaum. And it was now dark, and Jesus was not come to them.

Joh 6:18 And the sea arose by reason of a great wind that blew.

Joh 6:19 So when they had rowed about five and twenty or thirty furlongs *(Jesus walked about 3 miles @25 furlongs),* they see Jesus, walking on the sea, and drawing nigh unto the ship: and they were afraid.

Joh 6:20 But he saith unto them; "It is I; be not afraid."

Joh 6:21 Then they willingly received him into the ship: and immediately the ship was at the land whither they went.

Joh 6:22 The day following, when the people which stood on the other side of the sea saw that there was none other boat there, save that one whereinto his disciples were entered, and that Jesus went not with his disciples into the boat, but that his disciples were gone away alone;

<u>Gennesaret</u>

<u>Jesus Makes Whole All that Touched Him.</u>

Mat 14:34 And when they were gone over, they came into the land of Gennesaret.

Mat 14:35 And when the men of that place had knowledge of him, they sent out into all that country round about, and brought unto him all that were diseased;

Mat 14:36 And besought him that they might only touch the hem of his garment: and <u>as many as touched were made perfectly whole.</u>

<u>Jesus Makes Whole All that Touched Him.</u>

Mar 6:53 And when they had passed over, they came into the land of Gennesaret, and drew to the shore.

Mar 6:54 And when they were come out of the ship, straightway they knew him,

Mar 6:55 And ran through that whole region round about, and began to carry about in beds those that were sick, where they heard he was.

Mar 6:56 And whithersoever he entered, into villages, or cities, or country, they laid the sick in the streets, and besought him that they might touch if it were but the border of his garment: and <u>as many as touched him were made whole.</u>

Back to Capernaum

<u>Jesus The Bread of Life</u>

Joh 6:23 (Howbeit there came other boats from Tiberias nigh unto the place where they did eat bread, after that the Lord had given thanks:)

Joh 6:24 When the people therefore saw that Jesus was not there, neither his disciples, they also took shipping, and came to Capernaum, seeking for Jesus.

Joh 6:25 And when they had found him on the other side of the sea, they said unto him; "Rabbi, when camest thou hither?"

<u>Teachings in Capernaum the Synagogue Joh 6:59.</u>

Joh 6:26 Jesus answered them and said; "Verily, verily, I say unto you; Ye seek me, not because ye saw the miracles, but because ye did eat of the loaves, and were filled. 27 Labour not for the meat which perisheth, but for that meat which endureth unto everlasting life, which the Son of man shall give unto you: for him hath God the Father sealed."

Joh 6:28 Then said they unto him; "What shall we do, that we might work the works of God? "

Joh 6:29 Jesus answered and said unto them; <u>"This is the work of God, that ye believe on him whom he hath sent."</u>

Joh 6:30 They said therefore unto him; "What sign shewest thou then, that we may see, and believe thee? What dost thou work? 31 Our fathers did eat manna in the desert; as it is written He gave them bread from heaven to eat." (Exo 16:4)

Joh 6:32 Then Jesus said unto them; "Verily, verily, I say unto you, Moses gave you not that bread from heaven; but my Father giveth you the true bread from heaven. 33 For the bread of God is he which cometh down from heaven, and giveth life unto the world."

Joh 6:34 Then said they unto him; "Lord, evermore give us this bread."

Joh 6:35 And Jesus said unto them; "I am the bread of life: he that cometh to me shall never hunger; and he that believeth on me shall never thirst. 36 But I said unto you; That ye also have seen me, and believe not. 37 All that the Father giveth me shall come to me; and him that cometh to me I will in no wise cast out. 38 For I came down from heaven, *(Eccl 12:7)* not to do mine own will, but the will of him that sent me. 39 And this is the Father's will which hath sent me, that of all which he hath given me I should lose nothing, but should raise it up again at the last day. 40 And this is the will of him that sent me, that everyone which seeth the Son, and believeth on him, may have everlasting life: and I will raise him up at the last day."

Joh 6:41 The Jews then murmured at him, because he said; "I am the bread which came down from heaven."

Joh 6:42 And they said; "Is not this Jesus, the son of Joseph, whose father and mother we know? how is it then that he saith, I came down from heaven?"

<u>Jesus will raise believers up on the Last day.</u> *Zec 12:8*

Rev 20:4-6, John 11:24, Mat 13; Wheat and Tares. Predestination relies <u>upon you</u> choosing Jesus and doing Gods will, it is Your Choice, but God chose you first. Jesus had to fight the flesh and so do we, baptism is for a reason. Salvation is by Grace through Faith, you can't earn it, it's a free Gift. Your works kick in because you want to please the Father, your works will never justify you. The Holy Spirit draws us but we have to succumb to His advances. Same as in all relationships. 1 Cor 15:46.

Joh 6:43 Jesus therefore answered and said unto them; "Murmur not among yourselves. 44 No man can come to me, except the Father which hath sent me draw him: and I will raise him up <u>at the last day</u>. 45 It is written in the prophets; And they shall be all taught of God *(Isa 54:13)*. Every man therefore that hath heard, and hath learned of the Father, cometh unto me. 46 Not that any man hath seen the Father, save he which is of God, he hath seen the Father. Verily, verily, I say unto you, He that believeth on me hath everlasting life. 48 I am that bread of life. 49 Your fathers did eat manna in the wilderness, and are dead. 50 This is the bread which cometh down from heaven, that a man may eat thereof, and not die. 51 I am the living bread which came down from heaven: if any man eat of this bread, he shall live for ever: and the bread that I will give is my flesh, which I will give for the life of the world."

Joh 6:52 The Jews therefore strove among themselves, saying; "How can this man give us his flesh to eat?"

Holy Communion

Joh 6:53 Then Jesus said unto them; "Verily, verily, I say unto you, except ye eat the flesh of the Son of man, and drink his blood, ye have no life in you. 54 Whoso eateth my flesh, and drinketh my blood, hath eternal life; and I will raise him up at the last day. 55 For my flesh is meat indeed, and my blood is drink indeed. 56 He that eateth my flesh, and drinketh my blood, dwelleth in me, and I in him. 57 As the living Father hath sent me, and I live by the Father: so he that eateth me, even he shall live by me. 58 This is that bread which came down from heaven: not as your fathers did eat manna, and are dead: he that eateth of this bread shall live for ever."

Joh 6:59 These things said he in the synagogue, as he taught in Capernaum.

Jesus Has the Words of Eternal Life

Joh 6:60 Many therefore of his disciples, when they had heard this, said; "This is a hard saying; who can hear it?"

Joh 6:61 When Jesus knew in himself that his disciples murmured at it, he said unto them; "Doth this offend you? 62 What and if ye shall see the Son of man ascend up where he was before? 63 It is the spirit that quickeneth; the flesh profiteth nothing: the words that I speak unto you, they are spirit, and they are life. 64 But there are some of you that believe not." For Jesus knew from the beginning who they were that believed not, and who should betray him.

Jesus Culls His Followers. Zac 13:7, Isa 60:15

Joh 6:65 And he said; "Therefore said I unto you, that no man can come unto me, except it were given unto him of my Father." *(Rev 13:18)*

Joh 6:66 From that time many of his disciples went back, and walked no more with him.

Joh 6:67 Then said Jesus unto the twelve; "Will ye also go away?"

Joh 6:68 Then Simon Peter answered him; "Lord, to whom shall we go? thou hast the words of eternal life. 69 And we believe and are sure that thou art that Christ, the Son of the living God."

Joh 6:70 Jesus answered them; "Have not I chosen you twelve, and one of you is a devil?"

Joh 6:71 He spake of Judas Iscariot the son of Simon: for he it was that should betray him, being one of the twelve.

Jesus Stays in Galilee Until the Feast has Started

Joh 7:1 After these things Jesus walked in Galilee: for he would not walk in Jewry, because the Jews sought to kill him.

Joh 7:2 Now the Jews' feast of tabernacles was at hand.

(Oct 7-13 approx. 6 months before His crucifixion.)

Joh 7:3 His brethren therefore said unto him; "Depart hence, and go into Judaea, that thy disciples also may see the works that thou doest. 4 For there is no man that doeth anything in secret, and he himself seeketh to be known openly. If thou do these things, shew thyself to the world."

Joh 7:5 For neither did his brethren believe in him. *(Ps 69:8)*

Joh 7:6 Then Jesus said unto them; "My time is not yet come: but your time is alway ready. 7 The world cannot hate you; but me it hateth, because I testify of it, that the works thereof are evil. 8 Go ye up unto this feast: I go not up yet unto this feast; for my time is not yet full come."

Joh 7:9 When he had said these words unto them, he abode *(stayed)* still in Galilee.

Pharisees complain

Mat 15:1 Then came to Jesus scribes and Pharisees, which were of Jerusalem, saying; 2 "Why do thy disciples transgress the tradition of the elders? for they wash not their hands when they eat bread."

Pharisees complain

Mar 7:1 Then came together unto him the Pharisees, and certain of the scribes, which came from Jerusalem.

Mar 7:2 And when they saw some of his disciples eat bread with defiled, that is to say, with <u>unwashen, hands</u>, they found fault.

Mar 7:3 For the Pharisees, and all the Jews, except they wash their hands oft, eat not, holding the tradition of the elders.

Mar 7:4 And when they come from the market, except they wash, they eat not. And many other things there be, which they have received to hold, as the washing of cups, and pots, brasen vessels, and of tables.

Mar 7:5 Then the Pharisees and scribes asked him; "Why Walk not thy disciples according to the tradition of the elders, but eat bread with <u>unwashen hands</u>?"

Jesus Rebukes the Lack of Honouring Parents

If you are paying tithe and offerings or giving to get protection, not out of your abundance and if your extended family is suffering, is not biblical, especially your parents. Rev 3:17.

Mat 15:3 But he answered and said unto them; "Why do ye also transgress the commandment of God by your tradition? 4 For God commanded, saying; "Honour thy father and mother: and, He that curseth father or mother, let him die the death." 5 But ye say whosoever shall say to his father or his mother; "It is a gift, by whatsoever thou mightest be profited by me;" 6 And honour not his father or his mother, he shall be free. Thus, have ye made the commandment of God of none effect by your tradition. 7 Ye hypocrites, well did Esaias prophesy of you, saying; 8 "This people draweth nigh unto me with their mouth, and honoureth me with their lips; but their heart is far from me. 9 But in vain they do worship me, teaching for doctrines the commandments of men."" *(Isa 29:13)*

Jesus Rebukes the Lack of Honouring Parents

Mar 7:6 He answered and said unto them; "Well hath Esaias prophesied of you hypocrites, as it is written, this people honoureth me with their lips, but their heart is far from me." *(Isaiah 29:13)*

Mar 7:7 "Howbeit in vain do they worship me, teaching for doctrines the commandments of men. 8 For laying aside the commandment of God, ye hold the tradition of men, as the washing of pots and cups: and many other such like things ye do." 9 And he said unto them; "Full well ye reject the commandment of God, that ye may keep your own tradition. 10 For Moses said, "Honour thy father and thy mother; and, whoso curseth father or mother, let him die the death:" 11 But ye say; "if a man shall say to his father or mother, it is Corban, that is to say, a gift, by whatsoever thou mightest be profited by me; he shall be free." 12 And ye suffer him no more to do ought for his father or his mother; 13 Making the word of God of none effect through your tradition, which ye have delivered: and many such like things do ye."

Evil Heart Defiles a Person, *Luk 6:45, Mat 12:34*

Mat 15:10 And he called the multitude, and said unto them; "Hear, and understand: 11 Not that which goeth into the mouth defileth a man; but that which cometh out of the mouth, this defileth a man."

Mat 15:12 Then came his disciples, and said unto him; "Knowest thou that the Pharisees were offended, after they heard this saying?"

Evil Heart Defiles a Person

Mar 7:14 And when he had called all the people unto him, he said unto them; "Hearken unto me every one of you, and understand: 15 There is nothing from without a man, that entering into him can defile him: but the things which come out of him, those are they that defile the man. 16 If any man have ears to hear, let him hear."

Mar 7:17 And when he was entered into the house from the people, his disciples asked him concerning the parable.

Works of the Flesh. *Luk 6:39*

Mat 15:13 But he answered and said; "Every plant, which my heavenly Father hath not planted, shall be rooted up. 14 Let them alone: they be blind leaders of the blind. And if the blind lead the blind, both shall fall into the ditch.

Mat 15:15 Then answered Peter and said unto him; "Declare unto us this parable."

Gen 3:6, 2 Tim 3:1-7, Rev 21:8, 1 John 2:16, and Gal 5:19-21. Without holiness you will not see God, Heb 12:14.

Mat 15:16 And Jesus said; "Are ye also yet without understanding? 17 Do not ye yet understand, that whatsoever entereth in at the mouth goeth into the belly, and is cast out into the draught? 18 But those things which proceed out of the mouth come forth from the heart; and they defile the man. 19 For out of the heart proceed evil thoughts, murders, adulteries, fornications, thefts, false witness, blasphemies: 20 These are the things which defile a man: but to eat with unwashen hands defileth not a man.

Works of the Flesh

Mar 7:18 And he saith unto them; "Are ye so without understanding also? Do ye not perceive, that whatsoever thing from without entereth into the man, it cannot defile him; 19 Because it entereth not into his heart, but into the belly, and goeth out into the draught, purging all meats?"

Mar 7:20 And he said, "That which cometh out of the man, that defileth the man. 21 For from within, out of the heart of men, proceed evil thoughts, adulteries, fornications, murders, 22 Thefts, covetousness, wickedness, deceit, lasciviousness, an evil eye, blasphemy, pride, foolishness: 23 All these evil things come from within, and defile the man."

Tyre and Sidon

The Syrophoenician Woman's Faith

Mat 15:21 Then Jesus went thence, and departed into the coasts of Tyre and Sidon.

Mat 15:22 And, behold, a woman of Canaan came out of the same coasts, and cried unto him, saying; "Have mercy on me, O Lord, thou Son of David; my daughter is grievously vexed with a devil."

Mat 15:23 But he answered her not a word. And his disciples came and besought him, saying, Send her away; for she crieth after us.

Mat 15:24 But he answered and said; "I am not sent but unto the lost sheep of the house of Israel."

Mat 15:25 Then came she and worshipped *(G4352, Proskuneo, Prostrate, kiss like a dog)* him, saying; "Lord, help me."

Mat 15:26 But he answered and said; "It is not meet to take the children's bread, and to cast it to dogs."

Mat 15:27 And she said; "Truth, Lord: yet the dogs eat of the crumbs which fall from their masters' table."

Mat 15:28 Then Jesus answered and said unto her; "O woman, great is thy faith: be it unto thee even as thou wilt." And her daughter was made whole from that very hour.

The Syrophoenician Woman's Faith

Mar 7:24 And from thence he arose, and went into the borders of Tyre and Sidon, and entered into an house, and would have no man know it: but he could not be hid.

Mar 7:25 For a certain woman, whose young daughter had an unclean spirit, heard of him, and came and fell at his feet:

Mar 7:26 The woman was a Greek, a Syrophenician by nation; and she besought him that he would cast forth the devil out of her daughter.

Mar 7:27 But Jesus said unto her; "Let the children first be filled: for it is not meet to take the children's bread, and to cast it unto the dogs."

Mar 7:28 And she answered and said unto him; "Yes, Lord: yet the dogs under the table eat of the children's crumbs."

Mar 7:29 And he said unto her; "For this saying go thy way; the devil is gone out of thy daughter."

Mar 7:30 And when she was come to her house, she found the devil gone out, and her daughter laid upon the bed.

Sea of Galilee, Decapolis.

Jesus Heals a Multitude

Mat 15:29 And Jesus departed from thence, and came nigh unto the sea of Galilee; and went up into a mountain, and sat down there.

Mat 15:30 And great multitudes came unto him, having with them those that were lame, blind, dumb, maimed, and many others, and cast them down at Jesus' feet; and he healed them:

Mat 15:31 Insomuch that the multitude wondered, when they saw the dumb to speak, the maimed to be whole, the lame to walk, and the blind to see: and they glorified the God of Israel.

Jesus Heals a Deaf Man

Mar 7:31 And again, departing from the coasts of Tyre and Sidon, he came unto the sea of Galilee, through the midst of the coasts of Decapolis.

Mar 7:32 And they bring unto him one that was deaf, and had an impediment in his speech; and they beseech him to put his hand upon him.

Mar 7:33 And he took him aside from the multitude, and put his fingers into his ears, and he spit, and touched his tongue;

Mar 7:34 And looking up to heaven, he sighed, and saith unto him, "Ephphatha," *(G2188 Chaldee from Babylon, not Aramaic)* that is, Be opened.

Mar 7:35 And straightway his ears were opened, and the string of his tongue was loosed, and he spake plain.

Mar 7:36 And he charged them that they should tell no man: but the more he charged them, so much the more a great deal they published it;

Mar 7:37 And were beyond measure astonished, saying; "He hath done all things well: he maketh both the deaf to hear, and the dumb to speak."

Jesus Feeds the Four Thousand

Mat 15:32 Then Jesus called his disciples unto him, and said; "I have compassion on the multitude, because they continue with me now three days, and have nothing to eat: and I will not send them away fasting, lest they faint in the way."

Mat 15:33 And his disciples say unto him; "Whence should we have so much bread in the wilderness, as to fill so great a multitude?"

Mat 15:34 And Jesus saith unto them; "How many loaves have ye?" And they said; "Seven, and a few little fishes."

Mat 15:35 And he commanded the multitude to sit down on the ground.

Mat 15:36 And he took the seven loaves and the fishes, and gave thanks, and brake them, and gave to his disciples, and the disciples to the multitude.

Mat 15:37 And they did all eat, and were filled: and they took up of the broken meat that was left seven baskets full.

Mat 15:38 And they that did eat were four thousand men, beside women and children.

Mat 15:39 And he sent away the multitude, and took ship, and came into the coasts of Magdala.

Jesus Feeds the Four Thousand

Mar 8:1 In those days the multitude being very great, and having nothing to eat, Jesus called his disciples unto him, and saith unto them;

Mar 8:2 "I have compassion on the multitude, because they have now been with me three days, and have nothing to eat: 3 And if I send them away fasting to their own houses, they will faint by the way: for divers of them came from far."

Mar 8:4 And his disciples answered him; "From whence can a man satisfy these men with bread here in the wilderness?"

Mar 8:5 And he asked them; "How many loaves have ye?" And they said; "Seven."

Mar 8:6 And he commanded the people to sit down on the ground: and he took the seven loaves, and gave thanks, and brake, and gave to his disciples to set before them; and they did set them before the people.

Mar 8:7 And they had a few small fishes: and he blessed, and commanded to set them also before them.

Mar 8:8 So they did eat, and were filled: and they took up of the broken meat that was left seven baskets.

Mar 8:9 And they that had eaten were about four thousand: and he sent them away.

Coasts of Magdala, Dalmanutha

Discerning the Face of the Sky. Demanding a Sign.

Mat 16:1 The Pharisees also with the Sadducees came, and tempting desired him that he would shew them a sign from heaven.

Mat 16:2 He answered and said unto them; "When it is evening, ye say; "It will be fair weather: for the sky is red." 3 And in the morning; "It will be foul weather today: for the sky is red and lowring." O ye hypocrites, <u>ye can discern the face of the sky</u>; but can ye not discern the signs of the times? 4 A wicked and adulterous generation seeketh after a sign; and there shall no sign be given unto it, but the sign of the prophet Jonas." And he left them, and departed.

The Pharisees Demand a Sign

Mar 8:10 And straightway he entered into a ship with his disciples, and came into the parts of Dalmanutha.

Mar 8:11 And the Pharisees came forth, and began to question with him, seeking of him a sign from heaven, tempting him.

Mar 8:12 And he sighed deeply in his spirit, and saith; "Why doth this generation seek after a sign? verily I say unto you; There shall no sign be given unto this generation."

Mar 8:13 And he left them, and entering into the ship again departed to the other side.

Discerning the Face of the Sky. Demanding a Sign

Luk 12:54 And he said also to the people; "When ye see a cloud rise out of the west, straightway ye say, there cometh a shower; and so, it is. 55 And when ye see the south wind blow, ye say, there will be heat; and it cometh to pass. 56 Ye hypocrites, ye can discern the face of the sky and of the earth; but how is it that ye do not discern this time?"

Leaving Dalmanutha, West side of the Sea of Galilee

Beware The Leaven of the Pharisees and Sadducees.

Mat 16:5 And when his disciples were come to the other side, they had forgotten to take bread.

Mat 16:6 Then Jesus said unto them; "Take heed and beware of the leaven of the Pharisees and of the Sadducees."

Mat 16:7 And they reasoned among themselves, saying; "It is because we have taken no bread."

Mat 16:8 Which when Jesus perceived, he said unto them; "O ye of little faith, why reason ye among yourselves, because ye have brought no bread? 9 Do ye not yet understand, neither remember the five loaves of the five thousand, and how many baskets ye took up? 10 Neither the seven loaves of the four thousand, and how many baskets ye took up? 11 How is it that ye do not understand that I spake it not to you concerning bread, that ye should beware of the leaven of the Pharisees and of the Sadducees?"

Mat 16:12 Then understood they how that he bade them not beware of the leaven of bread, but of the doctrine of the Pharisees and of the Sadducees.

Beware The Leaven of the Pharisees and Herod

Mar 8:14 Now the disciples had forgotten to take bread, neither had they in the ship with them more than one loaf.

Mar 8:15 And he charged them, saying; "Take heed, beware of the leaven of the Pharisees, and of the leaven of Herod."

Mar 8:16 And they reasoned among themselves, saying; "It is because we have no bread?

Mar 8:17 And when Jesus knew it, he saith unto them; "Why reason ye, because ye have no bread? perceive ye not yet, neither understand? have ye your heart yet hardened? 18 Having eyes, see ye not? and having ears, hear ye not? and do ye not remember? 19 When I brake the five loaves among five thousand, how many baskets full of fragments took ye up?" They say unto him; "Twelve."

Mar 8:20 "And when the seven among four thousand, how many baskets full of fragments took ye up?" And they said; "Seven."

Mar 8:21 And he said unto them; "How is it that ye do not understand?"

Beware of the Leaven of the Pharisees.

Preaching near Bethany and Jerusalem. This is similar to Mark and Matthew but being in a boat is not mentioned.

Luk 12:1 In the meantime, when there were gathered together an innumerable multitude of people, insomuch that they trode one upon another, he began to say unto his disciples first of all, Beware ye of the leaven of the Pharisees, which is hypocrisy.

Luk 12:2 For there is nothing covered, that shall not be revealed; neither hid, that shall not be known.

Luk 12:3 Therefore whatsoever ye have spoken in darkness shall be heard in the light; and that which ye have spoken in the ear in closets shall be proclaimed upon the housetops

Jesus Heals a Blind Man at Bethsaida

Mar 8:22 And he cometh to Bethsaida; and they bring a blind man unto him, and besought him to touch him.

Mar 8:23 And he took the blind man by the hand, and led him out of the town; and when he had spit on his eyes, and put his hands upon him, he asked him if he saw ought.

Mar 8:24 And he looked up, and said; "I see men as trees, walking."

Mar 8:25 After that he put his hands again upon his eyes, and made him look up: and he was restored, and saw every man clearly.

Mar 8:26 And he sent him away to his house, saying; "Neither go into the town, nor tell it to any in the town."

Coasts of Caesarea Philippi.

Peter confesses Jesus as the Christ

Mat 16:13 When Jesus came into the coasts of Caesarea Philippi, he asked his disciples, saying; "Whom do men say that I the Son of man am?"

Mat 16:14 And they said; "Some say that thou art John the Baptist: some, Elias; and others, Jeremias, or one of the prophets."

Mat 16:15 He saith unto them; "But whom say ye that I am?"

Mat 16:16 And Simon Peter answered and said; "Thou art the Christ, the Son of the living God.

Mat 16:17 And Jesus answered and said unto him; "Blessed art thou, Simon Barjona: for flesh and blood hath not revealed it unto thee, but my Father which is in heaven. 18 And I say also unto thee, that thou art Peter *(Petros G4074)*, and upon this rock *(Petra G4073)* I will build my church *(Ekklesia G1577)*; and the gates of hell *(G86 Hades)* shall not prevail against it. 19 And I will give unto thee the keys of the kingdom of heaven: and whatsoever thou shalt bind on earth shall be bound in heaven: and whatsoever thou shalt loose on earth shall be loosed in heaven." *(Confirmation of John 1:42 Take a look at*

Job where the word rock is used as an analogy of steadfast and solid Job 39:28 and Ps 18:2)

Mat 16:20 Then charged he his disciples that they should tell no man that he was Jesus the Christ.

Mat 16:21 From that time forth began Jesus to shew unto his disciples, how that he must go unto Jerusalem, and suffer many things of the elders and chief priests and scribes, and be killed, and be raised again the third day. *(Hosea 6:2)*

Peter Confesses Jesus as the Christ

Mar 8:27 And Jesus went out, and his disciples, into the towns of Caesarea Philippi: and by the way he asked his disciples, saying unto them; "Whom do men say that I am?"

Mar 8:28 And they answered; "John the Baptist: but some say, Elias; and others, One of the prophets."

Mar 8:29 And he saith unto them; "But whom say ye that I am?" And Peter answereth and saith unto him; "Thou art the Christ."

Mar 8:30 And he charged them that they should tell no man of him.

Mar 8:31 And he began to teach them, that the Son of man must suffer many things, and be rejected of the elders, and of the chief priests, and scribes, and be killed, and after three days rise again.

Peter Confesses Jesus as the Christ

Luk 9:18 And it came to pass, as he was alone praying, his disciples were with him: and he asked them, saying; "Whom say the people that I am?"

Luk 9:19 They answering said; "John the Baptist; but some say, Elias; and others say, that one of the old prophets is risen again."

Luk 9:20 He said unto them; "But whom say ye that I am?" Peter answering said; "The Christ of God."

Luk 9:21 And he straitly charged them, and commanded them to tell no man that thing;

Luk 9:22 Saying; "The Son of man must suffer many things, and be rejected of the elders and chief priests and scribes, and be slain, and <u>be raised the third day</u>."

Jesus Rebukes satan through Peter

Mat 16:22 Then Peter took him, and began to rebuke him, saying; "Be it far from thee, Lord: this shall not be unto thee."

Mat 16:23 But he turned, and said unto Peter; "Get thee behind me, satan: thou art an offence unto me: for thou savourest not the things that be of God, but those that be of men."

Jesus Rebukes satan through Peter

Mar 8:32 And he spake that saying openly. And Peter took him, and began to rebuke him.

Mar 8:33 But when he had turned about and looked on his disciples, he rebuked Peter, saying; "Get thee behind me, satan: for thou savourest not the things that be of God, but the things that be of men."

Mar 8:34 And when he had called the people unto him with his disciples also, he said unto them; "Whosoever will come after me, let him deny himself, and take up his cross, and follow me. 35 For whosoever will save his life shall lose it; but whosoever shall lose his life for my sake and the gospel's, the same shall save it. 36 For what shall it profit a man, if he shall gain the whole world, and lose his own soul? 37 Or what shall a man give in exchange for his soul? 38 Whosoever therefore shall be ashamed of me and of my words in this adulterous and sinful generation; of him also shall the Son of man be ashamed, when he cometh in the glory of his Father with the holy angels."

Mar 9:1 And he said unto them; "Verily I say unto you; That there be some of them that stand here, which shall not taste of death, till they have seen the kingdom of God come with power." *(Luke 17:20, Rom 14:18, Acts 1:8)*

Take Up Your Cross and Follow Jesus. (Rom 8:29)

Mat 16:24 Then said Jesus unto his disciples; "If any man will come after me, let him deny himself, and take up his cross, and follow me. 25 For whosoever will save his life shall lose it: and whosoever will lose his life for my sake shall find it. 26 For what is a man profited, if he shall gain the whole world, and lose his own soul? or what shall a man give in exchange for his soul? 27 For the Son of man shall come in the glory of his Father with his angels; and then he shall reward every man according to his works. 28 Verily I say unto you, there be some standing here, which shall not taste of death, till they see the Son of man coming in his kingdom." *(Luke 17:20, Rom 14:18, Acts 1:8)*

Take Up Your Cross and Follow Jesus

Luk 9:23 And he said to them all; "<u>If any man will come after me</u>, let him deny himself, and take up his cross daily, and follow me. 24 For whosoever will save his life shall lose it: but whosoever will lose his life for my sake, the same shall save it. 25 For what is a man advantaged, if he gains the whole world, and lose himself, or be cast away? 26 For whosoever shall be ashamed of me and of my words, of him shall the Son of man be ashamed, when he shall come in his own glory, and in his Father's, and of the holy angels. 27 But I tell you of a truth, there be some standing here, which shall not taste of death, till they see the kingdom of God.

<u>Abiding in Galilee</u>

The Transfiguration on the Mount

Mat 17:1 And after six days Jesus taketh Peter, James, and John his brother, and bringeth them up into an high mountain apart,

Mat 17:2 And was transfigured before them: and his face did shine as the sun, and his raiment was white as the light.

Mat 17:3 And, behold, there appeared unto them Moses and Elias talking with him.

Mat 17:4 Then answered Peter, and said unto Jesus; "Lord, it is good for us to be here: if thou wilt, let us make here three tabernacles; one for thee, and one for Moses, and one for Elias."

Mat 17:5 While he yet spake, behold, a bright cloud overshadowed them: and behold a voice out of the cloud, which said, "THIS IS MY BELOVED SON, IN WHOM I AM WELL PLEASED; HEAR YE HIM".

Mat 17:6 And when the disciples heard it, they fell on their face, and were sore afraid.

Mat 17:7 And Jesus came and touched them, and said; "Arise, and be not afraid."

Mat 17:8 And when they had lifted up their eyes, they saw no man, save Jesus only.

Mat 17:9 And as they came down from the mountain, Jesus charged them, saying; "Tell the vision to no man, until the Son of man be risen again from the dead."

Mat 17:10 And his disciples asked him, saying; "Why then say the scribes that Elias must first come?"

Mat 17:11 And Jesus answered and said unto them; "Elias truly shall first come, and restore all things. 12 But I say unto you; That Elias is come already, and they knew him not, but have done unto him whatsoever they listed. Likewise, shall also the Son of man suffer of them."

Mat 17:13 Then the disciples understood that he spake unto them of John the Baptist.

<u>The Transfiguration on the Mount</u>

Mar 9:2 And after six days Jesus taketh with him Peter, and James, and John, and leadeth them up into an high mountain apart by themselves: and he was transfigured before them.

Mar 9:3 And his raiment became shining, exceeding white as snow; so as no fuller on earth can white them.

Mar 9:4 And there appeared unto them Elias with Moses: and they were talking with Jesus.

Mar 9:5 And Peter answered and said to Jesus; "Master, it is good for us to be here: and let us make three tabernacles; one for thee, and one for Moses, and one for Elias."

Mar 9:6 For he wist not what to say; for they were sore afraid.

Mar 9:7 And there was a cloud that overshadowed them: and a voice came out of the cloud, saying; "<u>THIS IS MY BELOVED SON: HEAR HIM</u>."

Mar 9:8 And suddenly, when they had looked round about, they saw no man any more, save Jesus only with themselves.

Mar 9:9 And as they came down from the mountain, he charged them that they should tell no man what things they had seen, till the Son of man were risen from the dead.

Mar 9:10 And they kept that saying with themselves, questioning one with another what the rising from the dead should mean.

Mar 9:11 And they asked him, saying; "Why say the scribes that Elias must first come?" 12 And he answered and told them; "Elias verily cometh first, and restoreth all things; and how it is written of the Son of man, that he must suffer many things, and be set at nought. 13 But I say unto you, That Elias is indeed come, and they have done unto him whatsoever they listed, as it is written of him."

The Transfiguration on the Mount

Luk 9:28 And it came to pass about an eight days after these sayings, he took Peter and John and James, and went up into a mountain to pray.

Luk 9:29 And as he prayed, the fashion of his countenance was altered, and his raiment was white and glistering.

Luk 9:30 And, behold, there talked with him two men, which were Moses and Elias:

Luk 9:31 Who appeared in glory, and spake of his decease which he should accomplish at Jerusalem.

Luk 9:32 But Peter and they that were with him were heavy with sleep: and when they were awake, they saw his glory, and the two men that stood with him.

Luk 9:33 And it came to pass, as they departed from him, Peter said unto Jesus; "Master, it is good for us to be here: and let us make three tabernacles; one for thee, and one for Moses, and one for Elias.", not knowing what he said.

Luk 9:34 While he thus spake, there came a cloud, and overshadowed them: and they feared as they entered into the cloud.

Luk 9:35 And there came a voice out of the cloud, saying; "<u>THIS IS MY BELOVED SON, HEAR YE HIM.</u>"

Luk 9:36 And when the voice was past, Jesus was found alone. And they kept it close and told no man in those days any of those things which they had seen.

Jesus Cast Out a devil from a Boy

Mat 17:14 And when they were come to the multitude, there came to him a certain man, kneeling down to him, and saying;

Mat 17:15 "Lord, have mercy on my son: for he is lunatick, and sore vexed: for ofttimes he falleth into the fire, and oft into the water. 16 And I brought him to thy disciples, and they could not cure him."

Mat 17:17 Then Jesus answered and said; "<u>O faithless and perverse generation</u>, how long shall I be with you? how long shall I suffer you? bring him hither to me."

Mat 17:18 And Jesus rebuked the devil, and he departed out of him: and the child was cured from that very hour.

<u>Pray and Fast and you will cast out devils Also.</u> *<u>Zec 4:6, John 14:12, James 4:7,</u>* *<u>Mat 6:33.</u>*

Mat 17:19 Then came the disciples to Jesus apart, and said; "Why could not we cast him out?"

Mat 17:20 And Jesus said unto them; "Because of your unbelief: for verily I say unto you; If ye have faith as a grain of mustard seed, ye shall say unto this mountain; Remove hence to yonder place; and it shall remove; and nothing shall be impossible unto you. 21 Howbeit this kind goeth not out but by prayer and fasting."

Jesus Casts out a Dumb Spirit from a Boy

Mar 9:14 And when he came to his disciples, he saw a great multitude about them, and the scribes questioning with them.

Mar 9:15 And straightway all the people, when they beheld him, were greatly amazed, and running to him saluted him.

Mar 9:16 And he asked the scribes; "What question ye with them? "

Mar 9:17 And one of the multitude answered and said; "Master, I have brought unto thee my son, which hath a dumb spirit; 18 And wheresoever he taketh him, he teareth him: and he foameth, and gnasheth with his teeth, and pineth away: and I spake to thy disciples that they should cast him out; and <u>they could not</u>."

Mar 9:19 He answereth him, and saith; "<u>O faithless generation</u>, how long shall I be with you? how long shall I suffer you? bring him unto me."

Mar 9:20 And they brought him unto him: and when he saw him, straightway the spirit tare him; and he fell on the ground, and wallowed foaming.

Mar 9:21 And he asked his father; "How long is it ago since this came unto him?" And he said; "Of a child. 22 And ofttimes it hath cast him into the fire, and into the waters, to destroy him: but if thou canst do anything, have compassion on us, and help us."

Mar 9:23 Jesus said unto him; "If thou canst believe, all things are possible to him that believeth."

Mar 9:24 And straightway the father of the child cried out, and said with tears; "Lord, I believe; help thou mine unbelief."

Mar 9:25 When Jesus saw that the people came running together, he rebuked the foul spirit, saying unto him; "Thou dumb and deaf spirit, I charge thee, come out of him, and enter no more into him."

Mar 9:26 And the spirit cried, and rent him sore, and came out of him: and he was as one dead; insomuch that many said, He is dead.

Mar 9:27 But Jesus took him by the hand, and lifted him up; and he arose.

<u>Pray and Fast and you will cast out devils also.</u> *Zec 4:6, John 14:12, Mat 6:33*

Mar 9:28 And when he was come into the house, his disciples asked him privately; "Why could not we cast him out?"

Mar 9:29 And he said unto them; "This kind can come forth by nothing, but by prayer and fasting."

<u>Jesus Casts Out a Dumb Spirit from a Boy</u>

Luk 9:37 And it came to pass, that on the next day, when they were come down from the hill, much people met him.

Luk 9:38 And, behold, a man of the company cried out, saying; "Master, I beseech thee, look upon my son: for he is my only child. 39 And, lo, a spirit taketh him, and he suddenly crieth out; and it teareth him that he foameth again and bruising him hardly departeth from him. 40 And I besought thy disciples to cast him out; and they could not."

Luk 9:41 And Jesus answering said; "<u>O faithless and perverse generation</u>, how long shall I be with you, and suffer you? Bring thy son hither."

Luk 9:42 And as he was yet a coming, the devil threw him down, and tare him. And Jesus rebuked the unclean spirit, and healed the child, and delivered him again to his father.

Galilee

Jesus Reveals his Death and Resurrection, *Mic 7:8, Hos 6:2. Mat 12:38*

Mat 17:22 And while they abode in Galilee, Jesus said unto them; "The Son of man shall be betrayed into the hands of men: 23 And they shall kill him, and the third day he shall be raised again." And they were exceeding sorry.

Jesus Reveals his Death and Resurrection

Mar 9:30 And they departed thence, and passed through Galilee; and he would not that any man should know it.

Mar 9:31 For he taught his disciples, and said unto them; "The Son of man is delivered into the hands of men, and they shall kill him; and after that he is killed, he shall rise the third day. "

Mar 9:32 But they understood not that saying, and were afraid to ask him.

Jesus Reveals His Death and Resurrection

Luk 9:43 And they were all amazed at the mighty power of God. But while they wondered everyone at all things which Jesus did, he said unto his disciples;

Luk 9:44 "Let these sayings sink down into your ears: for the Son of man shall be delivered into the hands of men."

Luk 9:45 But they understood not this saying, and it was hid from them, that they perceived it not: and they feared to ask him of that saying.

Capernaum, Galilee, In House

The Kings Children are Exempt

Mat 17:24 And when they were come to Capernaum, they that received tribute money came to Peter, and said; "Doth not your master pay tribute?"

Mat 17:25 He saith; "Yes." And when he was come into the house, Jesus prevented him, saying; "What thinkest thou, Simon? Of whom do the kings of the earth take custom or tribute? Of their own children, or of strangers?"

Mat 17:26 Peter saith unto him; "Of strangers." Jesus saith unto him; "Then are the children free. 27 Notwithstanding, lest we should offend them, go thou to the sea, and cast an hook, and take up the fish that first cometh up; and when thou hast opened his mouth, thou shalt find a piece of money: that take, and give unto them for me and thee."

Children are most precious.

Mat 18:1 At the same time came the disciples unto Jesus, saying; "<u>Who is the greatest</u> in the kingdom of heaven?"

Mat 18:2 And Jesus called a little child unto him, and set him in the midst of them,

Children are most precious.

Mar 9:33 And he came to Capernaum: and being in the house he asked them; "What was it that ye disputed among yourselves by the way?"

Mar 9:34 But they held their peace: for by the way they had disputed among themselves, <u>who should be the greatest.</u>

Mar 9:35 And he sat down, and called the twelve, and saith unto them; "If any man desire to be first, the same shall be last of all, and servant of all."

Mar 9:36 And he took a child, and set him in the midst of them: and when he had taken him in his arms, he said unto them;

Mar 9:37 "Whosoever shall receive one of such children in my name, receiveth me: and whosoever shall receive me, receiveth not me, but him that sent me."

Children are most precious.

Luk 9:46 Then there arose a reasoning among them, <u>which of them should be greatest</u>.

Luk 9:47 And Jesus, perceiving the thought of their heart, took a child, and set him by him,

Luk 9:48 And said unto them; "Whosoever shall receive this child in my name receiveth me: and whosoever shall receive me receiveth him that sent me: for he that is least among you all, the same shall be great."

Millstone is better

Mat 18:3 And said; "Verily I say unto you, except ye be converted, and become as little children, ye shall not enter into the kingdom of heaven. 4 Whosoever therefore shall humble himself as this little child, the same is greatest in the kingdom of heaven. 5 And whoso shall receive one such little child in my name receiveth me. 6 But whoso shall offend one of these little ones which believe in me, it were better for him that a <u>millstone</u> were hanged about his neck, and that he were drowned in the depth of the sea."

Millstone is better

Mar 9:42 And whosoever shall offend one of these little ones that believe in me, it is better for him that a <u>millstone</u> were hanged about his neck, and he were cast into the sea.

Millstone is better

Luk 17:1 Then said he unto the disciples; "It is impossible but that offences will come: but woe unto him, through whom they come! 2 It were better for him that a <u>millstone</u> was hanged about his neck, and he cast into the sea, than that he should offend one of these little ones.

Forbid not, one casting out devils. *Mat 10:42*

Mar 9:38 And John answered him, saying; "Master, we saw one casting out devils in thy name, and he followeth not us: and we forbad him, because he followeth not us."

Mar 9:39 But Jesus said; "Forbid him not: for there is no man which shall do a miracle in my name, that can lightly speak evil of me. 40 For he that is not against us is on our part. 41 For whosoever shall give you a cup of water to drink in my name, because ye belong to Christ, verily I say unto you, he shall not lose his reward.

Forbid not, one casting out devils

Luk 9:49 And John answered and said; "Master, we saw one casting out devils in thy name; and we forbad him, because he followeth not with us."

Luk 9:50 And Jesus said unto him; "Forbid him not: for he that is not against us is for us."

Jesus sets his face toward Jerusalem, Isaiah 50:7.

A Samaritan Village Rejects Jesus, Disciples get Offended

Luk 9:51 And it came to pass, when the time was come that he should be received up, he stedfastly set his face to go to Jerusalem,

Luk 9:52 And sent messengers before his face: and they went, and entered into a village of the Samaritans, to make ready for him.

Luk 9:53 And they did not receive him, because his face was as though he would go to Jerusalem.

Luk 9:54 And when his disciples James and John saw this, they said; "Lord, wilt thou that we command fire to come down from heaven, and consume them, even as Elias (Elijah. 2 Kings 1:10) did?"

Luk 9:55 But he turned, and rebuked them, and said; "Ye know not what manner of spirit ye are of. 56 For the Son of man is not come to destroy men's lives, but to save them." And they went to another village.

Cut off anything that holds you back from the presence of God

Mat 18:7 "Woe unto the world because of offences! for it must needs be that offences come; but woe to that man by whom the offence cometh! 8 Wherefore if thy hand or thy foot offend thee, cut them off, and cast them from thee: it is better for thee to enter into life halt or maimed, rather than having two hands or two feet to be cast into everlasting fire. 9 And if thine eye offend thee, pluck it out, and cast it from thee: it is better for thee to enter into life with one eye, rather than having two eyes to be cast into hell fire."

Cut off anything that holds you back from the presence of God

Mar 9:43 "And if thy hand offend thee, cut it off: it is better for thee to enter into life maimed, than having two hands to go into hell, into the fire that never shall be quenched: 44 Where their worm dieth not, and the fire is not quenched. 45 <u>And if thy foot offend thee, cut it off</u>: it is better for thee to enter halt into life, than having two feet to be cast into hell, into the fire that never shall be quenched: 46 Where their worm dieth not, and the fire is not quenched. 47 And if thine eye offend thee, pluck it out: it is better for thee to enter into the kingdom of God with one eye, than having two eyes to be cast into hell fire: 48 Where their worm dieth not, and the fire is not quenched.

The Parable of the Lost Sheep

Mat 18:10 "Take heed that ye despise not one of these little ones; for I say unto you; That in heaven their angels do always behold the face of my Father which is in heaven. 11 For the Son of man is come to save that which was lost. 12 How think ye? if a man have an hundred sheep, and one of them be gone astray, <u>doth he not leave the ninety and nine</u>, and goeth into the mountains, and seeketh that which is gone astray? 13 And if so be that he find it, verily I say unto you, he rejoiceth more of that sheep, than of the ninety and nine which went not astray. 14 Even so it is not the will of your Father which is in heaven, that one of these little ones should perish."

The Parable of the Lost Sheep

Luk 15:1 Then drew near unto him all the publicans and sinners for to hear him.

Luk 15:2 And the Pharisees and scribes murmured, saying; "This man receiveth sinners, and eateth with them."

Luk 15:3 And he spake this parable unto them, saying; 4 "What man of you, having an hundred sheep, if he lose one of them, <u>doth not leave the ninety and nine</u> in the wilderness, and go after that which is lost, until he find it? 5 And when he hath found it, he layeth it on his shoulders, rejoicing. 6 And when he cometh home, he calleth together his friends and neighbours, saying unto them; "Rejoice with me; for I have found my sheep which was lost." 7 I say unto you, that likewise joy shall be in heaven over one sinner that repenteth, more than over ninety and nine just persons, which need no repentance."

Go to your brother first.

Mat 18:15 "Moreover if thy brother shall trespass against thee, go and tell him his fault between thee and him alone: if he shall hear thee, thou hast gained thy brother. 16 But if he will not hear thee, then take with thee one or two more, that in the mouth of two or three witnesses every word may be established. 17 And if he shall neglect to hear them, tell it unto the church: but if he neglect to hear the church, let him be unto thee as an heathen man *(G1482 gentile)* and a publican. *(G5057 tax collector)*

Loosing and Binding on Earth. The Keys. (Mat 16:19)

Mat 18:18 "Verily I say unto you; Whatsoever ye shall bind on earth shall be bound in heaven: and whatsoever ye shall loose on earth shall be loosed in heaven. 19 Again I say unto you. That if two of you shall agree on earth as touching anything that they shall ask, it shall be done for them of my Father which is in heaven. 20 For where two or three are gathered together in my name, there am I in the midst of them."

Forgiving 70 x 7 per day; if they repent, Forgive from the Heart.

(Gen 4:15 and Gen 4:24 Forgiving 70 x 7.)

Mat 18:21 Then came Peter to him, and said; "Lord, how oft shall my brother sin against me, and I forgive him? till seven times?"

Mat 18:22 Jesus saith unto him; "I say not unto thee, Until seven times: but, Until seventy times seven. 23 Therefore is the kingdom of heaven likened unto a certain king, which would take account of his servants. 24 And when he had begun to reckon, one was brought unto him, which owed him ten thousand talents. 25 But forasmuch as he had not to pay, his lord commanded him to be sold, and his wife, and children, and all that he had, and payment to be made. 26 The servant therefore fell down, and worshipped him, saying; "Lord, have patience with me, and I will pay thee all." 27 Then the lord of that servant was moved with compassion, and loosed him, and forgave him the debt. 28

But the same servant went out, and found one of his fellowservants, which owed him an hundred pence: and he laid hands on him, and took him by the throat, saying; "Pay me that thou owest." 29 And his fellowservant fell down at his feet, and besought him, saying; "Have patience with me, and I will pay thee all." 30 And he would not: but went and cast him into prison, till he should pay the debt. 31 So when his fellowservants saw what was done, they were very sorry, and came and told unto their lord all that was done. 32 Then his lord, after that he had called him, said unto him; "O thou wicked servant, I forgave thee all that debt, because thou desiredst me: 33 Shouldest not thou also have had compassion on thy fellowservant, even as I had pity on thee?" 34 And his lord was wroth, and delivered him to the tormentors, till he should pay all that was due unto him. 35 So likewise shall my heavenly Father do also unto you, if ye from your hearts forgive not everyone his brother their trespasses." *(G3900 Paraptoma, falls, faults deliberate errors. We get our word parachute. James 5:16, same word used but different to the word used for sins we confess our sins to Jesus, 1Joh 1:9. Sins, Hamartia G266.)*

Forgive seven times if Repents Seven Times

Luk 17:3 "Take heed to yourselves: If thy brother trespass against thee, rebuke him; and if he repent, forgive him. 4 And if he trespass against thee seven times in a day, and seven times in a day turn again to thee, saying; "I repent;" thou shalt forgive him."

Moving Through the Coasts of Judea from Galilee.

Divorce, Remarriage can be Adultery Explained. *Matt 5:31*

Mat 19:1 And it came to pass, that when Jesus had finished these sayings, he departed from Galilee, and came into the coasts of Judaea beyond Jordan;

Mat 19:2 And great multitudes followed him; and he healed them there.

Mat 19:3 The Pharisees also came unto him, tempting him, and saying unto him; "Is it lawful for a man to put away his wife for every cause?"

Mat 19:4 And he answered and said unto them; "Have ye not read, that he which made them at the beginning made them male and female; 5 And said; "For this cause shall a man leave father and mother, and shall cleave to his wife: and they twain shall be one flesh?" *(Gen 2:24)* 6 Wherefore they are no more twain, but one flesh. What therefore God hath joined together, let not man put asunder."

Mat 19:7 They say unto him; "Why did Moses then command to give a writing of divorcement, and to put her away?"

Mat 19:8 He saith unto them; "<u>Moses because of the hardness of your hearts suffered you</u> to put away your wives: but from the beginning it was not so. 9 And I say unto you, whosoever shall put away his wife, except it be for fornication, and shall marry another, committeth adultery: and whoso marrieth her which is put away doth commit adultery."

Mat 19:10 His disciples say unto him; "If the case of the man be so with his wife, it is not good to marry."

The Gift of being a Eunuch.

Mat 19:11 But he said unto them; "All men cannot receive this saying, save they to whom it is given. 12 For there are some eunuchs, which were so born from their mother's womb: and there are some eunuchs, which were made eunuchs of men: and there be eunuchs, which have made themselves eunuchs for the kingdom of heaven's sake. He that is able to receive it, let him receive it."

Divorce and Remarriage can be Adultery

Mar 10:1 And he arose from thence, and cometh into the coasts of Judaea by the farther side of Jordan: and the people resort unto him again; and, as he was wont, he taught them again.

Mar 10:2 And the Pharisees came to him, and asked him; "Is it lawful for a man to put away his wife?" tempting him.

Mar 10:3 And he answered and said unto them; "What did Moses command you?"

Mar 10:4 And they said; "Moses suffered to write a bill of divorcement, and to put her away."

Mar 10:5 And Jesus answered and said unto them; "<u>For the hardness of your heart he wrote you this precept.</u> 6 But from the beginning of the creation God made them male and female. 7 For this cause shall a man leave his father and mother, and cleave to his wife; 8 And they twain shall be one flesh: so then they are no more twain, but one flesh. 9 What therefore God hath joined together, let not man put asunder."

Mar 10:10 And in the house his disciples asked him again of the same matter.

Mar 10:11 And he saith unto them; "Whosoever shall put away his wife, and marry another, committeth adultery against her. 12 And if a woman shall put away her husband, and be married to another, she committeth adultery."

<u>Divorce and Remarrying can be Adultery</u>

Luk 16:18 "Whosoever putteth away his wife, and marrieth another, committeth adultery: and whosoever marrieth her that is put away from her husband committeth adultery."

<u>Strive to Enter, The Strait Gate.</u> *Isa 35:8*

Luk 13:22 And he went through the cities and villages, teaching, and journeying toward Jerusalem.

Luk 13:23 Then said one unto him; "Lord, are there few that be saved? And he said unto them;

Luk 13:24 "Strive to enter in at the strait gate: for many, I say unto you, will seek to enter in, and shall not be able. 25 When once the master of the house is risen up, and hath shut to the door, and ye begin to stand without, and to knock at the door, saying; "Lord, Lord, open unto us;" and he shall answer and say unto you; "I know you not whence ye are": 26 Then shall ye begin to say; "we have eaten and drunk in thy presence, and thou hast taught in our streets." 27 But he shall say; "I tell you, I know you not whence ye are; depart from me, all ye workers of iniquity." *(Ps 6:8)* 28 There shall be weeping and gnashing of teeth, when ye shall see Abraham, and Isaac, and Jacob, and all the prophets, in the kingdom of God, and you yourselves thrust out. 29 And they shall come from the east, and from the west, and from the north, and from the south, and shall sit down in the kingdom of God. 30 And, behold, there are last which shall be first, and there are first which shall be last."

A Chief Pharisees House

Healing of a Man with Dropsy on the Sabbath

Luk 14:1 And it came to pass, as he went into the house of one of the chief Pharisees to eat bread on the sabbath day, that they watched him.

Luk 14:2 And, behold, there was a certain man before him which had the dropsy.

Luk 14:3 And Jesus answering spake unto the lawyers and Pharisees, saying, "Is it lawful to heal on the sabbath day?" *(Also repeated in Mat 12:10, Mar 3:1, Luk 6:9)*

Luk 14:4 And they held their peace. And he took him, and healed him, and let him go;

Luk 14:5 And answered them, saying, "Which of you shall have an ass or an ox fallen into a pit, and will not straightway pull him out on the sabbath day?"

Luk 14:6 And they could not answer him again to these things.

The Parable of the Wedding Feast

Luk 14:7 And he put forth a parable to those which were bidden, when he marked how they chose out the chief rooms; saying unto them;

Luk 14:8 "When thou art bidden of any man to a wedding, sit not down in the highest room; lest a more honourable man than thou be bidden of him; 9 And he that bade thee and him come and say to thee, give this man place; and thou begin with shame to take the lowest room. 10 But when thou art bidden, go and sit down in the lowest room; that when he that bade thee cometh, he may say unto thee, Friend, go up higher: then shalt thou have worship in the presence of them that sit at meat with thee. 11 For whosoever exalteth himself shall be abased; and he that humbleth himself shall be exalted."

Call the Poor to the Great Banquet. *Ps 23:5, Zeph 1:7, Rev 19:6-10.*

Luk 14:12 Then said he also to him that bade him; "When thou makest a dinner or a supper, call not thy friends, nor thy brethren, neither thy kinsmen, nor thy rich neighbours; lest they also bid thee again, and a recompence be made thee. 13 But when thou makest a feast, call the poor, the maimed, the lame, the blind: 14 And thou shalt be blessed; for they cannot recompense thee: for thou shalt be recompensed at the resurrection of the just."

Luk 14:15 And when one of them that sat at meat with him heard these things, he said unto him; "Blessed is he that shall eat bread in the kingdom of God."

Luk 14:16 Then said he unto him; "A certain man made a great supper, and bade many: 17 And sent his servant at supper time to say to them that were bidden, come; for all things are now ready. 18 And they all with one consent began to make excuse. The first said unto him; "I have bought a piece of ground, and I must needs go and see it: I pray thee have me excused." 19 And another said; "I have bought five yoke of oxen, and I go to prove them: I pray thee have me excused." 20 And another said; "I have married a wife, and therefore I cannot come." 21 So that servant came, and shewed his lord these things. Then the master of the house being angry said to his servant; "Go out quickly into the streets and lanes of the city, and bring in hither the poor, and the maimed, and the halt, and the blind." 22 And the servant said; "Lord, it is done as thou hast commanded, and yet there is room." 23 And the lord said unto the servant; "Go out into the highways and hedges, and compel them to come in, that my house may be filled. 24 For I say unto you, that none of those men which were bidden shall taste of my supper.""

The Price of Discipleship

Luk 14:25 And there went great multitudes with him: and he turned, and said unto them;

Luk 14:26 "If any man come to me, and hate *(G3404 love less)* not his father, and mother, and wife, and children, and brethren, and sisters, yea, and his own life also, he cannot be my disciple. 27 And whosoever doth not bear his cross, and come after me, cannot be my disciple. 28 For which of you, intending to build a tower, sitteth not down first, and counteth the cost, whether he have sufficient to finish it? 29 Lest haply, after he hath laid the foundation, and is not able to finish it, all that behold it begin to mock him, 30 Saying, this man began to build, and was not able to finish. 31 Or what king, going to make war against another king, sitteth not down first, and consulteth whether he be able with ten thousand to meet him that cometh against him with twenty thousand? 32 Or else, while the other is yet a great way off, he sendeth an ambassage, and desireth conditions of peace. 33 So likewise, whosoever he be of you that forsaketh not all that he hath, he cannot be my disciple."

14:34 salt losing its taste Mat 5:13

15:1 parable lost sheep Mat 18:10

The Parable of the Lost Coin

Luk 15:8 "Either what woman having ten pieces of silver, if she lose one piece, doth not light a candle, and sweep the house, and seek diligently till she find it? 9 And when she hath found it, she calleth her friends and her neighbours together, saying" Rejoice with me; for I have found the piece which I had lost." 10 Likewise, I say unto you; There is joy in the presence of the angels of God over one sinner that repenteth."

The Parable of the Prodigal Son

Luk 15:11 And he said; "A certain man had two sons, 12 And the younger of them said to his father; "Father, give me the portion of goods that falleth to me". And he divided unto them his living. 13 And not many days after the younger son gathered all together, and took his journey into a far country, and there wasted his substance with riotous living. 14 And when he had spent all, there arose a mighty famine in that land; and he began to be in want. 15 And he went and joined himself to a citizen of that country; and he sent him into his fields to feed swine. 16 And he would fain have filled his belly with the husks that the swine did eat: and no man gave unto him. 17 And when he came to himself, he said; "How many hired servants of my fathers have bread enough and to spare, and I perish with hunger! 18 I will arise and go to my father, and will say unto him, Father, I have sinned against heaven, and before thee, 19 And am no more worthy to be called thy son: make me as one of thy hired servants." And he arose, and came to his father. But when he was yet a great way off, his father saw him, and had compassion, and ran, and fell on his neck, and kissed him. 21 And the son said unto him; "Father, I have sinned against heaven, and in thy sight, and am no more worthy to be called thy son." 22 But the father said to his servants; "Bring forth the best robe, and put it on him; and put a ring on his hand, and shoes on his feet: 23 And bring hither the fatted calf, and kill it; and let us eat, and be merry: 24 For this my son was dead, and is alive again; he was lost, and is found." And they began to be merry. 25 Now his elder son was in the field: and as he came and drew nigh to the house, he heard music and dancing. 26 And he called one of the servants, and asked what these things meant. 27 And he said unto him; "Thy brother is come; and thy father hath killed the fatted calf, because he hath received him safe and sound." 28 And he was angry, and would not go in: therefore, came his father out, and intreated him. 29 And he answering said to his father; "Lo, these many years do I serve thee, neither transgressed I at any time thy commandment: and yet thou never gavest me a kid, that I might make merry with my friends: 30 But as soon as this thy son was come, which hath devoured thy living with harlots, thou hast killed for him the fatted calf." 31 And he said unto him; "Son, thou art ever with me, and all that I have is thine. 32 It was meet that we should make merry, and be glad: for this thy brother was dead, and is alive again; and was lost, and is found.""

The Parable of the Dishonest Manager

Luk 16:1 And he said also unto his disciples; "There was a certain rich man, which had a steward; and the same was accused unto him that he had wasted his goods. 2 And he called him, and said unto him; "How is it that I hear this of thee? Give an account of thy stewardship; for thou mayest be no longer steward." 3 Then the steward said within himself; "What shall I do? For my lord taketh away from me the stewardship: I cannot dig; to beg I am ashamed. 4 I am resolved what to do, that, when I am put out of the stewardship, they may receive me into their houses." 5 So he called every one of his lord's debtors unto him, and said unto the first; "How much owest thou unto my lord?" 6 And he said; "An hundred measures of oil." And he said unto him; "Take thy bill, and sit down quickly, and write fifty." 7 Then said he to another;

"And how much owest thou?" And he said; "An hundred measures of wheat." And he said unto him; "Take thy bill, and write fourscore." 8 And the lord commended the unjust steward, because he had done wisely: for the children of this world are in their generation wiser than the children of light. 9 And I say unto you; Make to yourselves friends of the mammon of unrighteousness; that, when ye fail, they may receive you into everlasting habitations."

16:10 Faithful in Little Mat 6:19

16:14 The Law Passing Mat 5:17

16:18 Divorce and Remarriage. Mat 19:1

The Rich Man and Lazarus

This is not a parable but a true story because Jesus said a "Certain Beggar Named Lazarus." He was very possibly talking about "The Lazarus, Mary`s and Martha`s brother, as God shows Jesus what is happening in the Spirit before it happens and while it happens". Spend time in God's presence and He will do the same for you. Joh 16:13.

Luk 16:19 "There was a certain rich man, which was clothed in purple and fine linen, and fared sumptuously every day: 20 And there was a certain beggar named Lazarus, which was laid at his gate, full of sores, 21 And desiring to be fed with the crumbs which fell from the rich man's table: moreover, the dogs came and licked his sores. 22 And it came to pass, that the beggar died, and was carried by the angels into Abraham's bosom: the rich man also died, and was buried; 23 And in hell he lifted up his eyes, being in torments, and seeth Abraham afar off, and Lazarus in his bosom. 24 And he cried and said; "Father Abraham, have mercy on me, and send Lazarus, that he may dip the tip of his finger in water, and cool my tongue; for I am tormented in this flame." 25 But Abraham said; "Son, remember that thou in thy lifetime receivedst thy good things, and likewise Lazarus evil things: but now he is comforted, and thou art tormented. 26 And beside all this, between us and you there is a great gulf fixed: so that they which would pass from hence to you cannot; neither can they pass to us, that would come from thence." 27 Then he said; "I pray thee therefore, father, that thou wouldest send him to my father's house: 28 For I have five brethren; that he may testify unto them, lest they also come into this place of torment." 29 Abraham saith unto him; "They have Moses and the prophets; let them hear them." 30 And he said; "Nay, father Abraham: but if one went unto them from the dead, they will repent." 31 And he said unto him; "If they hear not Moses and the prophets, neither will they be persuaded, though one rose from the dead.""

On the way to Jerusalem through Samaria

17:1 Millstone is Better Mat. 18:3

17:3 Forgive seven times if Repents Seven Times. Mat 18:15

17:5 Faith like a Mustard seed Matt 13:31

Jesus Cleanses Ten Lepers, no touching, no prayer, just Obedience to His Instructions.

Luk 17:11 And it came to pass, as he went to Jerusalem, that he passed through the midst of Samaria and Galilee.

Luk 17:12 And as he entered into a certain village, there met him ten men that were lepers, which stood afar off:

Luk 17:13 And they lifted up their voices, and said; "Jesus, Master, have mercy on us."

Luk 17:14 And when he saw them, he said unto them; "Go shew yourselves unto the priests." And it came to pass, that, as they went, they were cleansed.

Luk 17:15 And one of them, when he saw that he was healed, turned back, and with a loud voice glorified God,

Luk 17:16 And fell down on his face at his feet, giving him thanks: and he was a Samaritan.

Luk 17:17 And Jesus answering said; "Were there not ten cleansed? but where are the nine? 18 There are not found that returned to give glory to God, save this stranger."

Luk 17:19 And he said unto him, "Arise, go thy way: thy faith hath made thee whole."

The Kingdom of God is within you (Mat 6:33 and Rom 14:17)

Luk 17:20 And when he was demanded of the Pharisees, when the kingdom of God should come, he answered them and said; "The kingdom of God cometh not with observation: 21 Neither shall they say, Lo here! or, lo there! for, behold, the kingdom of God is within you."

17:22 As in the days of Noah Mat 24:36

17:37 Eagles Gathered Mat 24:25

The Parable of the Persistent Widow and Judge

Luk 18:1 And he spake a parable unto them to this end, that men ought always to pray, and not to faint;

Luk 18:2 Saying; "There was in a city a judge, which feared not God, neither regarded man: 3 And there was a widow in that city; and she came unto him, saying; "Avenge me of mine adversary." 4 And he would not for a while: but afterward he said within himself; "Though I fear not God, nor regard man; 5 Yet because this widow troubleth me, I will avenge her, lest by her continual coming she weary me." 6 And the Lord said; "Hear what the unjust judge saith. 7 And shall not God avenge his own elect, which cry day and night unto him, though he bear long with them? 8 I tell you that he will avenge them speedily. Nevertheless, when the Son of man cometh, shall he find faith *(Pistis, G4102. Gods' truthfulness)* on the earth?"

The Pharisee and the Tax Collector

Luk 18:9 And he spake this parable unto certain which trusted in themselves that they were righteous, and despised others:

Luk 18:10 "Two men went up into the temple to pray; the one a Pharisee, and the other a publican. 11 The Pharisee stood and prayed thus with himself: "God, I thank thee, that I am not as other men are, extortioners, unjust, adulterers, or even as this publican. 12 I fast twice in the week, I give tithes of all that I possess." 13 And the publican, standing afar off, would not lift up so much as his eyes unto heaven, but smote upon his breast, saying; "God be merciful to me a sinner." 14 I tell you, this man went down to his house justified rather than the other: for every one that exalteth himself shall be abased; and he that humbleth himself shall be exalted."

Suffer the Children Come to Me

Mat 19:13 Then were there brought unto him little children, that he should put his hands on them, and pray: and the disciples rebuked them.

Mat 19:14 But Jesus said; "Suffer little children, and forbid them not, to come unto me: for of such is the kingdom of heaven."

Mat 19:15 And he laid his hands on them, and departed thence.

Suffer the Children Come to Me

Mar 10:13 And they brought young children to him, that he should touch them: and his disciples rebuked those that brought them.

Mar 10:14 But when Jesus saw it, he was much displeased, and said unto them, "Suffer the little children to come unto me, and forbid them not: for of such is the kingdom of God. 15 Verily I say unto you, whosoever shall not receive the kingdom of God as a little child, he shall not enter therein."

Mar 10:16 And he took them up in his arms, put his hands upon them, and blessed them.

Suffer the Children Come to Me

Luk 18:15 And they brought unto him also infants, that he would touch them: but when his disciples saw it, they rebuked them.

Luk 18:16 But Jesus called them unto him, and said; "Suffer little children to come unto me, and forbid them not: for of such is the kingdom of God. 17 Verily I say unto you; Whosoever shall not receive the kingdom of God as a little child shall in no wise enter therein."

The Rich Young Ruler. Deut 6:5. *Lev 19:18 and 19:34*

Mat 19:16 And, behold, one came and said unto him; "Good Master, what good thing shall I do, that I may have eternal life?"

Mat 19:17 And he said unto him; "Why callest thou me good? there is none good but one, that is, God: but if thou wilt enter into life, keep the commandments."

Mat 19:18 He saith unto him; "Which?" Jesus said; "Thou shalt do no murder. Thou shalt not commit adultery. Thou shalt not steal. Thou shalt not bear false witness. 19 Honour thy father and thy mother: and, thou shalt love thy neighbour as thyself."

Mat 19:20 The young man saith unto him; "All these things have I kept from my youth up: what lack I yet?"

Mat 19:21 Jesus said unto him; "If thou wilt be perfect, go and sell that thou hast, and give to the poor, and thou shalt have treasure in heaven: and come and follow me."

Mat 19:22 But when the young man heard that saying, he went away sorrowful: for he had great possessions.

Mat 19:23 Then said Jesus unto his disciples; "Verily I say unto you; That a rich man shall hardly enter into the kingdom of heaven. 24 And again I say unto you; It is easier for a camel to go through the eye of a needle, than for a rich man to enter into the kingdom of God."

(Jesus was talking figuratively and truthfully. If He would have been referring to a particular gate, He would have said "The Eye of <u>The</u> Needle," naming the entry. There is no historical evidence that an entry named "Eye of a needle", for afterhours ever existed in Jerusalem. I believe the eye of the needle story is made up to justify a narrative what people think Jesus really meant. What He said is what He meant. People are always trying and bring God down to our level. Nothing is impossible when you are with God.)

Mat 19:25 When his disciples heard it, they were exceedingly amazed, saying; "Who then can be saved?"

Mat 19:26 But Jesus beheld them, and said unto them; "With men this is impossible; but with God all things are possible."

Mat 19:27 Then answered Peter and said unto him; "Behold, we have forsaken all, and followed thee; what shall we have therefore?"

Mat 19:28 And Jesus said unto them; "Verily I say unto you; That ye which have followed me, in the regeneration when the Son of man shall sit in the throne of his glory, ye also shall sit upon twelve thrones, judging the twelve tribes of Israel. 29 And every one that hath forsaken houses, or brethren, or sisters, or father, or mother, or wife, or children, or lands, for my name's sake, shall receive an hundredfold, and shall inherit everlasting life. 30 But many that are first shall be last; and the last shall be first."

The Rich Young Ruler

Mar 10:17 And when he was gone forth into the way, there came one running, and kneeled to him, and asked him; "Good Master, what shall I do that I may inherit eternal life?"

Mar 10:18 And Jesus said unto him; "Why callest thou me good? there is none good but one, that is, God. 19 Thou knowest the commandments. Do not commit adultery. Do not kill. Do not steal. Do not bear false witness. Defraud not. Honour thy father and mother."

Mar 10:20 And he answered and said unto him, "Master, all these have I observed from my youth."

Mar 10:21 Then Jesus beholding him loved him, and said unto him; "One thing thou lackest: go thy way, sell whatsoever thou hast, and give to the poor, and thou shalt have treasure in heaven: and come, take up the cross, and follow me."

Mar 10:22 And he was sad at that saying, and went away grieved: for he had great possessions.

Mar 10:23 And Jesus looked round about, and saith unto his disciples; "How hardly shall they that have riches enter into the kingdom of God!"

Mar 10:24 And the disciples were astonished at his words. But Jesus answereth again, and saith unto them; "Children, how hard is it for them that trust in riches to enter into the kingdom of God! 25 It is easier for a camel to go through the eye of a needle, than for a rich man to enter into the kingdom of God."

Mar 10:26 And they were astonished out of measure, saying among themselves; "Who then can be saved??

(What can God do with a man fully Surrendered to Him? 2 Chron 16:9, Isa 41:10.)

Mar 10:27 And Jesus looking upon them saith; "With men it is impossible, but not with God: for with *(Ou, G3844, next to)* God all things are possible."

Mar 10:28 Then Peter began to say unto him; "<u>Lo, we have left all</u>, and have followed thee."

Mar 10:29 And Jesus answered and said; "Verily I say unto you, there is no man that hath left house, or brethren, or sisters, or father, or mother, or wife, or children, or lands, for my sake, and the gospel's, 30 But he shall receive an hundredfold now in this time, houses, and brethren, and sisters, and mothers, and children, and lands, with persecutions; and in the world to come eternal life. 31But many that are <u>first shall be last</u>; and the last first."

The Rich Young Ruler

Luk 18:18 And a certain ruler asked him, saying; "<u>Good Master,</u> what shall I do to inherit eternal life?"

Luk 18:19 And Jesus said unto him; "Why callest thou me good? none is good, save one, that is, God. 20 Thou knowest the commandments, do not commit adultery, do not kill, do not steal, do not bear false witness, Honour thy father and thy mother."

Luk 18:21 And he said; "All these have I kept from my youth up."

Luk 18:22 Now when Jesus heard these things, he said unto him; "Yet lackest thou one thing: sell all that thou hast, and distribute unto the poor, and thou shalt have treasure in heaven: and come, follow me."

Luk 18:23 And when he heard this, he was very sorrowful: for he was very rich.

Luk 18:24 And when Jesus saw that he was very sorrowful, he said; "How hardly shall they that have riches enter into the kingdom of God! 25 For it is easier for a camel to go through a needle's eye, than for a rich man to enter into the kingdom of God."

Luk 18:26 And they that heard it said; "Who then can be saved?"

Luk 18:27 And he said; "The things which are impossible with men are possible with God."

Luk 18:28 Then Peter said; "<u>Lo, we have left all</u>, and followed thee."

Luk 18:29 And he said unto them; "Verily I say unto you; There is no man that hath left house, or parents, or brethren, or wife, or children, for the kingdom of God's sake, 30 Who shall not receive manifold more in this present time, and in the world to come life everlasting."

Vineyard Parable. Many are Called, few Chosen.

Mat 20:1 "For the kingdom of heaven is like unto a man that is an householder, which went out early in the morning to hire labourers into his vineyard. 2 And when he had agreed with the labourers for a penny a day, he sent them into his vineyard. 3 And he went out about the third hour, and saw others standing idle in the marketplace, 4 And said unto them; "Go ye also into the vineyard, and whatsoever is right I will give you." And they went their way. 5 Again he went out about the sixth and ninth hour, and did likewise. 6 And about the eleventh hour he went out, and found others standing idle, and saith unto them; "Why stand ye here all the day idle?" 7 They say unto him; "Because no man hath hired us." He saith unto them; "Go ye also into the vineyard; and whatsoever is right, that shall ye receive." 8 So when even was come, the lord of the vineyard saith unto his steward; "Call the labourers, and give them their hire, beginning from the last unto the first." 9 And when they came that were hired about the eleventh hour, they received every man a penny. 10 But when the first came, they supposed that they should have received more; and they likewise received every man a penny. 11 And when they had received it, they murmured against the goodman of the house, saying; "These last have wrought but one hour, and thou hast made them equal unto us, which have borne the burden and heat of the day." 13 But he answered one of them, and said; "Friend, I do thee no wrong: didst not thou agree with me for a penny? 14 Take that thine is, and go thy way: I will give unto this last, even as unto thee. 15 Is it not lawful for me to do what I will with mine own? Is thine eye evil, because I am good?" 16 So the last shall be first, and the first last: for many be called, but few chosen."

Heading to Jerusalem through Jericho

Jesus Tells His Resurrection a Third Time. Hosea 6:2

Mat 20:17 And Jesus going up to Jerusalem took the twelve disciples apart in the way, and said unto them; 18 "Behold, we go up to Jerusalem; and the Son of man shall be betrayed unto the chief priests and unto the scribes, and they shall condemn him to death, 19 And shall deliver him to the Gentiles to mock, and to scourge, and to crucify him: and the third day he shall rise again."

Jesus Tells His Resurrection a Third Time

Mar 10:32 And they were in the way going up to Jerusalem; and Jesus went before them: and they were amazed; and as they followed, they were afraid. And he took again the twelve, and began to tell them what things should happen unto him;

Mar 10:33 Saying; "Behold, we go up to Jerusalem; and the Son of man shall be delivered unto the chief priests, and unto the scribes; and they shall condemn him to death, and shall deliver him to the Gentiles: 34 And they shall mock him, and shall scourge him, and shall spit upon him, and shall kill him: and the third day he shall rise again."

Jesus Tells His Resurrection a Third Time

Luk 18:31 Then he took unto him the twelve, and said unto them; "Behold, we go up to Jerusalem, and all things that are written by the prophets concerning the Son of man shall be accomplished. 32 For he shall be delivered unto the Gentiles, and shall be mocked, and spitefully entreated, and spitted on: 33 And they shall scourge him, and put him to death: and the third day he shall rise again."

Luk 18:34 And they understood none of these things: and this saying was hid from them, neither knew they the things which were spoken.

A Mother's Request

Mat 20:20 Then came to him the mother of Zebedee's children with her sons, worshipping him, and desiring a certain thing of him.

Mat 20:21 And he said unto her; "What wilt thou?" She saith unto him; "Grant that these my two sons may sit, the one on thy right hand, and the other on the left, in thy kingdom."

Mat 20:22 But Jesus answered and said; "Ye know not what ye ask. Are ye able to drink of the cup that I shall drink of, and to be baptized with the baptism that I am baptized with?" They say unto him; "We are able."

Mat 20:23 And he saith unto them; "Ye shall drink indeed of my cup, and be baptized with the baptism that I am baptized with: but to sit on my right hand, and on my left, is not mine to give, but it shall be given to them for whom it is prepared of my Father."

Mat 20:24 And when the ten heard it, they were moved with indignation against the two brethren.

Mat 20:25 But Jesus called them unto him, and said; "Ye know that the princes of the Gentiles exercise dominion over them, and they that are great exercise authority upon them. 26 But it shall not be so among you: but whosoever will be great among you, let him be your minister; 27 And whosoever will be chief among you, let him be your servant: 28 Even as the Son of man came not to be ministered unto, but to minister, and to give his life a ransom for many."

The Disciples Request.

Mark must have heard about the request and didn't mention it was through their mother; putting full accountability back onto the disciples themselves. Mark was the only one that mentioned Jesus named the boys "The Sons of Thunder," Mark 3:17. There was rivalry between John and Peter, even down to the point of John mentioning what Jesus said about them in the last chapter of John, possibly hinting Jesus loved him more.

Mar 10:35 And James and John, the sons of Zebedee, come unto him, saying; "Master, we would that thou shouldest do for us whatsoever we shall desire."

Mar 10:36 And he said unto them; "What would ye that I should do for you?"

Mar 10:37 They said unto him; "Grant unto us that we may sit, one on thy right hand, and the other on thy left hand, in thy glory."

Mar 10:38 But Jesus said unto them; "Ye know not what ye ask: can ye drink of the cup that I drink of? and be baptized with the baptism that I am baptized with?"

Mar 10:39 And they said unto him; "We can." And Jesus said unto them; "Ye shall indeed drink of the cup that I drink of; and with the baptism that I am baptized withal shall ye be baptized: 40 But to sit on my right hand and on my left hand is not mine to give; but it shall be given to them for whom it is prepared."

Mar 10:41 And when the ten heard it, they began to be much displeased with James and John.

Mar 10:42 But Jesus called them to him, and saith unto them; "Ye know that they which are accounted to rule over the Gentiles exercise lordship over them; and their great ones exercise authority upon them. 43 But so shall it not be among you: but whosoever will be great among you, shall be your minister: 44 And whosoever of you will be the chiefest, shall be servant of all. 45 For even the Son of man came not to be ministered unto, but to minister, and to give his life a ransom for many."

Passing through and Departing Jericho

Jericho is N/E of Jerusalem approx 35 klms

Jesus Heals Two Blind Men.

Mat 20:29 And as they departed from Jericho, a great multitude followed him.

Mat 20:30 And, behold, two blind men sitting by the way side, when they heard that Jesus passed by, cried out, saying; "Have mercy on us, O Lord, thou Son of David."

Mat 20:31 And the multitude rebuked them, because they should hold their peace: but they cried the more, saying; "Have mercy on us, O Lord, thou Son of David."

Mat 20:32 And Jesus stood still, and called them, and said; "What will ye that I shall do unto you?"

Mat 20:33 They say unto him; "Lord, that our eyes may be opened."

Mat 20:34 So Jesus had compassion on them, and touched their eyes: and immediately their eyes received sight, and they followed him.

Jesus Heals Bartimaeus

Mar 10:46 And they came to Jericho: and as he went out of Jericho with his disciples and a great number of people, blind Bartimaeus, the son of Timaeus, sat by the highway side begging.

Mar 10:47 And when he heard that it was Jesus of Nazareth, he began to cry out, and say; "Jesus, thou Son of David, have mercy on me."

Mar 10:48 And many charged him that he should hold his peace: but he cried the more a great deal, "Thou Son of David, have mercy on me."

Mar 10:49 And Jesus stood still, and commanded him to be called. And they call the blind man, saying unto him; "Be of good comfort, rise; he calleth thee."

Mar 10:50 And he, casting away his garment, rose, and came to Jesus.

Mar 10:51 And Jesus answered and said unto him; "What wilt thou that I should do unto thee?" The blind man said unto him, "Lord, that I might receive my sight."

Mar 10:52 And Jesus said unto him; "Go thy way; thy faith hath made thee whole." And immediately he received his sight, and followed Jesus in the way.

Jesus Heals Bartimaeus

Luk 18:35 And it came to pass, that as he was come nigh unto Jericho, a certain blind man sat by the way side begging:

Luk 18:36 And hearing the multitude pass by, he asked what it meant.

Luk 18:37 And they told him, that Jesus of Nazareth passeth by.

Luk 18:38 And he cried, saying; "Jesus, thou Son of David, have mercy on me."

Luk 18:39 And they which went before rebuked him, that he should hold his peace: but he cried so much the more; "<u>Thou Son of David, have mercy on me</u>."

Luk 18:40 And Jesus stood, and commanded him to be brought unto him: and when he was come near, he asked him,

Luk 18:41 Saying; "<u>What wilt thou that I shall do unto thee?</u>" And he said; "Lord, that I may receive my sight."

Luk 18:42 And Jesus said unto him; "Receive thy sight: thy faith hath saved thee."

Luk 18:43 And <u>immediately he received his sight, and followed him,</u> glorifying God: and all the people, when they saw it, gave praise unto God.

Jesus calls Zacchaeus and he Truly Repents

Luk 19:1 And Jesus entered and passed through Jericho.

Luk 19:2 And, behold, there was a man named Zacchaeus, which was the chief among the publicans, and he was rich.

Luk 19:3 And he sought to see Jesus who he was; and could not for the press, because he was little of stature.

Luk 19:4 And he ran before, and climbed up into a sycamore tree to see him: for he was to pass that way.

Luk 19:5 And when Jesus came to the place, he looked up, and saw him, and said unto him; "Zacchaeus, make haste, and come down; for today I must abide at thy house."

Luk 19:6 And he made haste, and came down, and received him joyfully.

Luk 19:7 And when they saw it, they all murmured, saying; "That he was gone to be guest with a man that is a sinner."

Luk 19:8 And Zacchaeus stood, and said unto the Lord; "Behold, Lord, the half of my goods I give to the poor; and if I have taken anything from any man by false accusation, I restore him fourfold."

Luk 19:9 And Jesus said unto him; "This day is salvation come to this house, forsomuch as he also is a son of Abraham. 10 For the Son of man is come to seek and to save that which was lost."

<u>Near to Jerusalem.</u>

<u>Parable of the return of the Jesus</u>

Luke records that Jesus uses the word Minah, meaning a certain weight. The gifts of the Holy Spirit and presence are termed as weightiness, same as the burden of Jesus is Love. When the Holy Spirit witnesses to us there is a fire that burns just like a weight, we have to act upon the prompting and calling to relieve that weight or it will be taken from us and the door closed having our conscience seared if we don't repent. In my life the presence of God has come in waves, some big and some small. Ps 39:3, Amos 3:8, 2Chron 5:14, 2Tim 4:2.

Luk 19:11 And as they heard these things, he added and spake a parable, because he was nigh to Jerusalem, and because they thought that the kingdom of God should immediately appear.

Luk 19:12 He said therefore; "A certain nobleman went into a far country to receive for himself a kingdom, and to return. 13 And he called his ten servants, and delivered them ten pounds *(G3414, Minah, a certain weight)*, and said unto them; "Occupy till I come." *(Mat 28:19, Mark 16:15)* 14 But his citizens hated him, and sent a message after him, saying; "We will not have this man to reign over us." *(Isah 14:14)*. 15 And it came to pass, that when he was returned, having received the kingdom, *(Matt 13:30, Matt 28:18)* then he commanded these servants to be called unto him, to whom he had given the money, that he might know how much every man had gained by trading *(G1281 to earn in business)*. 16 Then came the first, saying; "Lord, thy pound hath gained ten pounds." 17 And he said unto him; "Well, thou good servant: because thou hast been faithful in a very little, have thou authority over ten cities." 18 And the second came, saying; "Lord, thy pound hath gained five pounds." 19 And he said likewise to him; "Be thou also over five cities." 20 And another came, saying; "Lord, behold, here is thy pound, which I have kept laid up in a napkin: 21 For I feared thee, because thou art an austere man: thou takest up that thou layedst not down, and reapest that thou didst not sow." 22 And he saith unto him; "Out of thine own mouth will I judge thee, thou wicked servant. Thou knewest that I was an austere man, taking up that I laid not down, and reaping that I did not sow: 23 Wherefore then gavest not thou my money into the bank, that at my coming I might have required mine own with usury?" 24 And he said unto them that stood by; "Take from him the pound, and give it to him that hath ten pounds." 25 And they said unto him; "Lord, he hath ten pounds." 26 For I say unto you, that unto every one which hath shall be given; and from him that hath not, even that he hath shall be taken away from him. 27 But those mine enemies, which would not that I should reign over them, bring hither, and slay them before me."

Jerusalem.

<u>Jesus Secretly Goes into the Feast in Jerusalem</u>

Joh 7:10 But when his brethren were gone up, then went he also up unto the feast, not openly, but as it were in secret.

Joh 7:11 Then the Jews sought him at the feast, and said; "Where is he?"

Joh 7:12 And there was much murmuring among the people concerning him: for some said; "He is a good man": others said; "Nay; but he deceiveth the people."

Joh 7:13 Howbeit no man spake openly of him for fear of the Jews.

Joh 7:14 Now about the midst of the feast Jesus went up into the temple, and taught.

Joh 7:15 And the Jews marvelled, saying; "How knoweth this man letters, having never learned?"

Joh 7:16 Jesus answered them, and said; "My doctrine is not mine, but his that sent me. 17 If any man will do his will, he shall know of the doctrine, whether it be of God, or whether I speak of myself. 18 He that speaketh of himself seeketh his own glory: but he that seeketh his glory that sent him, the same is true, and no unrighteousness is in him. 19 Did not Moses give you the law, and yet none of you keepeth the law? Why go ye about to kill me?"

Judge Righteously

Joh 7:20 The people answered and said; "Thou hast a devil: who goeth about to kill thee?"

Joh 7:21 Jesus answered and said unto them; "I have done one work, and ye all marvel. 22 Moses therefore gave unto you circumcision; (not because it is of Moses, but of the fathers;) and ye on the sabbath day circumcise a man. 23 If a man on the sabbath day receive circumcision, that the law of Moses should not be broken; are ye angry at me, because I have made a man every whit whole on the sabbath day? 24 Judge not according to the appearance, but judge righteous judgment."

This Be the Christ?

Joh 7:25 Then said some of them of Jerusalem; "Is not this he, whom they seek to kill? 26 But, lo, he speaketh boldly, and they say nothing unto him. Do the rulers know indeed that this is the very Christ? 27 Howbeit we know this man whence he is: but when Christ cometh, no man knoweth whence he is."

Joh 7:28 Then cried Jesus in the temple as he taught, saying; "Ye both know me, and ye know whence I am: and I am not come of myself, but he that sent me is true, whom ye know not. 29 But I know him: for I am from him, and he hath sent me."

Joh 7:30 Then they sought to take him: but no man laid hands on him, because his hour was not yet come.

Joh 7:31 And many of the people believed on him, and said; "When Christ cometh, will he do more miracles than these which this man hath done?"

Officers Sent to Arrest Jesus

Joh 7:32 The Pharisees heard that the people murmured such things concerning him; and the Pharisees and the chief priests sent officers to take him.

Joh 7:33 Then said Jesus unto them; "Yet a little while am I with you, and then I go unto him that sent me. 34 Ye shall seek me, and shall not find me: and where I am, thither ye cannot come."

Joh 7:35 Then said the Jews among themselves; "Whither will he go, that we shall not find him? will he go unto the dispersed among the Gentiles, and teach the Gentiles? 36 What manner of saying is this that he said; "Ye shall seek me, and shall not find me: and where I am, thither ye cannot come?""

Last day of the Feast

Rivers of Living Water

Joh 7:37 In the last day, that great day of the feast, Jesus stood and cried, saying; "If any man thirst, let him come unto me, and drink. 38 He that believeth on me, as the scripture hath said, out of his belly shall flow rivers of living water." (Jer 2:13, Joel 2:28)

Joh 7:39 (But this spake he of the Spirit, which they that believe on him should receive: for the Holy Ghost was not yet given; because that Jesus was not yet glorified.)

Division Amongst the People

Joh 7:40 Many of the people therefore, when they heard this saying, said; "Of a truth this is the Prophet."

Joh 7:41 Others said; "This is the Christ." But some said; "Shall Christ come out of Galilee? 42 Hath not the scripture said; That Christ cometh of the seed of David, and out of the town of Bethlehem, where David was?"

Joh 7:43 So there was a division among the people because of him.

Arresting Officers astounded at Jesus` preaching

Joh 7:44 And some of them would have taken him; but no man laid hands on him.

Joh 7:45 Then came the officers to the chief priests and Pharisees; and they said unto them; "Why have ye not brought him?"

Joh 7:46 The officers answered; "Never man spake like this man."

Joh 7:47 Then answered them the Pharisees; "Are ye also deceived? 48 Have any of the rulers or of the Pharisees believed on him? 49 But this people who knoweth not the law are cursed."

Joh 7:50 Nicodemus saith unto them, (he that came to Jesus by night, being one of them,); 51 "Doth our law judge any man, before it hear him, and know what he doeth?" *(John 3:4)*

Joh 7:52 They answered and said unto him; "Art thou also of Galilee? Search, and look: for out of Galilee ariseth no prophet."

Joh 7:53 And every man went unto his own house.

Jesus teaches in Jerusalem by day and goes to the Mt of Olives by night

The Woman Caught in Adultery, Jesus looks away. Job 31:1

Joh 8:1 Jesus went unto the mount of Olives.

Joh 8:2 And early in the morning he came again into the temple, and all the people came unto him; and he sat down, and taught them.

Joh 8:3 And the scribes and Pharisees brought unto him a woman taken in adultery; and when they had set her in the midst,

Joh 8:4 They say unto him; "Master, this woman was taken in adultery, in the very act. 5 Now Moses in the law commanded us, that such should be stoned: but what sayest thou?"

Joh 8:6 This they said, tempting him, that they might have to accuse him. But Jesus stooped down, and with his finger wrote on the ground, as though he heard them not. (Job 31:1)

Joh 8:7 So when they continued asking him, he lifted up himself, and said unto them; "He that is without sin among you, let him first cast a stone at her."

Joh 8:8 And again he stooped down, and wrote on the ground.

Joh 8:9 And they which heard it, being convicted by their own conscience, went out one by one, beginning at the eldest, even unto the last: and Jesus was left alone, and the woman standing in the midst.

Joh 8:10 When Jesus had lifted up himself, and saw none but the woman, he said unto her; "Woman, where are those thine accusers? hath no man condemned thee?"

Joh 8:11 She said; "No man, Lord." And Jesus said unto her; "Neither do I condemn thee: go, and sin no more."

<u>Teaching at the Treasury in the Temple</u>

Imagine; if there was no sun, we wouldn't exist, nothing would. 1 Corr 15:46. Jesus used the natural things of the world to show forth the spiritual. 1 Cor 15:46.

<u>I Am the Light of the World</u>

Joh 8:12 Then spake Jesus again unto them, saying; "I am the light of the world: he that followeth me shall not walk in darkness, but shall have the light of life."

Joh 8:13 The Pharisees therefore said unto him; "Thou bearest record of thyself; thy record is not true."

Joh 8:14 Jesus answered and said unto them; "Though I bear record of myself, yet my record is true: for I know whence I came, and whither I go; but ye cannot tell whence I come, and whither I go. 15 Ye judge after the flesh; I judge no man. 16 And yet if I judge, my judgment is true: for I am not alone, but I and the Father that sent me. 17 It is also written in your law, that the testimony of two men is true. 18 I am one that bear witness of myself, and the Father that sent me beareth witness of me."

Joh 8:19 Then said they unto him; "Where is thy Father?" Jesus answered; "Ye neither know me, nor my Father: if ye had known me, ye should have known my Father also."

Joh 8:20 <u>These words spake Jesus in the treasury</u>, as he taught in the temple: and no man laid hands on him; for his hour was not yet come.

Joh 8:21 Then said Jesus again unto them; "I go my way, and ye shall seek me, and shall die in your sins: whither I go, ye cannot come."

Joh 8:22 Then said the Jews; "Will he kill himself? because he saith, Whither I go, ye cannot come." *(1 Corr 3:16,17)*

Joh 8:23 And he said unto them; "Ye are from beneath; I am from above: ye are of this world; I am not of this world. 24 I said therefore unto you, that ye shall die in your sins: for if ye believe not that I am he, ye shall die in your sins."

Joh 8:25 Then said they unto him; "Who art thou?" And Jesus saith unto them; "Even the same that I said unto you from the beginning. 26 I have many things to say and to judge of you: but he that sent me is true; and I speak to the world those things which I have heard of him."

Joh 8:27 They understood not that he spake to them of the Father.

Joh 8:28 Then said Jesus unto them; "When ye have lifted up the Son of man, then shall ye know that I am he, and that I do nothing of myself; but as my Father hath taught me, I speak these things. 29 And he that sent me is with me: the Father hath not left me alone; for I do always those things that please him."

Joh 8:30 As he spake these words, many believed on him.

The Truth Will Make You Free

Joh 8:31 Then said Jesus to those Jews which believed on him; "If ye continue in my word, then are ye my disciples indeed; 32 And ye shall know the truth, and the truth shall make *(G1659 Eleutheroo, deliver, make free)* you free."

Joh 8:33 They answered him; "We be Abraham's seed, and were never in bondage to any man: how sayest thou, Ye shall be made free?"

Joh 8:34 Jesus answered them; "Verily, verily, I say unto you, whosoever committeth sin is the servant of sin. 35 And the servant abideth not in the house for ever: but the Son abideth ever. 36 If the Son therefore shall make you free, ye shall be free indeed. 37 I know that ye are Abraham's seed; but ye seek to kill me, because my word hath no place in you. 38 I speak that which I have seen with my Father: and ye do that which ye have seen with your father."

Jesus Rebukes the Pharisees

Joh 8:39 They answered and said unto him; "Abraham is our father." Jesus saith unto them; "If ye were Abraham's children, ye would do the works of Abraham. 40 But now ye seek to kill me, a man that hath told you the truth, which I have heard of God: this did not Abraham. 41 Ye do the deeds of your father." Then said they to him; "we be not born of fornication; we have one Father, even God."

Joh 8:42 Jesus said unto them; "If God were your Father, ye would love (G25 Agapao) me: for I proceeded forth and came from God; neither came I of myself, but he sent me. 43 Why do ye not understand my speech? even because ye cannot hear my word. 44 Ye are of your father the devil, and the lusts of your father ye will do. He was a murderer from the beginning, and abode not in the truth, because there is no truth in him. When he speaketh a lie, he speaketh of his own: for he is a liar, and the father of it. 45 And because I tell you the truth, ye believe me not. 46 Which of you convinceth me of sin? And if I say the truth, why do ye not believe me? 47 He that is of God heareth God's words: ye therefore hear them not, because ye are not of God."

<u>Jews say Jesus is a Samaritan and has a devil. Matt 10:25, Matt 12:24, Mar 3:22, Luk 11:15.</u>

Joh 8:48 Then answered the Jews, and said unto him; "Say we not well that thou art a Samaritan, and hast a devil?"

Joh 8:49 Jesus answered; "I have not a devil; but I honour my Father, and ye do dishonour me. 50 And I seek not mine own glory: there is one that seeketh and judgeth. 51 Verily, verily, I say unto you; If a man keep my saying, he shall never see death."

Joh 8:52 Then said the Jews unto him; "Now we know that thou hast a devil. Abraham is dead, and the prophets; and thou sayest, "If a man keep my saying, he shall never taste of death". 53 Art thou greater than our father Abraham, which is dead? and the prophets are dead: whom makest thou thyself?"

Joh 8:54 Jesus answered; "If I honour myself, my honour is nothing: it is my Father that honoureth me; of whom ye say, that he is your God: 55 Yet ye have not known him; but I know him: and if I should say, I know him not, I shall be a liar like unto you: but I know him, and keep his saying. 56 Your father Abraham rejoiced to see my day: and he saw it, and was glad."

Joh 8:57 Then said the Jews unto him; "Thou art not yet fifty years old, and hast thou seen Abraham?"

Joh 8:58 Jesus said unto them; "Verily, verily, I say unto you, Before Abraham was, I am." *(Exo 3:14)*

Joh 8:59 Then took they up stones to cast at him: but Jesus hid himself, and went out of the temple, going through the midst of them, and so passed by.

<u>Walking through Jerusalem</u>

<u>Jesus Heals a Man Born Blind from birth</u>

Joh 9:1 And as Jesus passed by, he saw a man which was blind from his birth.

Joh 9:2 And his disciples asked him, saying; "Master, who did sin, this man, or his parents, that he was born blind?"

Joh 9:3 Jesus answered, "Neither hath this man sinned, nor his parents: but that the works of God should be made manifest in him. 4 I must work the works of him that sent me, while it is day: the night cometh, when no man can work. 5 As long as I am in the world, I am the light of the world."

Joh 9:6 When he had thus spoken, he spat on the ground, and made clay of the spittle, and he anointed the eyes of the blind man with the clay,

Joh 9:7 And said unto him; "Go, wash in the pool of Siloam", (which is by interpretation, Sent.) He went his way therefore, and washed, and came seeing. *(The distance is about 600 mts from the Temple.)*

Joh 9:8 The neighbours therefore, and they which before had seen him that he was blind, said; "Is not this he that sat and begged?"

Joh 9:9 Some said; "This is he:" others said; "He is like him": but he said; "I am he."

Joh 9:10 Therefore said they unto him; "How were thine eyes opened?"

Joh 9:11 He answered and said; "A man that is called Jesus made clay, and anointed mine eyes, and said unto me, go to the pool of Siloam, and wash: and I went and washed, and I received sight."

Joh 9:12 Then said they unto him; "Where is he?" He said; "I know not."

Pharisees Interrogate the Man

Joh 9:13 They brought to the Pharisees him that aforetime was blind.

Joh 9:14 And it was the sabbath day when Jesus made the clay, and opened his eyes.

Joh 9:15 Then again, the Pharisees also asked him how he had received his sight. He said unto them; "He put clay upon mine eyes, and I washed, and do see."

Joh 9:16 Therefore said some of the Pharisees; "This man is not of God, because he keepeth not the sabbath day." Others said; "How can a man that is a sinner do such miracles?" And there was a division among them.

Joh 9:17 They say unto the blind man again; "What sayest thou of him, that he hath opened thine eyes?" He said; "He is a prophet."

Interrogation of the Mans Parents

Joh 9:18 But the Jews did not believe concerning him, that he had been blind, and received his sight, until they called the parents of him that had received his sight.

Joh 9:19 And they asked them, saying; "Is this your son, who ye say was born blind? how then doth he now see?"

Joh 9:20 His parents answered them and said; "We know that this is our son, and that he was born blind: 21 But by what means he now seeth, we know not; or who hath opened his eyes, we know not: he is of age; ask him: he shall speak for himself."

Joh 9:22 These words spake his parents, because they feared the Jews: for the Jews had agreed already, that if any man did confess that he was Christ, he should be put out of the synagogue.

Joh 9:23 Therefore said his parents; "He is of age; ask him."

Joh 9:24 Then again called they the man that was blind, and said unto him; "Give God the praise: we know that this man is a sinner."

Joh 9:25 He answered and said; "Whether he be a sinner or no, I know not: one thing I know, that, whereas I was blind, now I see."

Joh 9:26 Then said they to him again; "What did he to thee? how opened he thine eyes?"

Joh 9:27 He answered them; "I have told you already, and ye did not hear: wherefore would ye hear it again? will ye also be his disciples?"

Joh 9:28 Then they reviled him, and said; "Thou art his disciple; but we are Moses' disciples. 29 We know that God spake unto Moses: as for this fellow, we know not from whence he is."

Joh 9:30 The man answered and said unto them; "Why herein is a marvellous thing, that ye know not from whence he is, and yet he hath opened mine eyes.

31 Now we know that God heareth not sinners: but if any man be a worshipper of God, and doeth his will, him he heareth. 32 Since the world began was it not heard that any man opened the eyes of one that was born blind. 33 If this man were not of God, he could do nothing."

Joh 9:34 They answered and said unto him; "Thou wast altogether born in sins, and dost thou teach us?" And they cast him out.

<u>Jesus reveals himself as the Son of God to the Outcast</u>

Joh 9:35 Jesus heard that they had cast him out; and when he had found him, he said unto him, "Dost thou believe on the Son of God?"

Joh 9:36 He answered and said; "Who is he, Lord, that I might believe on him?"

Joh 9:37 And Jesus said unto him; "Thou hast both seen him, and it is he that talketh with thee."

Joh 9:38 And he said; "Lord, I believe." And he worshipped him.

Joh 9:39 And Jesus said; "For judgment I am come into this world, that they which see not might see; and that they which see might be made blind."

Joh 9:40 And some of the Pharisees which were with him heard these words, and said unto him; "Are we blind also?"

Joh 9:41 Jesus said unto them; "If ye were blind, ye should have no sin: but now ye say, we see; therefore, your sin remaineth. 10:1 Verily, verily, I say unto you; He that entereth not by the door into the sheepfold, but climbeth up some other way, the same is a thief and a robber. 2 But he that entereth in by the door is the shepherd of the sheep. 3 To him the porter openeth; and the sheep hear his voice: and he calleth his own sheep by name, and leadeth them out. 4 And when he putteth forth his own sheep, he goeth before them, and the sheep follow him: for they know his voice. :5 And a stranger will they not follow, but will flee from him: for they know not the voice of strangers."

The Good Sheppard

Joh 10:6 This parable spake Jesus unto them: but they understood not what things they were which he spake unto them.

Joh 10:7 Then said Jesus unto them again; "Verily, verily, I say unto you, I am the door of the sheep. 8 All that ever came before me are thieves and robbers: but the sheep did not hear them. 9 I am the door: by me if any man enter in, he shall be saved, and shall go in and out, and find pasture. 10 The thief cometh not, but for to steal, and to kill, and to destroy: I am come that they might have life, and that they might have it more abundantly. 11 I am the good shepherd: the good shepherd giveth his life for the sheep. 12 But he that is an hireling, and not the shepherd; whose own the sheep are not, seeth the wolf coming, and leaveth the sheep, and fleeth: and the wolf catcheth them, and scattereth the sheep. 13 The hireling fleeth, because he is an hireling, and careth not for the sheep. 14 I am the good shepherd, and know my sheep, and am known of mine. 15 As the Father knoweth me, even so know I the Father: and I lay down my life for the sheep. 16 And other sheep I have, which are not of this fold: them also I must bring, and they shall hear my voice; and there shall be one-fold, and one shepherd. 17 Therefore doth my Father love me, because I lay down my life, that I might take it again. 18 No man taketh it from me, but I lay it down of myself. I have power to lay it down, and I have power to take it again. This commandment have I received of my Father."

Joh 10:19 There was a division therefore again among the Jews for these sayings.

Jesus accused of having a devil again

Joh 10:20 And many of them said; "He hath a devil, and is mad; why hear ye him?"

Joh 10:21 Others said; "These are not the words of him that hath a devil. Can a devil open the eyes of the blind?"

Jerusalem in winter feast of Dedication.

3rd year of ministry
(Approx 4 months before his crucifixion)

Hanukkah for the year 2025 is celebrated/ observed on sundown of December 14 ending at sundown on Monday, December 22. Festival of Lights.

I and the Father Are One

Joh 10:22 And it was at Jerusalem the feast of the dedication, and it was winter.

Joh 10:23 And Jesus walked in the temple in Solomon's porch.

Joh 10:24 Then came the Jews round about him, and said unto him; "How long dost thou make us to doubt? If thou be the Christ, tell us plainly."

My Sheep Hear my Voice

Joh 10:25 Jesus answered them; "I told you, and ye believed not: the works that I do in my Father's name, they bear witness of me. 26 But ye believe not, because ye are not of my sheep, as I said unto you. 27 My sheep hear my voice, and I know them, and they follow me: 28 And I give unto them eternal life; and they shall never perish, neither shall any man pluck them out of my hand. 29 My Father, which gave them me, is greater than all; and no man is able to pluck them out of my Father's hand. 30 I and my Father are one." *(Acts 2:22)*

Joh 10:31 Then the Jews took up stones again to stone him.

Joh 10:32 Jesus answered them; "Many good works have I shewed you from my Father; for which of those works do ye stone me?"

Joh 10:33 The Jews answered him, saying; "For a good work we stone thee not; but for blasphemy; and because that thou, being a man, makest thyself God."

Joh 10:34 Jesus answered them; "Is it not written in your law, I said, Ye are gods? *(Psa 82:6)* 35 If he called them gods, unto whom the word of God came, and the scripture cannot be broken; 36 Say ye of him, whom the Father hath sanctified, and sent into the world. Thou blasphemest; because I said, I am the Son of God? 37 If I do not the works of my Father, believe me not. 38 But if I do, though ye believe not me, believe the works: that ye may know, and believe, that the Father is in me, and I in him."

Jesus Escapes Back to Aenon

Joh 10:39 Therefore they sought again to take him: but he escaped out of their hand, 40 And went away again beyond Jordan into the place where John at first baptized; and there he abode.

Joh 10:41 And many resorted unto him, and said; "John did no miracle: but all things that John spake of this man were true."

Joh 10:42 And many believed on him there.

Back to Bethany near Jerusalem

The Death of Lazarus

Joh 11:1 Now a certain man was sick, named Lazarus, of Bethany, the town of Mary and her sister Martha.

Joh 11:2 (It was that Mary which anointed the Lord with ointment, and wiped his feet with her hair, whose brother Lazarus was sick.) *Luke 7:38*

Joh 11:3 Therefore his sisters sent unto him, saying; "Lord, behold, he whom thou lovest is sick."

Joh 11:4 When Jesus heard that, he said; "This sickness is not unto death, but for the glory of God, that the Son of God might be glorified thereby."

Joh 11:5 Now Jesus loved Martha, and her sister, and Lazarus.

Joh 11:6 When he had heard therefore that he was sick, he abode two days still in the same place where he was.

Joh 11:7 Then after that saith he to his disciples; "Let us go into Judaea again."

Joh 11:8 His disciples say unto him; "Master, the Jews of late sought to stone thee; and goest thou thither again?"

Joh 11:9 Jesus answered; "Are there not twelve hours in the day? If any man walk in the day, he stumbleth not, because he seeth the light of this world. 10 But if a man walk in the night, he stumbleth, because there is no light in him."

Joh 11:11 These things said he: and after that he saith unto them; "Our friend Lazarus sleepeth; but I go, that I may awake him out of sleep."

Joh 11:12 Then said his disciples; "Lord, if he sleep, he shall do well."

Joh 11:13 Howbeit Jesus spake of his death: But they thought that he had spoken of taking of rest in sleep.

Joh 11:14 Then said Jesus unto them plainly; "Lazarus is dead. 15 And I am glad for your sakes that I was not there, to the intent ye may believe; nevertheless, let us go unto him."

Joh 11:16 Then said Thomas, which is called Didymus, unto his fellow disciples; "Let us also go, that we may die with him." (speaking of Jesus)

Bethany near Jerusalem

I Am The Resurrection and The Life

Joh 11:17 Then when Jesus came, he found that he had lain in the grave four days already.

Joh 11:18 Now Bethany was nigh unto Jerusalem, about fifteen furlongs off: *(Just under 2 miles. 3.2 Klms)*

Joh 11:19 And many of the Jews came to Martha and Mary, to comfort them concerning their brother.

Joh 11:20 Then Martha, as soon as she heard that Jesus was coming, went and met him: but Mary sat still in the house.

Joh 11:21 Then said Martha unto Jesus; "Lord, if thou hadst been here, my brother had not died. 22 But I know, that even now, whatsoever thou wilt ask of God, God will give it thee."

Joh 11:23 Jesus saith unto her; "Thy brother shall rise again."

Resurrection Day. The First Resurrection. (1Thes 4:16, Rev 20:4-5, Joh 6:39-44, Jude 1:14)

Joh 11:24 Martha saith unto him; "I know that he shall rise again in the resurrection at the last day."

This is very important because Jesus does not correct her like he did the Sadducees for wrong doctrine. Matt 22:29,30, Joh 6:44. Jesus is not coming back twice, this last day will be the first resurrection and second return of Jesus for all to see, to rid the world of evil. Zech 14:5, Jude 1:14, Mat 13:40, 1Co 16:22. If any man love not the Lord Jesus Christ, let him be Anathema Maranatha. Rev 20:4-6. See Mat 13.

Joh 11:25 Jesus said unto her; "I am the resurrection, and the life: he that believeth in me, though he were dead, yet shall he live: 26 And whosoever liveth and believeth in me shall never die. Believest thou this?"

Joh 11:27 She saith unto him; "Yea, Lord: I believe that thou art the Christ, the Son of God, which should come into the world."

Jesus Weeps at Lazarus's grave

Joh 11:28 And when she had so said, she went her way, and called Mary her sister secretly, saying; "The Master is come, and calleth for thee."

Joh 11:29 As soon as she heard that, she arose quickly, and came unto him.

Joh 11:30 Now Jesus was not yet come into the town, but was in that place where Martha met him.

Joh 11:31 The Jews then which were with her in the house, and comforted her, when they saw Mary, that she rose up hastily and went out, followed her, saying; "She goeth unto the grave to weep there."

Joh 11:32 Then when Mary was come where Jesus was, and saw him, she fell down at his feet, saying unto him; "Lord, if thou hadst been here, my brother had not died."

Joh 11:33 When Jesus therefore saw her weeping, and the Jews also weeping which came with her, he groaned in the spirit, and was troubled,

Joh 11:34 And said; "Where have ye laid him?" They said unto him; "Lord, come and see."

Joh 11:35 Jesus wept. (*Shortest verse in the NT*)

Joh 11:36 Then said the Jews; "Behold how he loved him!"

Joh 11:37 And some of them said; "Could not this man, which opened the eyes of the blind, have caused that even this man should not have died?"

Jesus Raises Lazarus

Joh 11:38 Jesus therefore again groaning in himself cometh to the grave. It was a cave, and a stone lay upon it.

Joh 11:39 Jesus said; "Take ye away the stone." Martha, the sister of him that was dead, saith unto him; "Lord, by this time he stinketh: for he hath been dead four days."

Joh 11:40 Jesus saith unto her; "Said I not unto thee, that, if thou wouldest believe, thou shouldest see the glory of God?"

Joh 11:41 Then they took away the stone from the place where the dead was laid. And Jesus lifted up his eyes, and said; "Father, I thank thee that thou hast heard me. 42 And I knew that thou hearest me always: but because of the people which stand by I said it, that they may believe that thou hast sent me."

Joh 11:43 And when he thus had spoken, he cried with a loud voice; "Lazarus, come forth."

Joh 11:44 And he that was dead came forth, bound hand and foot with graveclothes: and his face was bound about with a napkin. Jesus saith unto them; "Loose him, and let him go."

Mary Preaches.

(This could also mean Mary`s Ex customers believed on Jesus because of Marys transformation.)

Joh 11:45 Then many of the Jews which came to Mary, and had seen the things which Jesus did, believed on him.

Joh 11:46 But some of them went their ways to the Pharisees, and told them what things Jesus had done.

The Pharisees Plot to Kill Jesus

Joh 11:47 Then gathered the chief priests and the Pharisees a council, and said; "What do we? for this man doeth many miracles. 48 If we let him thus alone, all men will believe on him: and the Romans shall come and take away both our place and nation." *(Isa 5:20, Rom 3:8)*

Joh 11:49 And one of them, named Caiaphas, being the high priest that same year, said unto them; "Ye know nothing at all, 50 Nor consider that it is expedient for us, that one man should die for the people, and that the whole nation perish not."

Joh 11:51 And this spake he not of himself: but being high priest that year, he prophesied that Jesus should die for that nation;

Joh 11:52 And not for that nation only, but that also he should gather together in one the children of God that were scattered abroad.

Joh 11:53 Then from that day forth they took counsel together for to put him to death.

Finding Refuge in Ephraim. North of Jerusalem. NE of Jericho

Joh 11:54 Jesus therefore walked no more openly among the Jews; but went thence unto a country near to the wilderness, into a city called Ephraim, and there continued with his disciples.

Meanwhile at Jerusalem, near Passover time

The Passover in 2025 is April 12th or the 14th day of the 1st month, Abib. Exodus 12.

Joh 11:55 And the Jews' passover was nigh at hand: and many went out of the country up to Jerusalem before the passover, to purify themselves.

Joh 11:56 Then sought they for Jesus, and spake among themselves, as they stood in the temple; "What think ye, that he will not come to the feast?"

Joh 11:57 Now both the chief priests and the Pharisees had given a commandment, that, if any man knew where he is, he should shew it, that they might take him.

Duplicated for study purposes. *Copied to Mat 26.*

At this point Matthew, Mark and Luke say that the anointing of Jesus by Mary, is after the Triumphal entry into Jerusalem but John says it happens before. John 12:12. Still, John was the eye witness and the facts are; it still happened, just because the time lines are out doesn't make false witnesses or contradictions As Jesus travelled to and from Jerusalem and Bethany many times in those last months. This is a classic confirmation of different witness testimonies confirming the truth by stating facts but in different orders and they weren't changed to suit a narrative.

Joh 12:1 Mary Anoints Jesus. *Copied to Mat 26:6*

Joh 12:1 Then Jesus six days before the passover came to Bethany, where Lazarus was which had been dead, whom he raised from the dead.

Joh 12:2 There they made him a supper; and Martha served: but Lazarus was one of them that sat at the table with him.

Joh 12:3 Then took Mary a pound of ointment of spikenard, very costly, and anointed the feet of Jesus, and wiped his feet with her hair: and the house was filled with the odour of the ointment.

Joh 12:4 Then saith one of his disciples, Judas Iscariot, Simon's son, which should betray him; 5 "Why was not this ointment sold for three hundred pence, and given to the poor?"

Joh 12:6 This he said; not that he cared for the poor; but because he was a thief, and had the bag, and bare what was put therein.

(Judas carried the money bag, selfish insecure people always try and have absolute control of what they have been put in charge of, like they own it. There is a fine line between being a good steward and control, stewards will always refer you to the authority above them for permission and to get permissions. Stealing is another matter. No, it is not better to ask forgiveness

than to ask permission, this thinking is from the world and overrides Gods authority, there is always a balance.)

Joh 12:7 Then said Jesus; "Let her alone: against the day of my burying hath she kept this. 8 For the poor always ye have with you; but me ye have not always."

Priests plot to Kill Lazarus *Mat 26:6*

Joh 12:9 Much people of the Jews therefore knew that he was there: and they came not for Jesus' sake only, but that they might see Lazarus also, whom he had raised from the dead.

Joh 12:10 But the chief priests consulted that they might put Lazarus also to death;

Joh 12:11 Because that by reason of him many of the Jews went away, and believed on Jesus.

Bethphage/Mt of Olives/Jerusalem

The Colt and The Triumphant Entry into Jerusalem

Jesus passed through the East Gate before it was sealed in 1541. Eze 44:2.

Mat 21:1 And when they drew nigh unto Jerusalem, and were come to Bethphage, unto the mount of Olives, then sent Jesus two disciples,

Mat 21:2 Saying unto them; "Go into the village over against you, and straightway ye shall find an ass tied, and a colt with her: loose them, and bring them unto me. 3 And if any man say ought unto you, ye shall say; "The Lord hath need of them;" and straightway he will send them."

Mat 21:4 All this was done, that it might be fulfilled which was spoken by the prophet, saying; 5 "Tell ye the daughter of Sion, Behold, thy King cometh unto thee, meek, and sitting upon an ass, and a colt the foal of an ass." *(Zec 9:9)*

Mat 21:6 And the disciples went, and did as Jesus commanded them,

Mat 21:7 And brought the ass, and the colt, and put on them their clothes, and they set him thereon.

Mat 21:8 And a very great multitude spread their garments in the way; others cut down branches from the trees, and strawed them in the way.

Mat 21:9 And the multitudes that went before, and that followed, cried, saying; "Hosanna to the Son of David: Blessed is he that cometh in the name of the Lord; Hosanna in the highest."

Mat 21:10 And when he was come into Jerusalem, all the city was moved, saying; "Who is this?"

Mat 21:11 And the multitude said; "This is Jesus the prophet of Nazareth of Galilee."

The Colt and The Triumphant Entry into Jerusalem

Mar 11:1 And when they came nigh to Jerusalem, unto Bethphage and Bethany, at the mount of Olives, he sendeth forth two of his disciples,

Mar 11:2 And saith unto them; "Go your way into the village over against you: and as soon as ye be entered into it, ye shall find a colt tied, whereon never man sat; loose him, and bring him. 3 And if any man say unto you; "Why do ye this?" say ye that the Lord hath need of him; and straightway he will send him hither."

Mar 11:4 And they went their way, and found the colt tied by the door without in a place where two ways met; and they loose him.

Mar 11:5 And certain of them that stood there said unto them; "What do ye, loosing the colt?"

Mar 11:6 And they said unto them even as Jesus had commanded: and they let them go.

Mar 11:7 And they brought the colt to Jesus, and cast their garments on him; and he sat upon him.

Mar 11:8 And many spread their garments in the way: and others cut down branches off the trees, and strawed them in the way.

Mar 11:9 And they that went before, and they that followed, cried, saying; "Hosanna; Blessed is he that cometh in the name of the Lord: 10 Blessed be the kingdom of our father David, that cometh in the name of the Lord: Hosanna in the highest."

Mar 11:11 And Jesus entered into Jerusalem, and into the temple: and when he had looked round about upon all things, and now the eventide was come, he went out unto Bethany with the twelve.

The Colt and Triumphant Entry into Jerusalem

Luk 19:28 And when he had thus spoken, he went before, ascending up to Jerusalem.

Luk 19:29 And it came to pass, when he was come nigh to Bethphage and Bethany, at the mount called the mount of Olives, he sent two of his disciples,

Luk 19:30 Saying, "Go ye into the village over against you; in the which at your entering ye shall find a colt tied, whereon yet never man sat: loose him, and bring him hither. 31 And if any man ask you; Why do ye loose him? thus shall ye say unto him; Because the Lord hath need of him."

Luk 19:32 And they that were sent went their way, and found even as he had said unto them.

Luk 19:33 And as they were loosing the colt, the owners thereof said unto them; "Why loose ye the colt?"

Luk 19:34 And they said; "The Lord hath need of him."

Luk 19:35 And they brought him to Jesus: and they cast their garments upon the colt, and they set Jesus thereon.

Luk 19:36 And as he went, they spread their clothes in the way.

Luk 19:37 And when he was come nigh, even now at the descent of the mount of Olives, the whole multitude of the disciples began to rejoice and praise God with a loud voice for all the mighty works that they had seen;

Luk 19:38 Saying, Blessed be the King that cometh in the name of the Lord: peace in heaven, and glory in the highest.

Luk 19:39 And some of the Pharisees from among the multitude said unto him, Master, rebuke thy disciples.

Luk 19:40 And he answered and said unto them, I tell you that, if these should hold their peace, the stones would immediately cry out.

<u>Jesus mourns over Jerusalem.</u>

Luk 19:41 And when he was come near, he beheld the city, and wept over it,

Luk 19:42 Saying; "If thou hadst known, even thou, at least in this thy day, the things which belong unto thy peace! but now they are hid from thine eyes. 43 For the days shall come upon thee, that thine enemies shall cast a trench about thee, and compass thee round, and keep thee in on every side, 44 And shall lay thee even with the ground, and thy children within thee; and they shall not leave in thee one stone upon another; because thou knewest not the time of thy visitation."

<u>The Colt and Triumphant Entry into Jerusalem</u>

Joh 12:14 And Jesus, when he had found a young ass, sat thereon; as it is written; (*Isaiah 62:11 and Zec 9:9*)

Joh 12:12 On the next day much people that were come to the feast, when they heard that Jesus was coming to Jerusalem,

Joh 12:13 Took branches of palm trees, and went forth to meet him, and cried: "Hosanna: Blessed is the King of Israel that cometh in the name of the Lord."

Joh 12:15 Fear not, daughter of Sion: behold, thy King cometh, sitting on an ass's colt.

Joh 12:16 These things understood not his disciples at the first: but when Jesus was glorified, then remembered they that these things were written of him, and that they had done these things unto him.

Joh 12:17 The people therefore that was with him when he called Lazarus out of his grave, and raised him from the dead, bare record.

Joh 12:18 For this cause the people also met him, for that they heard that he had done this miracle.

Joh 12:19 The Pharisees therefore said among themselves; "Perceive ye how ye prevail nothing? behold, the world is gone after him."

Visiting Greeks Seek Jesus

Joh 12:20 And there were certain Greeks among them that came up to worship at the feast:

Joh 12:21 The same came therefore to Philip, which was of Bethsaida of Galilee, and desired him, saying, "Sir, we would see Jesus."

Joh 12:22 Philip cometh and telleth Andrew: and again, Andrew and Philip tell Jesus.

Joh 12:23 And Jesus answered them, saying; "The hour is come, that the Son of man should be glorified. 24 Verily, verily, I say unto you. Except a corn of wheat fall into the ground and die, it abideth alone: but if it dies, it bringeth forth much fruit. 25 He that loveth his life shall lose it; and he that hateth his life in this world shall keep it unto life eternal. 26 If any man serves me, let him follow me; and where I am, there shall also my servant be: if any man serves me, him will my Father honour."

The Son of Man Must Be Lifted Up. *Ps102:10, Num 21:7-9.*

Joh 12:27 "Now is my soul troubled; and what shall I say? Father, save me from this hour: but for this cause came I unto this hour. 28 Father, glorify thy name. Then came there a voice from heaven, saying; "I HAVE BOTH GLORIFIED IT, AND I WILL GLORIFY IT AGAIN."

Joh 12:29 The people therefore, that stood by, and heard it, said that it thundered: others said; "An angel spake to him."

Joh 12:30 Jesus answered and said; "This voice came not because of me, but for your sakes. 31 Now is the judgment of this world: now shall the prince of this world be cast out *(Isa 14:12)*. 32 And I, if I be lifted up from the earth, will draw all men unto me." (Ps102:10, Num 21:7-9.)

Note; satan has been cast out, Rev 12:7-12. Jesus saw it in the Spirit, satan is now in time and can't revisit heaven like he did in Job; Job 1:6, as the head of the Earth that he stole from Adam, he is now just the accuser of the brethren, Rev 17:8. Jesus conquered satan and received all authority from the Father. Satan is now in time and is governed by time and that is why the devils said to Jesus, "have you come to torment us before the time" Mat 8:29. Because satan is now in time he can't go back in time and that is why weapons have to be formed against us and can't prosper, Isa 54:17.

Yes, we still have people doing satanic things, thus the worlds system. God has already factored our Victory through Jesus Christ, His Son. Ps 27. And when Jesus was presented to God and cleansed the Heavenly Temple, Exo 25:40, Joh 20:17. He entered eternity, Isa 57:15 and cleansed it all, right from the beginning of time., Rev 13:8. If God be for you Nothing can be against you. Rom 8:31, no spells witchcraft or any evil. Satan has no power at all,

Joh 12:33 This he said, signifying what death he should die.

Joh 12:34 The people answered him; "We have heard out of the law that Christ abideth for ever: and how sayest thou, The Son of man must be lifted up? who is this Son of man?"

Joh 12:35 Then Jesus said unto them; "Yet a little while is the light with you. Walk while ye have the light, lest darkness come upon you: for he that walketh in darkness knoweth not whither he goeth. 36 While ye have light, believe in the light, that ye may be the children of light."

Probably back to Bethany

<u>The Unbelief of the People</u>

These things spake Jesus, and departed, and did hide himself from them.

Joh 12:37 But though he had done so many miracles before them, yet they believed not on him:

Joh 12:38 That the saying of Esaias the prophet might be fulfilled, which he spake; "Lord, who hath believed our report? and to whom hath the arm of the Lord been revealed?" *(Isaiah 53:1)*

Joh 12:39 <u>Therefore they could not believe</u>, because that <u>Esaias said</u> again;

(This is a strange statement to say, because the Lord God had prophesied, it is impossible to change Gods word, but said in Truth. 2 Chron 20:20, Isa 46:10)

Joh 12:40 "He hath blinded their eyes, and hardened their heart; that they should not see with their eyes, nor understand with their heart, and be converted, and I should heal them." *(Isaiah 6:10)*

Joh 12:41 These things said Esaias, when he saw his glory, and spake of him.

Joh 12:42 Nevertheless among the chief rulers also many believed on him; but because of the Pharisees they did not confess him, lest they should be put out of the synagogue:

Joh 12:43 For they loved the praise of men more than the praise of God. *(Prov 29:25)*

(This is a pivotal point in our Christianity not to worry about what your church thinks, stand up for righteousness and if you need to get on your knees or lift your hands in praise, do it all for Jesus from your heart. Psa 149, Psa 150. And the right dividing of Scripture is 1 Corr 14:40. Don't disrupt the service, the Lord will give you opportunity if it is from Him. If He can get a pregnant lady to Bethlehem to fulfil a scripture during a hostile takeover of a nation by the Romans, I am sure your gift will make room for you. Prov 18:16.)

<u>Jesus Came to Save the World</u>

Joh 12:44 Jesus cried and said; "He that believeth on me, believeth not on me, but on him that sent me. 45 And he that seeth me seeth him that sent me. 46 I am come a light into the world, that whosoever believeth on me should not abide in darkness. 47 And if any man hear my words, and believe not, I judge him not: for I came not to judge the world, but to save the world. 48 He that rejecteth me, and receiveth not my words, hath one that judgeth him: the word that I have spoken, the same shall judge him in the last day. 49 For I have not spoken of myself; but the Father which sent me, he gave me a commandment, what I should say, and what I should speak. 50 And I know that his commandment is life everlasting: whatsoever I speak therefore, even as the Father said unto me, so I speak."

Jerusalem then to Bethany

Jesus Cleanses the Temple Again. *(First time in John 2:15)*

Mat 21:12 And Jesus went into the temple of God, and cast out all them that sold and bought in the temple, and overthrew the tables of the moneychangers, and the seats of them that sold doves,

Mat 21:13 And said unto them; "It is written; My house shall be called the house of prayer; but ye have made it a den of thieves."

Mat 21:14 And the blind and the lame came to him in the temple; and he healed them.

Mat 21:15 And when the chief priests and scribes saw the wonderful things that he did, and the children crying in the temple, and saying; "Hosanna to the Son of David"; they were sore displeased,

Mat 21:16 And said unto him; "Hearest thou what these say?" And Jesus saith unto them, "Yea; have ye never read; Out of the mouth of babes and sucklings thou hast perfected praise?" *(Psalms 8:2)*

Mat 21:17 And he left them, and went out of the city into Bethany; and he lodged there.

Jesus Cleanses the Temple Again

Mar 11:15 And they come to Jerusalem: and Jesus went into the temple, and began to cast out them that sold and bought in the temple, and overthrew the tables of the moneychangers, and the seats of them that sold doves;

Mar 11:16 And would not suffer that any man should carry any vessel through the temple.

Mar 11:17 And he taught, saying unto them; "Is it not written; My house shall be called of all nations the house of prayer? But ye have made it a den of thieves." *(Isa 56:7)*

Mar 11:18 And the scribes and chief priests heard it, and sought how they might destroy him: for they feared him, because all the people was astonished at his doctrine.

Mar 11:19 And when even was come, he went out of the city.

Jesus Cleanses the Temple Again

Luk 19:45 And he went into the temple, and began to cast out them that sold therein, and them that bought;

Luk 19:46 Saying unto them; "It is written; My house is the house of prayer: but ye have made it a den of thieves."

Luk 19:47 And he taught daily in the temple. But the chief priests and the scribes and the chief of the people sought to destroy him,

Luk 19:48 And could not find what they might do: for all the people were very attentive to hear him.

Returning to Jerusalem from Bethany

Jesus Curses the Fig Tree

Mat 21:18 Now in the morning as he returned into the city, he hungered.

Mat 21:19 And when he saw a fig tree in the way, he came to it, and found nothing thereon, but leaves only, and said unto it; "Let no fruit grow on thee henceforward for ever." And presently the fig tree withered away.

Mat 21:20 And when the disciples saw it, they marvelled, saying; "How soon is the fig tree withered away! "

Mat 21:21 Jesus answered and said unto them; "Verily I say unto you; If ye have faith, and doubt not, ye shall not only do this which is done to the fig tree, but also if ye shall say unto this mountain, Be thou removed, and be thou cast into the sea; it shall be done. 22 And all things, whatsoever ye shall ask in prayer, believing, ye shall receive."

Jesus Curses the Fig Tree

Mar 11:12 And on the morrow, when they were come from Bethany, he was hungry:

Mar 11:13 And seeing a fig tree afar off having leaves, he came, if haply he might find anything thereon: and when he came to it, he found nothing but leaves; for the time of figs was not yet.

Mar 11:14 And Jesus answered and said unto it; "No man eat fruit of thee hereafter for ever." And his disciples heard it.

Mar 11:20 And in the morning, as they passed by, they saw the fig tree dried up from the roots.

Mar 11:21 And Peter calling to remembrance saith unto him; "Master, behold, the fig tree which thou cursedst is withered away."

Believe and it Will Happen

Mar 11:22 And Jesus answering saith unto them; "Have faith in God. 23 For verily I say unto you; That whosoever shall say unto this mountain; Be thou removed, and be thou cast into the sea; and shall not doubt in his heart, but shall believe that those things which he saith shall come to pass; he shall have whatsoever he saith. 24 Therefore I say unto you; What things soever ye desire, when ye pray, believe that ye receive them, and ye shall have them. 25 And when ye stand praying, forgive, if ye have ought against any: that your Father also which is in heaven may forgive you your trespasses. 26 But if ye do not forgive, neither will your Father which is in heaven forgive your trespasses."

Teachings in the Temple at Jerusalem

The Authority of Jesus Questioned

Mat 21:23 And when he was come into the temple, the chief priests and the elders of the people came unto him as he was teaching, and said; "By what authority doest thou these things? and who gave thee this authority?"

Mat 21:24 And Jesus answered and said unto them; "I also will ask you one thing, which if ye tell me, I in likewise will tell you by what authority I do these things. 25 The baptism of John, whence was it? from heaven, or of men?" And they reasoned with themselves, saying; "If we shall say; "From heaven;" he will say unto us; "Why did ye not then believe him?" 26 But if we shall say; Of men; we fear the people; for all hold John as a prophet."

Mat 21:27 And they answered Jesus, and said; "We cannot tell." And he said unto them; "Neither tell I you by what authority I do these things."

The Authority of Jesus Questioned

Mar 11:27 And they come again to Jerusalem: and as he was walking in the temple, there come to him the chief priests, and the scribes, and the elders,

Mar 11:28 And say unto him; "By what authority doest thou these things? and who gave thee this authority to do these things?"

Mar 11:29 And Jesus answered and said unto them; "I will also ask of you one question, and answer me, and I will tell you by what authority I do these things. 30 The baptism of John, was it from heaven, or of men? answer me."

Mar 11:31 And they reasoned with themselves, saying; "If we shall say; "From heaven;" he will say; "Why then did ye not believe him?" 32 But if we shall say; "Of men;"" They feared the people: for all men counted John, that he was a prophet indeed.

Mar 11:33 And they answered and said unto Jesus; "We cannot tell." And Jesus answering saith unto them; "Neither do I tell you by what authority I do these things."

The Authority of Jesus Questioned

Luk 20:1 And it came to pass, that on one of those days, as he taught the people in the temple, and preached the gospel, the chief priests and the scribes came upon him with the elders,

Luk 20:2 And spake unto him, saying; "Tell us, by what authority doest thou these things? or who is he that gave thee this authority?"

Luk 20:3 And he answered and said unto them; "I will also ask you one thing; and answer me: 4 The baptism of John, was it from heaven, or of men?"

Luk 20:5 And they reasoned with themselves, saying, "If we shall say; "From heaven;" he will say; "Why then believed ye him not?" 6 But and if we say;

"Of men;" all the people will stone us:" for they be persuaded that John was a prophet.

Luk 20:7 And they answered, that they could not tell whence it was.

Luk 20:8 And Jesus said unto them; "Neither tell I you by what authority I do these things."

The Parable of the Two disobedient Sons

Mat 21:28 "But what think ye? A certain man had two sons; and he came to the first, and said; "Son, go work today in my vineyard." 29 He answered and said, "I will not:" but afterward he repented, and went. 30 And he came to the second, and said likewise. And he answered and said; "I go, sir:" and went not. 31 Whether of them twain did the will of his father?" They say unto him; "The first." Jesus saith unto them; "Verily I say unto you; That the publicans and the harlots go into the kingdom of God before you. 32 For John came unto you in the way of righteousness, and ye believed him not: but the publicans and the harlots believed him: and ye, when ye had seen it, repented not afterward, that ye might believe him."

The Parable of the Wicked Tenants. *Isaiah Ch 5, Job 1:10.*

Mat 21:33 "Hear another parable: There was a certain householder, which planted a vineyard, *(sown the word)* and hedged it round about, and digged a winepress in it, and built a tower, and let it out to husbandmen, *(Mankind)* and went into a far country *(Heaven):* 34 And when the time of the fruit drew near, he sent his servants *(the Prophets, 2kings 21:10)* to the husbandmen, that they might receive the fruits of it. 35 And the husbandmen took his servants, and beat one, and killed another, and stoned another. 36 Again, he sent other servants more than the first: and they did unto them likewise. 37 But last of all he sent unto them his son *(Jesus)*, saying; "They will reverence my son." 38 But when the husbandmen saw the son, they said among themselves; "This is the heir; come, let us kill him, and let us seize on his inheritance." 39 And they caught him, and cast him out of the vineyard *(Jerusalem)*, and slew him. 40 When the lord therefore of the vineyard cometh, what will he do unto those husbandmen?"

Mat 21:41 They say unto him; "He will miserably destroy those wicked men, and will let out his vineyard unto other husbandmen, which shall render him the fruits in their seasons." *(Ps 2:8,9, Rev 2:27, Zec 14:4, Mal 4, Rev 19.)*

Mat 21:42 Jesus saith unto them; "Did ye never read in the scriptures; "The stone which the builders rejected, the same is become the head of the corner: this is the Lord's doing, and it is marvellous in our eyes?" *(Isa 8:14, Ps 118:22,23)* 43 Therefore say I unto you; The kingdom of God shall be taken from you, and given to a nation bringing forth the fruits thereof. 44 And whosoever shall fall on this stone shall be broken: but on whomsoever it shall fall, it will grind him to powder."

Mat 21:45 And when the chief priests and Pharisees had heard his parables, they perceived that he spake of them.

Mat 21:46 But when they sought to lay hands on him, they feared the multitude, because they took him for a prophet.

The Parable of the Wicked Tenants

Mar 12:1 And he began to speak unto them by parables. "A certain man planted a vineyard, and set an hedge about it, and digged a place for the winefat, and built a tower, and let it out to husbandmen, and went into a far country. 2 And at the season he sent to the husbandmen a servant, that he might receive from the husbandmen of the fruit of the vineyard. 3 And they caught him, and beat him, and sent him away empty. 4 And again he sent unto them another servant; and at him they cast stones, and wounded him in the head, and sent him away shamefully handled. 5 And again he sent another; and him they killed, and many others; beating some, and killing some. 6 Having yet therefore one son, his well-beloved, he sent him also last unto them, saying; "They will reverence my son." 7 But those husbandmen said among themselves; "This is the heir; come, let us kill him, and the inheritance shall be ours." 8 And they took him, and killed him, and cast him out of the vineyard. 9 What shall therefore the lord of the vineyard do? He will come and destroy the husbandmen, and will give the vineyard unto others. 10 And have ye not read this scripture; The stone which the builders rejected is become the head of the corner: 11 This was the Lord's doing, and it is marvellous in our eyes?" *(Ps 118:23)*

Mar 12:12 And they sought to lay hold on him, but feared the people: for they knew that he had spoken the parable against them: and they left him, and went their way.

The Parable of the Wicked Tenants

Luk 20:9 Then began he to speak to the people this parable; "A certain man planted a vineyard, and let it forth to husbandmen, and went into a far country for a long time. 10 And at the season he sent a servant to the husbandmen, that they should give him of the fruit of the vineyard: but the husbandmen beat him, and sent him away empty. 11 And again he sent another servant: and they beat him also, and entreated him shamefully, and sent him away empty. 12 And again he sent a third: and they wounded him also, and cast him out. 13 Then said the lord of the vineyard, what shall I do? I will send my beloved son: it maybe they will reverence him when they see him. 14 But when the husbandmen saw him, they reasoned among themselves, saying, this is the heir: come, let us kill him, that the inheritance may be ours. 15 So they cast him out of the vineyard, and killed him. What therefore shall the lord of the vineyard do unto them? 16 He shall come and destroy these husbandmen, and shall give the vineyard to others." And when they heard it, they said; "God forbid."

Luk 20:17 And he beheld them, and said; "What is this then that is written; The stone which the builders rejected, the same is become the head of the corner? 18 Whosoever shall fall upon that stone shall be broken; but on whomsoever it shall fall, it will grind him to powder." *(Isa 8:14, Psa 118:22)*

Luk 20:19 And the chief priests and the scribes the same hour sought to lay hands on him; and they feared the people: for they perceived that he had spoken this parable against them.

The Heavenly Wedding Feast. Many called, few Chosen.

Mat 22:1 And Jesus answered and spake unto them again by parables, and said;

Mat 22:2 "The kingdom of heaven is like unto a certain king, which made a marriage for his son, 3 And sent forth his servants to call them that were bidden to the wedding: and they would not come. 4 Again, he sent forth other servants, saying; "Tell them which are bidden, Behold, I have prepared my dinner: my oxen and my fatlings are killed, and all things are ready: come unto the marriage." 5 But they made light of it, and went their ways, one to his farm, another to his merchandise: 6 And the remnant took his servants, and entreated them spitefully, and slew them. 7 But when the king heard thereof, he was wroth: and he sent forth his armies, and destroyed those murderers, and burned up their city. 8 Then saith he to his servants; "The wedding is ready, but they which were bidden were not worthy. 9 Go ye therefore into the highways, and as many as ye shall find, bid to the marriage." 10 So those servants went out into the highways, and gathered together all as many as they found, both bad and good: and the wedding was furnished with guests. 11 And when the king came in to see the guests, he saw there a man which had not on a wedding garment: 12 And he saith unto him; "Friend, how camest thou in hither not having a wedding garment?" And he was speechless. 13 Then said the king to the servants; "Bind him hand and foot, and take him away, and cast him into outer darkness;" there shall be weeping and gnashing of teeth. 14 For many are called, but few are chosen."

Paying Taxes to Caesar

Mat 22:15 Then went the Pharisees, and took counsel how they might entangle him in his talk.

Mat 22:16 And they sent out unto him their disciples with the Herodians, saying; "Master, we know that thou art true, and teachest the way of God in truth, neither carest thou for any man: for thou regardest not the person of men. 17 Tell us therefore, What thinkest thou? Is it lawful to give tribute unto Caesar, or not?"

Mat 22:18 But Jesus perceived their wickedness, and said; "Why tempt ye me, ye hypocrites? 19 Shew me the tribute money." And they brought unto him a penny.

Mat 22:20 And he saith unto them; "Whose is this image and superscription?"

Mat 22:21 They say unto him; "Caesar's." Then saith he unto them; "Render therefore unto Caesar the things which are Caesar's; and unto God the things that are God's."

Mat 22:22 When they had heard these words, they marvelled, and left him, and went their way.

Paying Taxes to Caesar

Mar 12:13 And they send unto him certain of the Pharisees and of the Herodians, to catch him in his words.

Mar 12:14 And when they were come, they say unto him; "Master, we know that thou art true, and carest for no man: for thou regardest not the person of men, but teachest the way of God in truth: Is it lawful to give tribute to Caesar, or not? 15 Shall we give, or shall we not give?" But he, knowing their hypocrisy, said unto them; "Why tempt ye me? bring me a penny, that I may see it."

Mar 12:16 And they brought it. And he saith unto them; "Whose is this image and superscription?" And they said unto him; "Caesar's."

Mar 12:17 And Jesus answering said unto them; "Render to Caesar the things that are Caesar's, and to God the things that are God's." And they marvelled at him.

Paying Taxes to Caesar

Luk 20:20 And they watched him, and sent forth spies, which should feign themselves just men, that they might take hold of his words, that so they might deliver him unto the power and authority of the governor.

Luk 20:21 And they asked him, saying; "Master, we know that thou sayest and teachest rightly, neither acceptest thou the person of any, but teachest the way of God truly: 22 Is it lawful for us to give tribute unto Caesar, or no?"

Luk 20:23 But he perceived their craftiness, and said unto them; "Why tempt ye me? 24 Shew me a penny. Whose image and superscription hath it?" They answered and said; "Caesar's."

Luk 20:25 And he said unto them; "Render therefore unto Caesar the things which be Caesar's, and unto God the things which be God's."

Luk 20:26 And they could not take hold of his words before the people: and they marvelled at his answer, and held their peace.

Sadducees Dispute the Resurrection and are Rebuked.

(Reference Lukes genealogy. Luke 3:23

Mat 22:23 The same day came to him the Sadducees, which say that there is no resurrection, and asked him,

Mat 22:24 Saying; "Master, Moses said; "If a man die, having no children, his brother shall marry his wife, and raise up seed unto his brother." 25 Now there were with us seven brethren: and the first, when he had married a wife, deceased, and, having no issue, left his wife unto his brother: 26 Likewise the second also, and the third, unto the seventh. 27 And last of all the woman died also. 28 Therefore in the resurrection whose wife shall she be of the seven? for they all had her."

Mat 22:29 Jesus answered and said unto them; "Ye do err, not knowing the scriptures, nor the power of God. 30 For in the resurrection they neither marry, nor are given in marriage, but are as the angels of God in heaven. 31 But as touching the resurrection of the dead, have ye not read that which was spoken unto you by God, saying, 32 I am the God of Abraham, and the God of Isaac, and the God of Jacob? God is not the God of the dead, but of the living."

Mat 22:33 And when the multitude heard this, they were astonished at his doctrine.

Sadducees Dispute the Resurrection and are Rebuked

Mar 12:18 Then come unto him the Sadducees, which say there is no resurrection; and they asked him, saying;

Mar 12:19 "Master, Moses wrote unto us; "If a man's brother die, and leave his wife behind him, and leave no children, that his brother should take his wife, and raise up seed unto his brother." 20 Now there were seven brethren: and the first took a wife, and dying left no seed. 21 And the second took her, and died, neither left he any seed: and the third likewise. 22 And the seven had her, and left no seed: last of all the woman died also. 23 In the resurrection therefore, when they shall rise, whose wife shall she be of them? for the seven had her to wife."

Mar 12:24 And Jesus answering said unto them; "Do ye not therefore err, because ye know not the scriptures, neither the power of God? 25 For when they shall rise from the dead, they neither marry, nor are given in marriage; but are as the angels which are in heaven. 26 And as touching the dead, that they rise: Have ye not read in the book of Moses, how in the bush God spake unto him, saying, I am the God of Abraham, and the God of Isaac, and the God of Jacob? 27 He is not the God of the dead, but the God of the living: ye therefore do greatly err."

Sadducees Dispute the Resurrection and are Rebuked

Luk 20:27 Then came to him certain of the Sadducees, which deny that there is any resurrection; and they asked him,

Luk 20:28 Saying; "Master, Moses wrote unto us; "<u>If any man's brother die</u>, having a wife, and he die without children, that his brother should take his wife, and raise up seed unto his brother." 29 There were therefore seven brethren: and the first took a wife, and died without children. 30 And the second took her to wife, and he died childless. 31 And the third took her; and in like manner the seven also: and they left no children, and died. 32 Last of all the woman died also. 33 Therefore in the resurrection whose wife of them is she? for seven had her to wife."

Luk 20:34 And Jesus answering said unto them; "The children of this world marry, and are given in marriage: 35 But they which shall be accounted worthy to obtain that world, and the resurrection from the dead, neither marry, nor are given in marriage: 36 Neither can they die any more: for they are equal unto the angels; and are the children of God, being the children of the resurrection. 37 Now that the dead are raised, even Moses shewed at the bush, when he calleth the Lord the God of Abraham, and the God of Isaac, and the God of Jacob. 38 For he is not a God of the dead, but of the living: for all live unto him."

Luk 20:39 Then certain of the scribes answering said; "Master, thou hast well said."

Luk 20:40 And after that they durst not ask him any question at all.

A Lawyer Temps Jesus

Mat 22:34 But when the Pharisees had heard that he had put the Sadducees to silence, they were gathered together.

Mat 22:35 Then one of them, which was a lawyer, asked him a question, tempting him, and saying; 36 "Master, which is the great commandment in the law?"

Mat 22:37 Jesus said unto him; "Thou shalt love the Lord thy God with all thy heart, and with all thy soul, and with all thy mind. 38 This is the first and great commandment. 39 And the second is like unto it. Thou shalt love thy neighbour as thyself. 40 On these two commandments hang all the law and the prophets."

A Lawyer Temps Jesus

Mar 12:28 And one of the scribes came, and having heard them reasoning together, and perceiving that he had answered them well, asked him; "Which is the first commandment of all?"

Mar 12:29 And Jesus answered him; "The first of all the commandments is, Hear, O Israel; The Lord our God is one Lord: 30 And thou shalt love the Lord thy God with all thy heart, and with all thy soul, and with all thy mind, and with all thy strength: this is the first commandment. 31 And the second is like, namely this; Thou shalt love thy neighbour as thyself. There is none other commandment greater than these."

Mar 12:32 And the scribe said unto him; "Well, Master, thou hast said the truth: for there is one God; and there is none other but he: 33 And to love him with all the heart, and with all the understanding, and with all the soul, and with all the strength, and to love his neighbour as himself, is more than all whole burnt offerings and sacrifices."

Mar 12:34 And when Jesus saw that he answered discreetly, he said unto him; "Thou art not far from the kingdom of God." And no man after that durst ask him any question.

A Lawyer Temps Jesus

Luk 10:25 And, behold, a certain lawyer stood up, and tempted him, saying "Master, what shall I do to inherit eternal life?" 26 He said unto him; "What is written in the law? how readest thou?"

Luk 10:27 And he answering said; "<u>Thou shalt love the Lord thy God with all thy heart</u>, and with all thy soul, and with all thy strength, <u>and with all thy mind; and thy neighbour as thyself.</u>"

Luk 10:28 And he said unto him; "Thou hast answered right: this do and thou shalt live."

Luk 10:29 But he, willing to justify himself, said unto Jesus; "And who is my neighbour?" *(Lev 19:18)*

The Parable of the Good Samaritan

Luk 10:30 And Jesus answering said; "A certain man went down from Jerusalem to Jericho, and fell among thieves, which stripped him of his raiment, and wounded him, and departed, leaving him half dead. 31 And by chance there came down a certain priest that way: and when he saw him, he passed by on the other side. 32 And likewise a Levite, when he was at the place, came and looked on him, and passed by on the other side. 33 But a certain Samaritan, as he journeyed, came where he was: and when he saw him, he had compassion on him, 34 And went to him, and bound up his wounds, pouring in oil and wine, and set him on his own beast, and brought him to an inn, and took care of him. 35 And on the morrow when he departed, he took out two pence, and gave them to the host, and said unto him, take care of him; and whatsoever thou spendest more, when I come again, I will repay thee. 36 Which now of these three, thinkest thou, was neighbour unto him that fell among the thieves?

Luk 10:37 And he said; "He that shewed mercy on him." Then said Jesus unto him; "Go, and do thou likewise." *(Micah 6:8)*

Martha complains and Mary Receives her Ministry. *Ps 23:6, Ps 27:4, Ps 84:10.*

Luk 10:38 Now it came to pass, as they went, that he entered into a certain village *(Bethany)*: and a certain woman named Martha received him into her house.

Luk 10:39 And she had a sister called Mary, which also sat at Jesus' feet, and heard his word.

Luk 10:40 But Martha was cumbered about much serving, and came to him, and said; "Lord, dost thou not care that my sister hath left me to serve alone? bid her therefore that she help me!"

Luk 10:41 And Jesus answered and said unto her; "Martha, Martha, thou art careful and troubled about many things: 42 But one thing is needful: and Mary hath chosen that good part, which shall not be taken away from her."

Whose Son Is the Christ?

Mat 22:41 While the Pharisees were gathered together, Jesus asked them,

Mat 22:42 Saying; "What think ye of Christ? whose son is he?" They say unto him; "The Son of David."

Mat 22:43 He saith unto them; "How then doth David in spirit call him Lord, saying; 44 "The LORD said unto my Lord, sit thou on my right hand, till I make thine enemies thy footstool?" 45 If David then calls him Lord, how is he, his son?" *(Ps 110:1)*

Mat 22:46 And no man was able to answer him a word, neither durst any man from that day forth ask him any more questions.

Whose Son is the Christ? *(Ps 110:1)*

Mar 12:35 And Jesus answered and said, while he taught in the temple; "How say the scribes that Christ is the Son of David? 36 For David himself said by the Holy Ghost; "The LORD said to my Lord; Sit thou on my right hand, till I make thine enemies thy footstool." 37 David therefore himself calleth him Lord; and whence is he then his son?" And the common people heard him gladly.

Whose Son Is the Christ? *(Ps 110:1)*

Luk 20:41 And he said unto them; "How say they that Christ is David's son? 42 And David himself saith in the book of Psalms, The LORD said unto my Lord; <u>Sit thou on my right hand</u>, 43 Till I make thine enemies thy footstool. 44 David therefore calleth him Lord, how is he then his son?"

Seven Woes to the Scribes and Pharisees

Mat 23:1 Then spake Jesus to the multitude, and to his disciples,

Mat 23:2 Saying; "The scribes and the Pharisees sit in Moses' seat: 3 All therefore whatsoever they bid you observe, that observe and do; but do not ye after their works: for they say, and do not. 4 For they bind heavy burdens and grievous to be borne, and lay them on men's shoulders; but they themselves will not move them with one of their fingers. 5 But all their works they do for to be seen of men: they make broad their phylacteries, and enlarge the borders of their garments, 6 And love the uppermost rooms at feasts, and the chief seats in the synagogues, 7 And greetings in the markets, and to be called of men, Rabbi, Rabbi. 8 But be not ye called Rabbi: for one is your Master, even Christ; and all ye are brethren. 9 And call no man your father upon the earth: for one is your Father, which is in heaven. 10 Neither be ye called masters: for one is your Master, even Christ. 11 But he that is greatest among you shall be your servant. 12 And whosoever shall exalt himself shall be abased; and he that shall humble himself shall be exalted. 13 But woe unto you, scribes and Pharisees, hypocrites! for ye shut up the kingdom of heaven against men: for ye neither go in yourselves, neither suffer ye them that are entering to go in. 14 Woe unto you, scribes and Pharisees, hypocrites! for ye devour widows' houses, and for a pretence make long prayer: therefore, ye shall receive the greater damnation. 15 Woe unto you, scribes and Pharisees, hypocrites! for ye compass sea and land to make one proselyte, and when he is made, ye make him twofold more the child of hell than yourselves. 16 Woe unto you, ye blind guides, which say, whosoever shall swear by the temple, it is nothing; but whosoever shall swear by the gold of the temple, he is a debtor! 17 Ye fools and blind: for whether is greater, the gold, or the temple that sanctifieth the gold? 18 And whosoever shall swear by the altar, it is nothing; but whosoever sweareth by the gift that is upon it, he is guilty. 19 Ye fools and blind: for whether is greater, the gift, or the altar that sanctifieth the gift?"

Don't Make Oaths

Mat 23:20 "Whoso therefore shall swear by the altar, sweareth by it, and by all things thereon. 21 And whoso shall swear by the temple, sweareth by it, and by him that dwelleth therein. 22 And he that shall swear by heaven, sweareth by the throne of God, and by him that sitteth thereon. 23 Woe unto you, scribes and Pharisees, hypocrites! for ye pay tithe of mint and anise and cummin, and have omitted the weightier matters of the law, judgment, mercy, and faith: these ought ye to have done, and not to leave the other undone. 24 Ye blind guides, which strain at a gnat, and swallow a camel."

Woe to the Teachers and Leaders. *Lev 19:14*

Mat 23:25 "Woe unto you, scribes and Pharisees, hypocrites! for ye make clean the outside of the cup and of the platter, but within they are full of extortion and excess. 26 Thou blind Pharisee, cleanse first that which is within the cup and platter, that the outside of them may be clean also. 27 Woe unto you, scribes and Pharisees, hypocrites! for ye are like unto whited sepulchres, which indeed appear beautiful outward, but are within full of dead men's bones, and of all uncleanness. 28 Even so ye also outwardly appear righteous unto men, but within ye are full of hypocrisy and iniquity. 29 Woe unto you, scribes and Pharisees, hypocrites! because ye build the tombs of the prophets, and garnish the sepulchres of the righteous, 30 And say; "If we had been in the days of our fathers, we would not have been partakers with them in the blood of the prophets." 31 Wherefore ye be witnesses unto yourselves, that ye are the children of them which killed the prophets. 32 Fill ye up then the measure of your fathers. 33 Ye serpents, ye generation of vipers, how can ye escape the damnation of hell? 34 Wherefore, behold, I send unto you prophets, and wise men, and scribes: and some of them ye shall kill and crucify; and some of them shall ye scourge in your synagogues, and persecute them from city to city: 35 That upon you may come all the righteous blood shed upon the earth, from the blood of righteous Abel unto the blood of Zacharias son of Barachias, whom ye slew between the temple and the altar. 36 Verily I say unto you, all these things shall come upon this generation."

Pharisees Rebuked

Luk 11:37 And as he spake a certain Pharisee besought him to dine with him: and he went in, and sat down to meat.

Luk 11:38 And when the Pharisee saw it, he marvelled that he had not first washed before dinner.

Luk 11:39 And the Lord said unto him; "Now do ye Pharisees make clean the outside of the cup and the platter; but your inward part is full of ravening and wickedness. 40 Ye fools, did not he that made that which is without make that which is within also? 41 But rather give alms of such things as ye have; and, behold, all things are clean unto you. 42 But woe unto you, Pharisees! for ye tithe mint and rue and all manner of herbs, and pass over judgment and the love of God: these ought ye to have done, and not to leave the other undone. 43 Woe unto you, Pharisees! for ye love the uppermost seats in the synagogues, and greetings in the markets. 44 Woe unto you, scribes and Pharisees, hypocrites! for ye are as graves which appear not, and the men that walk over them are not aware of them."

Luk 11:45 Then answered one of the lawyers, and said unto him; "Master, thus saying thou reproachest us also."

Luk 11:46 And he said; "Woe unto you also, ye lawyers! for ye lade men with burdens grievous to be borne, and ye yourselves touch not the burdens with one of your fingers. 47 Woe unto you! for ye build the sepulchres of the prophets, and your fathers killed them. 48 Truly ye bear witness that ye allow the deeds of your fathers: for they indeed killed them, and ye build their sepulchres. 49 Therefore also said the wisdom of God, I will send them prophets and apostles, and some of them they shall slay and persecute: 50 That the blood of all the prophets, which was shed from the foundation of the world, may be required of this generation; 51 From the blood of Abel unto the blood of Zacharias, which perished between the altar and the temple: verily I say unto you, It shall be required of this generation. 52 Woe unto you, lawyers! for ye have taken away the key of knowledge: ye entered not in yourselves, and them that were entering in ye hindered."

Luk 11:53 And as he said these things unto them, the scribes and the Pharisees began to urge him vehemently, and to provoke him to speak of many things: 54 Laying wait for him, and seeking to catch something out of his mouth, that they might accuse him.

Jesus Mourns Over Jerusalem

Mat 23:37 "O Jerusalem, Jerusalem, thou that killest the prophets, and stonest them which are sent unto thee, <u>how often would I have gathered thy children together, even as a hen gathereth her chickens under her wings</u>, and ye would not! 38 Behold, your house is left unto you desolate. 39 For I say unto you, Ye shall not see me henceforth, till ye shall say, Blessed is he that cometh in the name of the Lord."

Jesus Mourns Over Jerusalem

Luk 13:31 The same day there came certain of the Pharisees, saying unto him; "Get thee out, and depart hence: for Herod will kill thee."

Luk 13:32 And he said unto them; "Go ye, and tell that fox, Behold, I cast out devils, and I do cures today and tomorrow, and the third day I shall be perfected. 33 Nevertheless I must walk to day, and tomorrow, and the day following: for it cannot be that a prophet perish out of Jerusalem. 34 O Jerusalem, Jerusalem, which killest the prophets, and stonest them that are sent unto thee; <u>how often would I have gathered thy children together, as a hen doth gather her brood under her wings</u>, and ye would not! 35 Behold, your house is left unto you desolate: and verily I say unto you, Ye shall not see me, until the time come when ye shall say; Blessed is he that cometh in the name of the Lord."

Beware of the Scribes

Mar 12:38 And he said unto them in his doctrine; "<u>Beware of the scribes</u>, which love to go in long clothing, and love salutations in the marketplaces, 39 And the chief seats in the synagogues, and the uppermost rooms at feasts: 40 Which devour widows' houses, and for a pretence make long prayers: these shall receive greater damnation."

Beware of the Scribes

Luk 20:45 Then in the audience of all the people he said unto his disciples;

Luk 20:46 "Beware of the scribes, which desire to walk in long robes, and love greetings in the markets, and the highest seats in the synagogues, and the chief rooms at feasts; 47 Which devour widows' houses, and for a shew make long prayers: the same shall receive greater damnation."

The Widow's Offering

Mar 12:41 And Jesus sat over against the treasury, and beheld how the people cast money into the treasury: and many that were rich cast in much.

Mar 12:42 And there came a certain poor widow, and she threw in two mites, which make a farthing. *(Quarter of a penny)*

Mar 12:43 And he called unto him his disciples, and saith unto them; "Verily I say unto you; That this poor widow hath cast more in, than all they which have cast into the treasury: 44 For all they did cast in of their abundance; but she of her want did cast in all that she had, even all her living."

The Widow's Offering

Luk 21:1 And he looked up, and saw the rich men casting their gifts into the treasury.

Luk 21:2 And he saw also a certain poor widow casting in thither two mites.

Luk 21:3 And he said; "Of a truth I say unto you, that this poor widow hath cast in more than they all: 4 For all these have of their abundance cast in unto the offerings of God: but she of her penury *(extreme poverty)* hath cast in all the living that she had."

Heading to the Mount of Olives

Jesus Prophesies the Destruction of the Temple

Mat 24:1 And Jesus went out, and departed from the temple: and his disciples came to him for to shew him the buildings of the temple.

Mat 24:2 And Jesus said unto them; "See ye not all these things? verily I say unto you; There shall not be left here one stone upon another, that shall not be thrown down."

Jesus Prophesies the Destruction of the Temple

Mar 13:1 And as he went out of the temple, one of his disciples saith unto him; "Master, see what manner of stones and what buildings are here!"

Mar 13:2 And Jesus answering said unto him; "Seest thou these great buildings? there shall not be left one stone upon another, that shall not be thrown down."

Jesus Prophesies the Destruction of the Temple

Luk 21:5 And as some spake of the temple, how it was adorned with goodly stones and gifts, he said;

Luk 21:6 "As for these things which ye behold, the days will come, in the which there shall not be left one stone upon another, that shall not be thrown down."

Luk 21:7 And they asked him, saying; "Master, but when shall these things be? and what sign will there be when these things shall come to pass?"

Seated on Mt of Olives

Signs of the End of the Age

Mat 24:3 And as he sat upon the mount of Olives, the disciples came unto him privately, saying; "Tell us, when shall these things be? and what shall be the sign of thy coming, and of the end of the world?"

Mat 24:4 And Jesus answered and said unto them; "Take heed that no man deceive you. 5 For many shall come in my name, saying, I am Christ *(I am anointed)*; and shall deceive many. 6 And ye shall hear of wars and rumours of wars: see that ye be not troubled: for all these things must come to pass, but the end is not yet. 7 For nation shall rise against nation, and kingdom against kingdom: and there shall be famines, and pestilences, and earthquakes, in divers **(many)** places. 8 All these are the beginning of sorrows.

9 Then shall they deliver you up to be afflicted, and shall kill you: and ye shall be hated of all nations for my name's sake. 10 And then shall many be offended, and shall betray one another, and shall hate one another. 11 And many false prophets shall rise, and shall deceive many. 12 And because iniquity shall abound, the love of many shall wax cold. 13 But he that shall endure unto the end, the same shall be saved. 14 And this gospel of the kingdom shall be preached in all the world for a witness unto all nations; and then shall the end come."

<u>Signs of the End of the Age.</u>

Mar 13:3 And as he sat upon the mount of Olives over against the temple, Peter and James and John and Andrew asked him privately;

Mar 13:4 "Tell us, when shall these things be? and what shall be the sign when all these things shall be fulfilled?"

Mar 13:5 And Jesus answering them began to say; "<u>Take heed lest any man deceive you:</u> 6 For many shall come in my name, saying, I am Christ; and shall deceive many. 7 And when ye shall hear of wars and rumours of wars, be ye not troubled: for such things must needs be; but the end shall not be yet. 8 For nation shall rise against nation, and kingdom against kingdom: and there shall be earthquakes in divers **(Various, Many)** places, and there shall be famines and troubles: these are the beginnings of sorrows. 9 But take heed to yourselves: <u>for they shall deliver you up to councils</u>; and in the synagogues ye shall be beaten: and ye shall be brought before rulers and kings for my sake, for a testimony against them. 10 And the gospel must first be published among all nations. 11 But when they shall lead you, and deliver you up, take no thought beforehand what ye shall speak, neither do ye premeditate: but whatsoever shall be given you in that hour, that speak ye: for it is not ye that speak, but the Holy Ghost. 12 Now the brother shall betray the brother to death, and the father the son; and children shall rise up against their parents, and shall cause them to be put to death. 13 And ye shall be hated of all men for my name's sake: but he that shall endure unto the end, the same shall be saved."

Signs of the End of the Age.

Luk 21:8 And he said; "Take heed that ye be not deceived: for many shall come in my name, saying, I am Christ *(Anointed)*; and the time draweth near: go ye not therefore after them. 9 But when ye shall hear of wars and commotions, be not terrified: for these things must first come to pass; but the end is not by and by."

Luk 21:10 Then said he unto them; "Nation shall rise against nation, and kingdom against kingdom: 11 And great earthquakes shall be in divers *(many)* places, and famines, and pestilences; and fearful sights and great signs shall there be from heaven. 12 But before all these, they shall lay their hands on you, and persecute you, delivering you up to the synagogues, and into prisons, being brought before kings and rulers for my name's sake. 13 And it shall turn to you for a testimony. 14 Settle it therefore in your hearts, not to meditate before what ye shall answer: 15 For I will give you a mouth and wisdom, which all your adversaries shall not be able to gainsay nor resist. 16 And ye shall be betrayed both by parents, and brethren, and kinsfolks, and friends; and some of you shall they cause to be put to death. 17 And ye shall be hated of all men for my name's sake. 18 But there shall not an hair of your head perish. 19 In your patience possess ye your souls."

Desolation of Jerusalem. (This has happened once already 70 A.D. by the Romans)

Luk 21:20 "And when ye shall see Jerusalem compassed with armies, then know that the desolation thereof is nigh. 21 Then let them which are in Judaea flee to the mountains; and let them which are in the midst of it depart out; and let not them that are in the countries enter thereinto. 22 For these be the days of vengeance, that all things which are written may be fulfilled. 23 But woe unto them that are with child, and to them that give suck, in those days! for there shall be great distress in the land, and wrath upon this people. 24 And they shall fall by the edge of the sword, and shall be led away captive into all nations: and Jerusalem shall be trodden down of the Gentiles, until the times of the Gentiles be fulfilled."

As Jesus said the blood of all the prophets were required of that generation in Luke 11:50 and as Daniel said the Rock made without hands spread throughout the whole earth, Dan 2:44. Israel was destroyed in 70 A.D. and the Christians spread throughout the whole known world; remembering that the first 3000 saved were from all parts of the known world, also confirming Mark 13:10 and Acts 1:8. Israel returned and became a state in 1948 after many world wars, being extremely persecuted in WW2, then comes the grace of God. Think about this; Did you know that Trump approved the attacked Iran on the 23 of Sivan the same day Esther got permission from the king to defend themselves from being exterminated?

The Abomination of Desolation (Dan 11:31)

Mat 24:15 "When ye therefore shall see the abomination of desolation, spoken of by Daniel the prophet, stand in the holy place, (whoso readeth, let him understand:) 16 Then let them which be in Judaea flee into the mountains: 17 Let him which is on the housetop not come down to take anything out of his house: 18 Neither let him which is in the field return back to take his clothes. 19 And woe unto them that are with child, and to them that give suck in those days! 20 But pray ye that your flight be not in the winter, neither on the sabbath day: 21 For then shall be great tribulation, such as was not since the beginning of the world to this time, no, nor ever shall be. 22 And except those days should be shortened, there should no flesh be saved: but for the elect's sake those days shall be shortened. 23 Then if any man shall say unto you; "Lo, here is Christ, or there;" believe it not. 24 For there shall arise false Christs, and false prophets, and shall shew great signs and wonders; insomuch that, if it were possible, they shall deceive the very elect."

(A false prophet is one that leads you away from Jesus and God, not the ones that stuff up and get it wrong, for we only see in part, 1 Corr 13:9) let him that has never been wrong cast the first stone. Look for the Holy Spirit and always confirm any prophesy with scripture.

The Abomination of Desolation. Dan 11:31

Mar 13:14 "But when ye shall see the abomination of desolation, spoken of by Daniel the prophet, standing where it ought not, (let him that readeth understand,) then let them that be in Judaea flee to the mountains: 15 And let him that is on the housetop not go down into the house, neither enter therein, to take anything out of his house: 16 And let him that is in the field not turn back again for to take up his garment. 17 But woe to them that are with child, and to them that give suck in those days! 18 And pray ye that your flight be not in the winter. 19 For in those days shall be affliction, such as was not from the beginning of the creation which God created unto this time, neither shall be. 20 And except that the Lord had shortened those days, no flesh should be saved: but for the elect's sake, whom he hath chosen, he hath shortened the days. 21 And then if any man shall say to you; "Lo, here is Christ"; or, "lo, he is there"; believe him not: 22 For false Christs and false prophets shall rise, and shall shew signs and wonders, to seduce, if it were possible, even the elect. 23 But take ye heed: behold, I have foretold you all things."

Eagles gathered.

(When Jesus returns it will be an open spectacle for the world will see, Mark 13:26, Luk 21:25)

Mat 24:25 "Behold, I have told you before." *(Luk 17:22, Mat 13,)*

Mat 24:26 "Wherefore if they shall say unto you; "Behold, he is in the desert"; go not forth: "Behold, he is in the secret chambers"; believe it not. 27 For as the lightning cometh out of the east, and shineth even unto the west; So shall also the coming of the Son of man be. 28 For wheresoever the carcase is, there will the eagles be gathered together."

Eagles Gathered

Luk 17:37 And they answered and said unto him; "Where, Lord?" And he said unto them, "Wheresoever the body is, thither will the eagles be gathered together."

The Return of Jesus After the Great Tribulation. *Mar 13:19*

Study References.

Gen 1:14, Isa 13:9-10, Isa 30:26, Joel 2:31, Joel 3:13-15, Zec 12:10, Mal 4:1-6, Jude Rev 6:11, Rev 7:13-14, Rev 20:4-6).

(Keep in mind that The Christians in the middle east have been suffering persecution since Jesus` time until now. Even the holocaust was persecution for the Jewish people as satan is still trying to wipe them out because of the Messiah. I have come to learn "Hurt people hurt people", satan comes to steal kill and destroy; to do as much hurt as possible to thwart the will of God but Jesus came to give life and life More Abundantly Joh 10:10, because He suffered more than us all and still forgave even without God helping Him. Mar 15:34, 2Chron 32:31.)

Mat 24:29 "Immediately after the tribulation of those days shall the sun be darkened, and the moon shall not give her light, and the stars shall fall from heaven, and the powers of the heavens shall be shaken: 30 And then shall appear the sign of the Son of man in heaven: and then shall all the tribes of the earth mourn, and they shall see the Son of man coming in the clouds of heaven with power and great glory. 31 And he shall send his angels with a great sound of a trumpet *(1 Corr 15:52),* and they shall gather together his elect from the four winds, from one end of heaven to the other."

(Matt 13:30, Matt 13:41)

The Return of Jesus after the main Tribulation

(Matt 13:30, Matt 13:41, Joel Ch 2&3, Rev 6-7, Rev 20:4-6)

Mar 13:24 "But in those days, after that tribulation, the sun shall be darkened, and the moon shall not give her light, 25 And the stars of heaven shall fall, and the powers that are in heaven shall be shaken. 26 And then shall they see the Son of man coming in the clouds with great power and glory. 27 And then shall he send his angels, and shall gather together his elect from the four winds, from the uttermost part of the earth to the uttermost part of heaven." *(Even Elon Musk`s crew will be called back from Mars and any person that has died in space.)*

The Return of Jesus after the Sun and Moon Darkened

Matt 13:30, Matt 13:41, Rev 20:4-6, Mar 13:19, Last trump 1cor 15:52. After the anti-Christ revealed 2 thess 2:3. First resurrection after the great Tribulation, Rev 20:4-5 as they had not worshipped nor received the mark of the beast.

Luk 21:25 "And there shall be signs in the sun, and in the moon, and in the stars; and upon the earth distress of nations, with perplexity; the sea and the waves roaring; 26 Men's hearts failing them for fear, and for looking after those things which are coming on the earth: for the powers of heaven shall be shaken. 27 And then shall they see the Son of man coming in a cloud with power and great glory. 28 And when these things begin to come to pass, then look up, and lift up your heads; for your redemption draweth nigh."

Behold the Fig Tree

Mat 24:32 "Now learn a parable of the fig tree; When his branch is yet tender, and putteth forth leaves, ye know that summer is nigh: 33 So likewise ye, when ye shall see all these things, know that it is near, even at the doors. 34 Verily I say unto you; This generation shall not pass, till all these things be fulfilled. 35 Heaven and earth shall pass away, but my words shall not pass away."

(Jesus said "It is finished" all of what is written of Jesus is complete. Rev 13:8 Alpha and Omega. God has won; Gods word returned to Him. John 1:14, Isaiah 55:11. Luk 18:8)

Behold the Fig Tree

Mar 13:28 "<u>Now learn a parable of the fig tree</u>; When her branch is yet tender, and putteth forth leaves, ye know that summer is near: 29 So ye in like manner, when ye shall see these things come to pass, know that it is nigh, even at the doors. 30 Verily I say unto you, that this generation shall not pass, till all these things be done. 31 Heaven and earth shall pass away: but my words shall not pass away."

Behold the Fig Tree

Luk 21:29 And he spake to them a parable; "<u>Behold the fig tree</u>, and all the trees; 30 When they now shoot forth, ye see and know of your own selves that summer is now nigh at hand. 31 So likewise ye, when ye see these things come to pass, know ye that the kingdom of God is nigh at hand. 32 Verily I say unto you, "This generation shall not pass away, till all be fulfilled. 33 Heaven and earth shall pass away: but my words shall not pass away. 34 And take heed to yourselves, lest at any time your hearts be overcharged with surfeiting, and drunkenness, and cares of this life, and so that day come upon you unawares. 35 For as a snare shall it come on all them that dwell on the face of the whole earth. 36 Watch ye therefore, and pray always, that ye may be accounted worthy to escape all these things that shall come to pass, and to stand before the Son of man."

Luk 21:37 And in the day time he was teaching in the temple; and at night he went out, and abode in the mount that is called the mount of Olives.

Luk 21:38 And all the people came early in the morning to him in the temple, for to hear him.

No Man nor Angel, Knows That Day or Hour.

Jesus is clearly defining here that God has kept somethings for Himself. Jesus is reigning as God and has all authority, if He now knows or not, I am not sure, being the same as the Father, we will find out when perfection comes, 1Cor 13:9. Acts 2.22, John 20:17, Ps 22, Luk 23:46. Note that Jesus is one with God, full of God and has been given all authority from God and that makes him as God, but not God, but God to us. Luk 6:40, Mat 10:25, John 20:28. The mystery of the Godhead. Acts 17:29, Rom 1:20, Col 2:9. The secret to the timing of Jesus second coming and the timing is in Rev 6:11. He is only coming back once.

(Dan 7:13,14, Rev 6:11 Rev 20, Matt 13:30, Matt 13:40-43, Luke 12:35)

Mat 24:36 "But of that day and hour knoweth no man, no, not the angels of heaven, but my Father only. 37 But as the days of Noe were, so shall also the coming of the Son of man be. 38 For as in the days that were before the flood they were eating and drinking, marrying and giving in marriage, until the day that Noe entered into the ark, 39 And knew not until the flood came, and took them all away, *(the Evil ones)*; So shall also the coming of the Son of man be. 40 Then shall two be in the field; the one shall be taken, and the other left. 41 Two women shall be grinding at the mill; the one shall be taken, and the other left. 42 Watch therefore: for ye know not what hour your Lord doth come."

No Man nor Angel Knows That Day or Hour

Mar 13:32 "But of that day and that hour knoweth no man, no, not the angels which are in heaven, neither the Son, but the Father. 33 Take ye heed, watch and pray: for ye know not when the time is. 34 For the Son of man is as a man taking a far journey, who left his house, and gave authority to his servants, and to every man his work, and commanded the porter to watch. 35 Watch ye therefore: for ye know not when the master of the house cometh, at even, or at midnight, or at the cockcrowing, or in the morning: 36 Lest coming suddenly he find you sleeping."

Mar 13:37 "And what I say unto you I say unto all, Watch."

As in the days of Noah.

(See Also Matt 24.25 The evil ones were caught by surprise and taken as in the days of Noe, also Mat 13:40-43)

Luk 17:22 And he said unto the disciples; "The days will come, when ye shall desire to see one of the days of the Son of man, and ye shall not see it. 23 And they shall say to you, see here; or, see there: go not after them, nor follow them. 24 For as the lightning, that lighteneth out of the one part under heaven, shineth unto the other part under heaven; so shall also the Son of man be in his day. 25 But first must he suffer many things, and be rejected of this generation. 26 And as it was in the days of Noe, so shall it be also in the days of the Son of man. 27 They did eat, they drank, they married wives, they were given in marriage, until the day that Noe entered into the ark, and the flood came, and destroyed them all. 28 Likewise also as it was in the days of Lot; they did eat, they drank, they bought, they sold, they planted, they builded; 29 But the same day that Lot went out of Sodom it rained fire and brimstone from heaven, and destroyed them all. 30 Even thus shall it be in the day when the Son of man is revealed. 31 In that day, he which shall be upon the housetop, and his stuff in the house, let him not come down to take it away: and he that is in the field, let him likewise not return back. 32 Remember Lot's wife. 33 Whosoever shall seek to save his life shall lose it; and whosoever shall lose his life shall preserve it. 34 I tell you, in that night there shall be two men in one bed; the one shall be taken, and the other shall be left. 35 Two women shall be grinding together; the one shall be taken, and the other left. 36 Two men shall be in the field; the one shall be taken, and the other left."

Thief in the Night

Mat 24:43 "But know this, that if the goodman of the house had known in what watch the thief would come, he would have watched, and would not have suffered his house to be broken up. 44 Therefore be ye also ready: for in such an hour as ye think not the Son of man cometh. 45 Who then is a faithful and wise servant, whom his lord hath made ruler over his household, to give them meat in due season? 46 Blessed is that servant, whom his lord when he cometh shall find so doing. 47 Verily I say unto you; That he shall make him ruler over all his goods. 48 But and if that evil servant shall say in his heart, My lord delayeth his coming; 49 And shall begin to smite his fellowservants, and to eat and drink with the drunken; 50 The lord of that servant shall come in a day when he looketh not for him, and in an hour that he is not aware of, 51 And shall cut him asunder, and appoint him his portion with the hypocrites: there shall be weeping and gnashing of teeth."

Thief in the Night

Luk 12:35 "Let your loins be girded about, and your lights burning; 36 And ye yourselves like unto men that wait for their lord, when he will return from the wedding; that when he cometh and knocketh, they may open unto him immediately. 37 Blessed are those servants, whom the lord when he cometh shall find watching: verily I say unto you, that he shall gird himself, and make them to sit down to meat, and will come forth and serve them. 38 And if he shall come in the second watch, or come in the third watch, and find them so, blessed are those servants. 39 And this know, that if the goodman of the house had known what hour the thief would come, he would have watched, and not have suffered his house to be broken through. 40 Be ye therefore ready also: for the Son of man cometh at an hour when ye think not."

Luk 12:41 Then Peter said unto him; "Lord, speakest thou this parable unto us, or even to all?"

Being a Faithful Steward. 2 Sam 7:14 (three sevens again)

Luk 12:42 And the Lord said; "Who then is that faithful and wise steward, whom his lord shall make ruler over his household, to give them their portion of meat in due season? 43 Blessed is that servant, whom his lord when he cometh shall find so doing. 44 Of a truth I say unto you, that he will make him ruler over all that he hath. 45 But and if that servant say in his heart, my lord delayeth his coming; and shall begin to beat the menservants and maidens, and to eat and drink, and to be drunken; 46 The lord of that servant will come in a day when he looketh not for him, and at an hour when he is not aware, and will cut him in sunder, and will appoint him his portion with the unbelievers. 47 And that servant, which knew his lord's will, and prepared not himself, neither did according to his will, shall be beaten with many stripes. 48 But he that knew not, and did commit things worthy of stripes, shall be beaten with few stripes. For unto whomsoever much is given, of him shall be much required: and to whom men have committed much, of him they will ask the more."

The Parable of the Ten Virgins. Be prepared. *Job 29:6, Ps 18:1, Prov 23:23, Isa 55:1.*

Mat 25:1 "Then shall the kingdom of heaven be likened unto ten virgins, which took their lamps, and went forth to meet the bridegroom. 2 And five of them were wise, and five were foolish. 3 They that were foolish took their lamps, and took no oil with them: 4 But the wise took oil in their vessels with their lamps. 5 While the bridegroom tarried, they all slumbered and slept. 6 And at midnight there was a cry made, Behold, the bridegroom cometh; go ye out to meet him. 7 Then all those virgins arose, and trimmed their lamps. 8 And the foolish said unto the wise; "Give us of your oil; for our lamps are gone out." 9 But the wise answered, saying; "Not so; lest there be not enough for us and you: but go ye rather to them that sell, and buy for yourselves." 10

And while they went to buy, the bridegroom came; and they that were ready went in with him to the marriage: and the door was shut. 11 Afterward came also the other virgins, saying; "Lord, Lord, open to us." 12 But he answered and said; "Verily I say unto you, I know you not." 13 Watch therefore, for ye know neither the day nor the hour wherein the Son of man cometh."

The Parable of the Talents Invested in us

Mat 25:14 "For the kingdom of heaven is as a man travelling into a far country, who called his own servants, and delivered unto them his goods. 15 And unto one he gave five talents, to another two, and to another one; to every man according to his several ability; and straightway took his journey. 16 Then he that had received the five talents went and traded with the same, and made them other five talents. 17 And likewise he that had received two, he also gained other two. 18 But he that had received one went and digged in the earth, and hid his lord's money. 19 After a long time the lord of those servants cometh, and reckoneth with them. 20 And so he that had received five talents came and brought other five talents, saying; "Lord, thou deliveredst unto me five talents: behold, I have gained beside them five talents more." 21 His lord said unto him; "Well done, thou good and faithful servant: thou hast been faithful over a few things, I will make thee ruler over many things: enter thou into the joy of thy lord." 22 He also that had received two talents came and said; "Lord, thou deliveredst unto me two talents: behold, I have gained two other talents beside them." 23 His lord said unto him; "Well done, good and faithful servant; thou hast been faithful over a few things, I will make thee ruler over many things: enter thou into the joy of thy lord." 24 Then he which had received the one talent came and said; "Lord, I knew thee that thou art an hard man, reaping where thou hast not sown, and gathering where thou hast not strawed: 25 And I was afraid, and went and hid thy talent in the earth: lo, there thou hast that is thine." 26 His lord answered and said unto him; "Thou wicked and slothful servant, thou knewest that I reap where I sowed not, and gather where I have not strawed: 27 Thou oughtest therefore to have put my money to the exchangers, and then at my coming I should have received mine own with usury *(interest)*. 28 Take therefore the talent from him, and give it unto him which hath ten talents." 29 For unto every one that hath shall be given, and he shall have abundance: but from him that hath not shall be taken away even that which he hath. 30 And cast ye the unprofitable servant into outer darkness: there shall be weeping and gnashing of teeth."

<u>Jesus`s Return and Final Judgment</u> *(Matt 13:30, Matt 13:40-43)*

Jesus never says to us, our doctrine is wrong, go burn in hell, but is looking for Gods truth in us. Goats don't teach Love they can be selfish destructive animals, cute, needy and always butting heads. But we are judged according to what Faith, (Gods truthfulness), we have; the words Jesus spoke, our obedience and compassion we have shown our, and His brethren that are in Him. Joh 13:35.

Back In those days there was no personal rights for prisoners, no 3 meals a day, showers and clothes, or visiting rights. To see a prisoner, you had to bribe your way in. The wellbeing of a prisoner was based on how many friends and family they had bringing food and supplies. Jesus is a friend to the rejected we are to be also.

Mat 25:31 "When the Son of man shall come in his glory, and all the holy angels with him, *(Matt 13:40-43)* then shall he sit upon the throne of his glory: 32 And before him shall be gathered all nations: and he shall separate them one from another, as a shepherd divideth his sheep from the goats: 33 And he shall set the sheep on his right hand, but the goats on the left. 34 Then shall the King say unto them on his right hand; "Come, ye blessed of my Father, inherit the kingdom prepared for you from the foundation of the world: 35 For I was an hungred, and ye gave me meat: I was thirsty, and ye gave me drink: I was a stranger, and ye took me in: 36 Naked, and ye clothed me: I was sick, and ye visited me: I was in prison, and ye came unto me." 37 Then shall the righteous answer him, saying; "Lord, when saw we thee an hungred, and fed thee? or thirsty, and gave thee drink? 38 When saw we thee a stranger, and took thee in? or naked, and clothed thee? 39 Or when saw we thee sick, or in prison, and came unto thee?" 40 And the King shall answer and say unto them; "Verily I say unto you; Inasmuch as ye have done it unto one of the least of these my brethren, ye have done it unto me." 41 Then shall he say also unto them on the left hand; "Depart from me, ye cursed, into everlasting fire, prepared for the devil and his angels: 42 For I was an hungred, and ye gave me no meat: I was thirsty, and ye gave me no drink: 43 I was a stranger, and ye took me not in: naked, and ye clothed me not: sick, and in prison, and ye visited me not." 44 Then shall they also answer him, saying; "Lord, when saw we thee an hungred, or athirst, or a stranger, or naked, or sick, or in prison, and did not minister unto thee?" 45 Then shall he answer them, saying; "Verily I say unto you; Inasmuch as ye did it not to one of the least of these, ye did it not to me." 46 And these shall go away into everlasting punishment: but the righteous into life eternal."

Two Days Before Passover.

(They must have been long Days for Jesus)

The Plot to Kill Jesus

Mat 26:1 And it came to pass, when Jesus had finished all these sayings, he said unto his disciples;

Mat 26:2 "Ye know that after two days is the feast of the passover, and the Son of man is betrayed to be crucified."

Mat 26:3 Then assembled together the chief priests, and the scribes, and the elders of the people, unto the palace of the high priest, who was called Caiaphas,

Mat 26:4 And consulted that they might take Jesus by subtilty, and kill him.

Mat 26:5 But they said; "Not on the feast day, lest there be an uproar among the people."

The Plot to Kill Jesus

Mar 14:1 After two days was the feast of the passover, and of unleavened bread: and the chief priests and the scribes sought how they might take him by craft, and put him to death.

Mar 14:2 But they said; "Not on the feast day, lest there be an uproar of the people."

The Plot to Kill Jesus

Luk 22:1 Now the feast of unleavened bread drew nigh, which is called the Passover.

Luk 22:2 And the chief priests and scribes sought how they might kill him; for they feared the people.

Bethany

Matthew (Mat 26:2) says Mary anointed Jesus approx 2 days before the passover and John says sometime after the 6th day (Joh 12:1) and John says they were in Mary's house but Matthew (Mat 26:6) and (Mark 14:3) say that they were in Simons the leper's house. I wonder if Simon was the father, related to Martha, Mary and Lazarus. Mary would have had to become a prostitute and that is why one says it was Simon's house and Mary's house also. Not Gospel, but would explain why the difference. Remember, they wrote down the scriptures 30 years after Jesus resurrection. Another point would be if Lazarus was the same Lazarus Jesus used in comparison with the rich man in hell, I think so.

Mary Anoints Jesus, Judas Offended

Mat 26:6 Now when Jesus was in Bethany, in the house of Simon the leper,

Mat 26:7 There came unto him a woman having an alabaster box of very precious ointment, and poured it on his head, as he sat at meat.

Mat 26:8 But when his disciples saw it, they had indignation, saying; "To what purpose is this waste? 9 For this ointment might have been sold for much, and given to the poor."

Mat 26:10 When Jesus understood it, he said unto them; "Why trouble ye the woman? for she hath wrought a good work upon me. 11 For ye have the poor always with you; but me ye have not always. 12 For in that she hath poured this ointment on my body, she did it for my burial. 13 Verily I say unto you. Wheresoever this gospel shall be preached in the whole world, there shall also this, that this woman hath done, be told for a memorial of her."

Mary Anoints Jesus, Judas Offended

Mar 14:3 And being in Bethany in the house of Simon the leper, as he sat at meat, there came a woman having an alabaster box of ointment of spikenard very precious; and she broke the box, and poured it on his head.

Mar 14:4 And there were some that had indignation within themselves, and said, "Why was this waste of the ointment made? 5 For it might have been sold for more than three hundred pence, and have been given to the poor." And they murmured against her.

Mar 14:6 And Jesus said; "Let her alone; why trouble ye her? she hath wrought a good work on me. 7 For ye have the poor with you always, and whensoever ye will ye may do them good: but me ye have not always. 8 She hath done what she could: she is come aforehand to anoint my body to the burying. 9 Verily I say unto you, wheresoever this gospel shall be preached throughout the whole world, this also that she hath done shall be spoken of for a memorial of her."

Bethany

6 days before Passover

Mary Anoints Jesus, Judas Offended

This plays with the timeline as John says it happens before the entry into Jersualem and 6 days before the passover I have copied John's account here for comparative studies, but also left his account in his timeline. Time stamp of Mat 21:1.

Joh 12:1 Then Jesus six days before the passover came to Bethany, where Lazarus was which had been dead, whom he raised from the dead.

Joh 12:2 There they made him a supper; and Martha served: but Lazarus was one of them that sat at the table with him.

Joh 12:3 Then took Mary a pound of ointment of spikenard, very costly, and anointed the feet of Jesus, and wiped his feet with her hair: and the house was filled with the odour of the ointment.

Joh 12:4 Then saith one of his disciples, Judas Iscariot, Simon's son, which should betray him; 5 "Why was not this ointment sold for three hundred pence, and given to the poor?"

Joh 12:6 This he said; not that he cared for the poor; but because he was a thief, and had the bag, and bare what was put therein.

Joh 12:7 Then said Jesus; "Let her alone: against the day of my burying hath she kept this. 8 For the poor always ye have with you; but me ye have not always."

The Chief Priests Plot to Kill Lazarus

Joh 12:9 Much people of the Jews therefore knew that he was there: and they came not for Jesus' sake only, but that they might see Lazarus also, whom he had raised from the dead.

Joh 12:10 But the chief priests consulted that they might put Lazarus also to death;

Joh 12:11 Because that by reason of him, *(Lazarus)* many of the Jews went away, and believed on Jesus.

Judas sets up to Betray Jesus

Mat 26:14 Then one of the twelve, called Judas Iscariot, went unto the chief priests,

Mat 26:15 And said unto them; "What will ye give me, and I will deliver him unto you?" And they covenanted with him for thirty pieces of silver.

Mat 26:16 And from that time he sought opportunity to betray him.

Judas sets up to Betray Jesus

Mar 14:10 And Judas Iscariot, one of the twelve, went unto the chief priests, to betray him unto them.

Mar 14:11 And when they heard it, they were glad, and promised to give him money. And he sought how he might conveniently betray him.

Judas sets up to Betray Jesus

Luk 22:3 Then entered Satan into Judas surnamed Iscariot, being of the number of the twelve.

Luk 22:4 And he went his way, and communed with the chief priests and captains, how he might betray him unto them.

Luk 22:5 And they were glad, and covenanted to give him money.

Luk 22:6 And he promised, and sought opportunity to betray him unto them in the absence of the multitude.

Preparing for The Passover with the Disciples (EX 12:6)

Modern references say that the feast of Unleavened Bread follows passover but Matthew, Mark and Luke clearly reference it before Passover. Jesus made sure the Disciples had somewhere to eat the passover that Friday night. after Jesus was crucified and rested on the seventh day.

Mat 26:17 Now the first day of the feast of unleavened bread the disciples came to Jesus, saying unto him; "Where wilt thou that we prepare for thee to eat the passover?"

Mat 26:18 And he said; "Go into the city to such a man, and say unto him; The Master saith; My time is at hand; I will keep the passover at thy house with my disciples."

Mat 26:19 And the disciples did as Jesus had appointed them; and they made ready the passover.

Preparing The Passover with the Disciples (EX 12:6)

Mar 14:12 And the first day of unleavened bread, when they killed the passover, his disciples said unto him; "Where wilt thou that we go and prepare that thou mayest eat the passover?"

Mar 14:13 And he sendeth forth two of his disciples, and saith unto them; "Go ye into the city, and there shall meet you a man bearing a pitcher of water: follow him. 14 And wheresoever he shall go in, say ye to the goodman of the house; The Master saith, where is the guest chamber, where I shall eat the passover with my disciples? 15 And he will shew you a large upper room furnished and prepared: there make ready for us."

Mar 14:16 And his disciples went forth, and came into the city, and found as he had said unto them: and they made ready the passover.

Mar 14:17 And in the evening he cometh with the twelve.

The Lamb was with the family for 3 and a half days before it was prepared to be sacrificed on the 14th day, Exo 12:1-11. The days were from 6pm-6pm. Due to the day starting at 6 pm evening, they wouldn't have been able to buy a lamb until the shops opened the next morning when trade started. If they raised it themselves it still had to be approved, be spotless and checked in full light. Being raised by the family It was loved and accepted by the children, just like Jesus was.

Being the 10th till 14th, less the first night = 3.5 days. We also assume the disciples went back to where they had the last supper, for the passover. Matt 26:18. Jesus ministered for approx 3.5 years bring to pass the prophesy of Ezekiel 4:6 a day for a year; this can also apply to the 40 days Jesus spent in the wilderness to break and overcome any disobedience of the flesh that the Israelites couldn't endure.

<u>Preparing The Passover with the Disciples</u>

Luk 22:7 Then came the day of unleavened bread, when the passover must be killed.

Luk 22:8 And he sent Peter and John; saying; "Go and prepare us the passover, that we may eat."

Luk 22:9 And they said unto him; "Where wilt thou that we prepare?"

Luk 22:10 And he said unto them; "Behold, when ye are entered into the city, there shall a man meet you, bearing a pitcher of water; follow him into the house where he entereth in. 11 And ye shall say unto the goodman of the house, The Master saith unto thee, where is the guest chamber, where I shall eat the passover with my disciples? 12 And he shall shew you a large upper room furnished: there make ready."

Luk 22:13 And they went, and found as he had said unto them: and they made ready the passover.

Betrayer revealed to the others

Mat 26:20 Now when the even was come, he sat down with the twelve.

Mat 26:21 And as they did eat, he said; "Verily I say unto you, that one of you shall betray me."

Mat 26:22 And they were exceeding sorrowful, and began every one of them to say unto him; "Lord, is it I?"

Mat 26:23 And he answered and said; "He that dippeth his hand with me in the dish, the same shall betray me. 24 The Son of man goeth as it is written of him: but woe unto that man by whom the Son of man is betrayed! it had been good for that man if he had not been born."

Mat 26:25 Then Judas, which betrayed him, answered and said; "Master, is it I?" He said unto him; "Thou hast said."

Betrayer revealed to the others

Mar 14:18 And as they sat and did eat, Jesus said; "Verily I say unto you; One of you which eateth with me shall betray me."

Mar 14:19 And they began to be sorrowful, and to say unto him one by one; "Is it I?" and another said; "Is it I?"

Mar 14:20 And he answered and said unto them; "It is one of the twelve, that dippeth with me in the dish. 21 The Son of man indeed goeth, as it is written of him: but woe to that man by whom the Son of man is betrayed! good were it for that man if he had never been born."

The Lord's Supper

Mat 26:26 And as they were eating, Jesus took bread, and blessed it, and brake it, and gave it to the disciples, and said; "Take, eat; this is my body."

Mat 26:27 And he took the cup, and gave thanks, and gave it to them, saying; "Drink ye all of it; 28 For this is my blood of the New Testament, which is shed for many for the remission of sins. 29 But I say unto you, I will not drink henceforth of this fruit of the vine, until that day when I drink it new with you in my Father's kingdom."

The Lord's Supper

Mar 14:22 And as they did eat, Jesus took bread, and blessed, and brake it, and gave to them, and said; "Take, eat: this is my body."

Mar 14:23 And he took the cup, and when he had given thanks, he gave it to them: and they all drank of it.

Mar 14:24 And he said unto them; "This is my blood of the New Testament, which is shed for many. 25 Verily I say unto you, I will drink no more of the fruit of the vine, until that day that I drink it new in the kingdom of God."

The Lord's Supper

Luk 22:14 And when the hour was come, he sat down, and the twelve apostles with him.

Luk 22:15 And he said unto them; "With desire I have desired to eat this passover with you before I suffer: 16 For I say unto you, I will not any more eat thereof, until it be fulfilled in the kingdom of God."

Luk 22:17 And he took the cup, and gave thanks, and said; "Take this, and divide it among yourselves: 18 For I say unto you, I will not drink of the fruit of the vine, until the kingdom of God shall come."

Luk 22:19 And he took bread, and gave thanks, and brake it, and gave unto them, saying; "This is my body which is given for you: this do in remembrance of me. 20 Likewise also the cup after supper, saying; "This cup is the New Testament in my blood, which is shed for you."

After Supper; Jesus Washes the Disciples' Feet. (Our Thursday night)

Joh 13:1 Now before the feast of the passover, when Jesus knew that his hour was come that he should depart out of this world unto the Father, having loved his own which were in the world, he loved them unto the end.

Joh 13:2 And supper being ended, the devil having now put into the heart of Judas Iscariot, Simon's son, to betray him;

Joh 13:3 Jesus knowing that the Father had given all things into his hands, and that he was come from God, and went to God;

Joh 13:4 He riseth from supper, and laid aside his garments; and took a towel, and girded himself.

Joh 13:5 After that he poureth water into a bason, and began to wash the disciples' feet, and to wipe them with the towel wherewith he was girded.

Joh 13:6 Then cometh he to Simon Peter: and Peter saith unto him; "Lord, dost thou wash my feet?"

Joh 13:7 Jesus answered and said unto him; "What I do thou knowest not now; but thou shalt know hereafter."

Joh 13:8 Peter saith unto him; "Thou shalt never wash my feet." Jesus answered him; "If I wash thee not, thou hast no part with me."

Joh 13:9 Simon Peter saith unto him; "Lord, not my feet only, but also my hands and my head."

Joh 13:10 Jesus saith to him; "He that is washed needeth not save to wash his feet, but is clean every whit: and ye are clean, but not all."

Joh 13:11 For he knew who should betray him; therefore, said he; "Ye are not all clean."

Joh 13:12 So after he had washed their feet, and had taken his garments, and was set down again, he said unto them; "Know ye what I have done to you? 13 Ye call me Master and Lord: and ye say well; for so I am. 14 If I then, your Lord and Master, have washed your feet; ye also ought to wash one another's feet. 15 For I have given you an example, that ye should do as I have done to you. 16 Verily, verily, I say unto you, the servant is not greater than his lord; neither he that is sent greater than he that sent him. 17 If ye know these things, happy are ye if ye do them. 18 I speak not of you all: I know whom I have chosen: but that the scripture may be fulfilled, He that eateth bread with me hath lifted up his heel against me. 19 Now I tell you before it come, that, when it is come to pass, ye may believe that I am he. 20 Verily, verily, I say unto you, He that receiveth whomsoever I send receiveth me; and he that receiveth me receiveth him that sent me."

A Betrayer Exposed to the Others

Luk 22:21 "But, behold, the hand of him that betrayeth me is with me on the table. 22 And truly the Son of man goeth, as it was determined: but woe unto that man by whom he is betrayed!"

Luk 22:23 And they began to enquire among themselves, which of them it was that should do this thing.

Betrayer Exposed to the Others

Joh 13:21 When Jesus had thus said, he was troubled in spirit, and testified, and said, Verily, verily, I say unto you, that one of you shall betray me.

Joh 13:22 Then the disciples looked one on another, doubting of whom he spake.

Joh 13:23 Now there was leaning on Jesus' bosom one of his disciples, whom Jesus loved.

Joh 13:24 Simon Peter therefore beckoned to him, that he should ask who it should be of whom he spake.

Joh 13:25 He then lying on Jesus' breast saith unto him; "Lord, who is it?"

Joh 13:26 Jesus answered; "He it is, to whom I shall give a sop, when I have dipped it." And when he had dipped the sop, he gave it to Judas Iscariot, the son of Simon.

Joh 13:27 And after the sop Satan entered into him. Then said Jesus unto him; "That thou doest, do quickly."

Joh 13:28 Now no man at the table knew for what intent he spake this unto him.

Joh 13:29 For some of them thought, because Judas had the bag, that Jesus had said unto him; Buy those things that we have need of against the feast; or, that he should give something to the poor.

Joh 13:30 He then having received the sop went immediately out: and it was night.

Who Is the Greatest? The disciples still bickering.

Mark 9:33, and Luke 9:46, Matt 18:1 (Previous disputes)

Luk 22:24 And there was also a strife among them, which of them should be accounted the greatest.

Luk 22:25 And he said unto them; "The kings of the Gentiles exercise lordship over them; and they that exercise authority upon them are called benefactors. 26 But ye shall not be so: but he that is greatest among you, let him be as the younger; and he that is chief, as he that doth serve. 27 For whether is greater, he that sitteth at meat, or he that serveth? is not he that sitteth at meat? but I am among you as he that serveth. 28 Ye are they which have continued with me in my temptations. 29 And I appoint unto you a kingdom, as my Father hath appointed unto me; 30 That ye may eat and drink at my table in my kingdom, and sit on thrones judging the twelve tribes of Israel."

To the Mt of Olives

A New Commandment

Joh 13:31 Therefore, when he was gone out, Jesus said; "Now is the Son of man glorified, and God is glorified in him. 32 If God be glorified in him, God shall also glorify him in himself, and shall straightway glorify him. 33 Little children, yet a little while I am with you. Ye shall seek me: and as I said unto the Jews, Whither I go, ye cannot come; so now I say to you. 34 A new commandment I give unto you; That ye love one another; as I have loved you, that ye also love one another. 35 By this shall all men know that ye are my disciples, if ye have love one to another."

To the Mt of Olives

Jesus Tells of Peter's Denial

Mat 26:30 And when they had sung a hymn, they went out into the mount of Olives.

Mat 26:31 Then saith Jesus unto them; "All ye shall be offended because of me this night: for it is written, I will smite the shepherd, and the sheep of the flock shall be scattered abroad. 32 But after I am risen again, I will go before you into Galilee." *(Zec 13:7)*

Mat 26:33 Peter answered and said unto him; "Though all men shall be offended because of thee, yet will I never be offended."

Mat 26:34 Jesus said unto him; "Verily I say unto thee, that this night, before the cock crow, thou shalt deny me thrice."

Mat 26:35 Peter said unto him; "Though I should die with thee, yet will I not deny thee." Likewise, also said all the disciples.

Jesus Tells of Peter's Denial

Mar 14:26 And when they had sung a hymn, they went out into the mount of Olives.

Mar 14:27 And Jesus saith unto them; 'All ye shall be offended because of me this night: for it is written, I will smite the shepherd, and the sheep shall be scattered. 28 But after that I am risen, I will go before you into Galilee." *(Zec 13:7)*

Mar 14:29 But Peter said unto him; "Although all shall be offended, yet will not I."

Mar 14:30 And Jesus saith unto him; "Verily I say unto thee, that this day, even in this night, before the cock crow twice, thou shalt deny me thrice."

Mar 14:31 But he spake the more vehemently; "If I should die with thee, I will not deny thee in any wise." Likewise, also said they all.

Jesus Tells Peter's Denial

Luk 22:31 And the Lord said; "Simon, Simon, behold, Satan hath desired to have you, that he may sift you as wheat: 32 But I have prayed for thee, that thy faith fail not: and when thou art converted, strengthen thy brethren."

Luk 22:33 And he said unto him; "Lord, I am ready to go with thee, both into prison, and to death."

Luk 22:34 And he said; "I tell thee, Peter, the cock shall not crow this day, before that thou shalt thrice deny that thou knowest me."

Jesus Tells of Peter's Denial

Joh 13:36 Simon Peter said unto him; "Lord, whither goest thou?" Jesus answered him, "Whither I go, thou canst not follow me now; but thou shalt follow me afterwards."

Joh 13:37 Peter said unto him; "Lord, why cannot I follow thee now? I will lay down my life for thy sake."

Joh 13:38 Jesus answered him; "Wilt thou lay down thy life for my sake? Verily, verily, I say unto thee, the cock shall not crow, till thou hast denied me thrice.

Joh 14:1 Let not your heart be troubled: ye believe in God, believe also in me. 2 In my Father's house are many mansions: if it were not so, I would have told you. I go to prepare a place for you. 3 And if I go and prepare a place for you, I will come again, and receive you unto myself; that where I am, there ye may be also. 4 And whither I go ye know, and the way ye know."

Joh 14:5 Thomas saith unto him; "Lord, we know not whither thou goest; and how can we know the way?"

The Way the Truth and the Life

Joh 14:6 Jesus saith unto him; "I am the way, the truth, and the life: no man cometh unto the Father, but by me. 7 If ye had known me, ye should have known my Father also: and from henceforth ye know him, and have seen him."

Joh 14:8 Philip saith unto him; "Lord, shew us the Father, and it sufficeth us."

One with the Father.

Joh 14:9 Jesus saith unto him; "Have I been so long time with you, and yet hast thou not known me, Philip? he that hath seen me hath seen the Father; and how sayest thou then, Shew us the Father? 10 Believest thou not that I am in the Father, and the Father in me? the words that I speak unto you I speak not of myself: but the Father that dwelleth in me, he doeth the works. 11 Believe me that I am in the Father, and the Father in me: or else believe me for the very works' sake. 12 Verily, verily, I say unto you, He that believeth on me, the works that I do shall he do also; and greater works than these shall he do; because I go unto my Father. 13 And whatsoever ye shall ask in my name, that will I do, that the Father may be glorified in the Son. 14 If ye shall ask any thing in my name, I will do it."

Jesus Promises the Holy Spirit

Joh 14:15 "If ye love me, keep my commandments. 16 And I will pray the Father, and he shall give you another Comforter, that he may abide with you for ever; 17 Even the Spirit of truth; whom the world cannot receive, because it seeth him not, neither knoweth him: but ye know him; for he dwelleth with you, and shall be in you. 18 I will not leave you comfortless: I will come to you. 19 Yet a little while, and the world seeth me no more; but ye see me: because I live, ye shall live also. 20 At that day ye shall know that I am in my Father, and ye in me, and I in you. 21 He that hath my commandments, and keepeth them, he it is that loveth me: and he that loveth me shall be loved of my Father, and I will love him, and will manifest myself to him."

Joh 14:22 Judas saith unto him, not Iscariot; "Lord, how is it that thou wilt manifest thyself unto us, and not unto the world?"

Love is obedience

Joh 14:23 Jesus answered and said unto him; "If a man love me, he will keep my words: and my Father will love him, and we will come unto him, and make our abode with him. 24 He that loveth me not keepeth not my sayings: and the word which ye hear is not mine, but the Father's which sent me. 25 These things have I spoken unto you, being yet present with you. 26 But the Comforter, which is the Holy Ghost, whom the Father will send in my name, he shall teach you all things, and bring all things to your remembrance, whatsoever I have said unto you."

Joh 14:27 "Peace I leave with you, my peace I give unto you: *(Ps 29:11)* not as the world giveth, give I unto you. Let not your heart be troubled, neither let it be afraid. 28 Ye have heard how I said unto you, I go away, and come again unto you. If ye loved me, ye would rejoice, because I said, I go unto the Father: for my Father is greater than I. 29 And now I have told you before it come to pass, that, when it is come to pass, ye might believe. 30 Hereafter I will not talk much with you: for the prince of this world cometh, and hath nothing in me. 31 But that the world may know that I love the Father; and as the Father gave me commandment, even so I do. Arise, let us go hence."

I Am the True Vine

Joh 15:1 "I am the true vine, and my Father is the husbandman. 2 Every branch in me that beareth not fruit he taketh away: and every branch that beareth fruit, he purgeth it, that it may bring forth more fruit. 3 Now ye are clean through the word which I have spoken unto you. 4 Abide in me, and I in you. As the branch cannot bear fruit of itself, except it abide in the vine; no more can ye, except ye abide in me. 5 I am the vine, ye are the branches: He that abideth in me, and I in him, the same bringeth forth much fruit: for without me ye can do nothing. 6 If a man abide not in me, he is cast forth as a branch, and is withered; and men gather them, and cast them into the fire, and they are burned. 7 If ye abide in me, and my words abide in you, ye shall ask what ye will, and it shall be done unto you. 8 Herein is my Father glorified, that ye bear much fruit; So, shall ye be my disciples."

The New commandment Reiterated.

Joh 15:9 "As the Father hath loved me, so have I loved you: continue ye in my love. 10 If ye keep my commandments, ye shall abide in my love; even as I have kept my Father's commandments, and abide in his love. 11 These things have I spoken unto you, that my joy might remain in you, and that your joy might be full. 12 This is my commandment; That ye love one another, as I have loved you. 13 Greater love hath no man than this, that a man lay down his life for his friends. 14 Ye are my friends, if ye do whatsoever I command you. 15

Henceforth I call you not servants; for the servant knoweth not what his lord doeth: but I have called you friends; for all things that I have heard of my Father I have made known unto you. 16 Ye have not chosen me, but I have chosen you, and ordained you, that ye should go and bring forth fruit, and that your fruit should remain: that whatsoever ye shall ask of the Father in my name, he may give it you. 17 These things I command you, that ye love one another."

Hated of the World

Joh 15:18 "If the world hates you, ye know that it hated me before it hated you. 19 If ye were of the world, the world would love his own: but because ye are not of the world, but I have chosen you out of the world, therefore the world hateth you. 20 Remember the word that I said unto you; The servant is not greater than his lord. If they have persecuted me, they will also persecute you; if they have kept my saying, they will keep yours also. 21 But all these things will they do unto you for my name's sake, because they know not him that sent me. 22 If I had not come and spoken unto them, they had not had sin: but now they have no cloke for their sin. 23 He that hateth me hateth my Father also. 24 If I had not done among them the works which none other man did, they had not had sin: but now have they both seen and hated both me and my Father. 25 But this cometh to pass, that the word might be fulfilled that is written in their law; They hated me without a cause.*(PS 69:4)* 26 But when the Comforter is come, whom I will send unto you from the Father, even the Spirit of truth, which proceedeth from the Father, he shall testify of me: 27 And ye also shall bear witness, because ye have been with me from the beginning.

Joh 16:1 These things have I spoken unto you, that ye should not be offended. 2 They shall put you out of the synagogues: yea, the time cometh, that whosoever killeth you will think that he doeth God service. 3 And these things will they do unto you, because they have not known the Father, nor me."

The Work of the Holy Spirit.

Joh 16:4 "But these things have I told you, that when the time shall come, ye may remember that I told you of them. And these things I said not unto you at the beginning, because I was with you. 5 But now I go my way to him that sent me; and none of you asketh me, whither goest thou? 6 But because I have said these things unto you, sorrow hath filled your heart. 7 Nevertheless I tell you the truth; It is expedient for you that I go away: for if I go not away, the Comforter will not come unto you; but if I depart, I will send him unto you. 8 And when he is come, he will reprove the world of sin, and of righteousness, and of judgment: 9 Of sin, because they believe not on me; 10 Of righteousness, because I go to my Father, and ye see me no more; 11 Of judgment, because the prince of this world is judged. 12 I have yet many things to say unto you, but ye cannot bear them now. 13 Howbeit when he, the Spirit of truth, is come, he will guide you into all truth: for he shall not speak of himself; but whatsoever he shall hear, that shall he speak: and he will shew you things to come. 14 He shall glorify me: for he shall receive of mine, and shall shew it unto you. 15 All things that the Father hath are mine: therefore, said I, that he shall take of mine, and shall shew it unto you."

Your Sorrow Will Turn into Joy

Joh 16:16 "A little while, and ye shall not see me: and again, a little while, and ye shall see me, because I go to the Father."

Joh16:17 Then said some of his disciples among themselves; "What is this that he saith unto us, A little while, and ye shall not see me: and again, a little while, and ye shall see me: and, Because I go to the Father?"

Joh 16:18 They said therefore; "What is this that he saith, A little while? we cannot tell what he saith."

Joh 16:19 Now Jesus knew that they were desirous to ask him, and said unto them; "Do ye enquire among yourselves of that I said, A little while, and ye shall not see me: and again, a little while, and ye shall see me? 20 Verily, verily, I say unto you; That ye shall weep and lament, but the world shall rejoice: and ye shall be sorrowful, but your sorrow shall be turned into joy. 21 A woman when she is in travail hath sorrow, because her hour is come: but as soon as she is delivered of the child, she remembereth no more the anguish, for joy that a man is born into the world. 22 And ye now therefore have sorrow: but I will see you again, and your heart shall rejoice, and your joy no man taketh from you. 23 And in that day ye shall ask me nothing. Verily, verily, I say unto you, Whatsoever ye shall ask the Father in my name, he will give it you. 24 Hitherto have ye asked nothing in my name: ask, and ye shall receive, that your joy may be full."

I Have Overcome the World

Joh 16:25 "These things have I spoken unto you in proverbs: but the time cometh, when I shall no more speak unto you in proverbs, but I shall shew you plainly of the Father. 26 At that day ye shall ask in my name: and I say not unto you, that I will pray the Father for you: 27 For the Father himself loveth you, because ye have loved me, and have believed that I came out from God. 28 I came forth from the Father, and am come into the world: again, I leave the world, and go to the Father."

Joh 16:29 His disciples said unto him; "Lo, now speakest thou plainly, and speakest no proverb. 30 Now are we sure that thou knowest all things, and needest not that any man should ask thee: by this we believe that thou camest forth from God."

Joh 16:31 Jesus answered them; "Do ye now believe? 32 Behold, the hour cometh, yea, is now come, that ye shall be scattered, every man to his own, and shall leave me alone: and yet I am not alone, because the Father is with me. 33 These things I have spoken unto you, that in me ye might have peace. In the world ye shall have tribulation: but be of good cheer; I have overcome the world."

Jesus Prayer Glorify Thou Me.

Joh 17:1 These words spake Jesus, and lifted up his eyes to heaven, and said; "Father, the hour is come; glorify thy Son, that thy Son also may glorify thee: 2 As thou hast given him power over all flesh, that he should give eternal life to as many as thou hast given him. 3 And this is life eternal, that they might know thee the only true God, and Jesus Christ, whom thou hast sent. 4 I have glorified thee on the earth: I have finished the work which thou gavest me to do. 5 And now, O Father, glorify thou me with thine own self with the glory which I had with thee before the world was. 6 I have manifested thy name unto the men which thou gavest me out of the world: thine they were, and thou gavest them me; and they have kept thy word. 7 Now they have known that all things whatsoever thou hast given me are of thee. 8 For I have given unto them the words which thou gavest me; and they have received them, and have known surely that I came out from thee, and they have believed that thou didst send me. 9 I pray for them: I pray not for the world, but for them which thou hast given me; for they are thine. 10 And all mine are thine, and thine are mine; and I am glorified in them. 11 And now I am no more in the world, but these are in the world, and I come to thee. Holy Father, keep through thine own name those whom thou hast given me, that they may be one, as we are. 12 While I was with them in the world, I kept them in thy name: those that thou gavest me I have kept, and none of them is lost, but the son of perdition; that the scripture might be fulfilled. 13 And now come I to thee; and these things I speak in the world, that they might have my joy fulfilled in themselves. 14 I have given them thy word; and the world hath hated them, because they are not of the world, even as I am not of the world."

<u>Jesus prays against the removal of the saints. Mar 13:37</u>

Joh 17:15 "<u>I pray not that thou shouldest take them out of the world</u>, but that thou shouldest keep them from the evil. 16 They are not of the world, even as I am not of the world. 17 Sanctify (*Make Holy, Sanctified*) them through thy truth: thy word is truth."

Joh 17:18 "As thou hast sent me into the world, even so have I also sent them into the world. 19 And for their sakes I sanctify (*Make Holy*) myself, that they also might be sanctified through the truth. 20 Neither pray I for these alone, but for them also which shall believe on me through their word; 21 That they all may be one; as thou, Father, art in me, and I in thee, that they also may be one in us: that the world may believe that thou hast sent me. 22 And the glory which thou gavest me I have given them; that they may be one, even as we are one: 23 I in them, and thou in me, that they may be made perfect in one; and that the world may know that thou hast sent me, and hast loved them, as thou hast loved me. 24 Father, I will that they also, whom thou hast given me, be with me where I am; that they may behold my glory, which thou hast given me: for thou lovedst me before the foundation of the world. 25 O righteous Father, the world hath not known thee: but I have known thee, and these have known that thou hast sent me. 26 And I have declared unto them thy name, and will declare it: that the love wherewith thou hast loved me may be in them, and I in them."

Scripture Must Be Fulfilled in Jesus

Luk 22:35 And he said unto them; "When I sent you without purse, and scrip, and shoes, lacked ye anything?" And they said, "Nothing."

Luk 22:36 Then said he unto them; "But now, he that hath a purse, let him take it, and likewise his scrip: and he that hath no sword, let him sell his garment, and buy one. 37 For I say unto you, that this that is written must yet be accomplished in me, and he was reckoned among the transgressors: for the things concerning me have an end."

Luk 22:38 And they said; "Lord, behold, here are two swords." And he said unto them, "It is enough."

The Garden Gethsemane

Jesus Prays

Mat 26:36 Then cometh Jesus with them unto a place called Gethsemane, and saith unto the disciples; "Sit ye here, while I go and pray yonder."

Mat 26:37 And he took with him Peter and the two sons of Zebedee, and began to be sorrowful and very heavy.

Mat 26:38 Then saith he unto them; "My soul is exceeding sorrowful, even unto death: tarry ye here, and watch with me."

Mat 26:39 And he went a little further, and fell on his face, and prayed, saying; "O my Father, if it be possible, let this cup pass from me: nevertheless, not as I will, but as thou wilt."

Mat 26:40 And he cometh unto the disciples, and findeth them asleep, and saith unto Peter; "What, could ye not watch with me one hour? 41 Watch and pray, that ye enter not into temptation: the spirit indeed is willing, but the flesh is weak."

Mat 26:42 He went away again the second time, and prayed, saying; "O my Father, if this cup may not pass away from me, except I drink it, thy will be done."

Mat 26:43 And he came and found them asleep again: for their eyes were heavy.

Mat 26:44 And he left them, and went away again, and prayed the third time, saying the same words.

Mat 26:45 Then cometh he to his disciples, and saith unto them; "Sleep on now, and take your rest: behold, the hour is at hand, and the Son of man is betrayed into the hands of sinners. 46 Rise, let us be going: behold, he is at hand that doth betray me."

Jesus Prays

Mar 14:32 And they came to a place which was named Gethsemane: and he saith to his disciples; "Sit ye here, while I shall pray."

Mar 14:33 And he taketh with him Peter and James and John, and began to be sore amazed, and to be very heavy;

Mar 14:34 And saith unto them; "My soul is exceeding sorrowful unto death: tarry ye here, and watch."

Mar 14:35 And he went forward a little, and fell on the ground, and prayed that, if it were possible, the hour might pass from him.

Mar 14:36 And he said; "Abba, Father, all things are possible unto thee; take away this cup from me: nevertheless, not what I will, but what thou wilt."

Mar 14:37 And he cometh, and findeth them sleeping, and saith unto Peter; "Simon, sleepest thou? couldest not thou watch one hour? 38 Watch ye and pray, lest ye enter into temptation. The spirit truly is ready, but the flesh is weak."

Mar 14:39 And again he went away, and prayed, and spake the same words.

Mar 14:40 And when he returned, he found them asleep again, (for their eyes were heavy,) neither wist they what to answer him.

Mar 14:41 And he cometh the third time, and saith unto them; "Sleep on now, and take your rest: it is enough, the hour is come; behold, the Son of man is betrayed into the hands of sinners. 42 Rise up, let us go; lo, he that betrayeth me is at hand."

Jesus Prays

Luk 22:39 And he came out, and went, as he was wont, to the mount of Olives; and his disciples also followed him.

Luk 22:40 And when he was at the place, he said unto them; "Pray that ye enter not into temptation.

Luk 22:41 And he was withdrawn from them about a stone's cast, and kneeled down, and prayed,

Luk 22:42 Saying; "Father, if thou be willing, remove this cup from me: nevertheless, not my will, but thine, be done."

Luk 22:43 And there appeared an angel unto him from heaven, strengthening him.

Luk 22:44 And being in an agony he prayed more earnestly: and his sweat was as it were great drops of blood falling down to the ground.

Luk 22:45 And when he rose up from prayer, and was come to his disciples, he found them sleeping for sorrow,

Luk 22:46 And said unto them; "Why sleep ye? rise and pray, lest ye enter into temptation."

Jesus Arrested

Mat 26:47 And while he yet spake, lo, Judas, one of the twelve, came, and with him a great multitude with swords and staves, from the chief priests and elders of the people.

Mat 26:48 Now he that betrayed him gave them a sign, saying; "Whomsoever I shall kiss, that same is he: hold him fast."

Mat 26:49 And forthwith he came to Jesus, and said; "Hail, master; and kissed him."

Mat 26:50 And Jesus said unto him; "Friend, wherefore art thou come?" Then came they, and laid hands-on Jesus, and took him.

Mat 26:51 And, behold, one of them which were with Jesus stretched out his hand, and drew his sword, and struck a servant of the high priests, and smote off his ear.

Mat 26:52 Then said Jesus unto him; "Put up again thy sword into his place: for all they that take the sword shall perish with the sword. 53 Thinkest thou that I cannot now pray to my Father, and he shall presently give me more than twelve legions of angels? *(2 kings 6:17)* 54 But how then shall the scriptures be fulfilled, that thus it must be?"

Mat 26:55 In that same hour said Jesus to the multitudes; "Are ye come out as against a thief with swords and staves for to take me? I sat daily with you teaching in the temple, and ye laid no hold on me."

Mat 26:56 But all this was done, that the scriptures of the prophets might be fulfilled. Then all the disciples forsook him, and fled.

Jesus Arrested

Mar 14:43 And immediately, while he yet spake, cometh Judas, one of the twelve, and with him a great multitude with swords and staves, from the chief priests and the scribes and the elders.

Mar 14:44 And he that betrayed him had given them a token, saying; "Whomsoever I shall kiss, that same is he; take him, and lead him away safely."

Mar 14:45 And as soon as he was come, he goeth straightway to him, and saith; "Master, master." *(Rhabbi Rhabbi);* and kissed him.

Mar 14:46 And they laid their hands on him, and took him.

Mar 14:47 And one of them that stood by drew a sword, and smote a servant of the high priest, and cut off his ear.

Mar 14:48 And Jesus answered and said unto them; "Are ye come out, as against a thief, with swords and with staves to take me? 49 I was daily with you in the temple teaching, and ye took me not: but the scriptures must be fulfilled."

Mar 14:50 And they all forsook him, and fled. (Zec 13:7)

Jesus Arrested

Luk 22:47 And while he yet spake, behold a multitude, and he that was called Judas, one of the twelve, went before them, and drew near unto Jesus to kiss him.

Luk 22:48 But Jesus said unto him; "Judas, betrayest thou the Son of man with a kiss?"

Luk 22:49 When they which were about him saw what would follow, they said unto him; "Lord, shall we smite with the sword?"

Luk 22:50 And one of them smote the servant of the high priest, and cut off his right ear.

Luk 22:51 And Jesus answered and said; "Suffer ye thus far." And he touched his ear, and healed him.

Luk 22:52 Then Jesus said unto the chief priests, and captains of the temple, and the elders, which were come to him; "Be ye come out, as against a thief, with swords and staves? 53 When I was daily with you in the temple, ye stretched forth no hands against me: but this is your hour, and the power of darkness."

Jesus Arrested

Joh 18:1 When Jesus had spoken these words, he went forth with his disciples over the brook Cedron *(1 kings 2:37)*, where was a garden, into the which he entered, and his disciples.

Joh 18:2 And Judas also, which betrayed him, knew the place: for Jesus ofttimes resorted thither with his disciples.

Joh 18:3 Judas then, having received a band of men and officers from the chief priests and Pharisees, cometh thither with lanterns and torches and weapons.

Joh 18:4 Jesus therefore, knowing all things that should come upon him, went forth, and said unto them; "Whom seek ye?"

Joh 18:5 They answered him; "Jesus of Nazareth." Jesus saith unto them; "I am he." And Judas also, which betrayed him, stood with them.

Joh 18:6 As soon then as he had said unto them; "I am he", they went backward, and fell to the ground.

Joh 18:7 Then asked he them again; "Whom seek ye?" And they said; "Jesus of Nazareth."

Joh 18:8 Jesus answered; "I have told you that I am he: if therefore ye seek me, let these go their way:"

Joh 18:9 That the saying might be fulfilled, which he spake, of them which thou gavest me have I lost none. (Joh 17:12)

Joh 18:10 Then Simon Peter having a sword drew it, and smote the high priest's servant, and cut off his right ear. The servant's name was Malchus.

Joh 18:11 Then said Jesus unto Peter; "Put up thy sword into the sheath: the cup which my Father hath given me, shall I not drink it?"

A Young Man Flees

Mar 14:51 And there followed him a certain young man, having a linen cloth cast about his naked body; and the young men laid hold on him: *(Possibly Mark himself.)*

Mar 14:52 And he left the linen cloth, and fled from them naked.

Jesus Before the council

Mat 26:57 And they that had laid hold on Jesus led him away to Caiaphas the high priest, where the scribes and the elders were assembled.

Mat 26:58 But Peter followed him afar off unto the high priest's palace, and went in, and sat with the servants, to see the end.

Mat 26:59 Now the chief priests, and elders, and all the council, sought false witness against Jesus, to put him to death;

Mat 26:60 But found none: yea, though many false witnesses came, yet found they none. At the last came two false witnesses,

Mat 26:61 And said; "This fellow said, I am able to destroy the temple of God, and to build it in three days."

Mat 26:62 And the high priest arose, and said unto him; "Answerest thou nothing? what is it which these witness against thee?"

Mat 26:63 But Jesus held his peace. And the high priest answered and said unto him; "I adjure thee by the living God, that thou tell us whether thou be the Christ, the Son of God."

Mat 26:64 Jesus saith unto him; "Thou hast said: nevertheless, I say unto you, Hereafter shall ye see the Son of man sitting on the right hand of power, and coming in the clouds of heaven."

Mat 26:65 Then the high priest rent his clothes, saying; "He hath spoken blasphemy; what further need have we of witnesses? behold, now ye have heard his blasphemy. 66 What think ye?" They answered and said; "He is guilty of death."

Mat 26:67 Then did they spit in his face, and buffeted him; and others smote him with the palms of their hands,

Mat 26:68 Saying; "Prophesy unto us, thou Christ. Who is he that smote thee?"

Jesus Before the Council

Mar 14:53 And they led Jesus away to the high priest: and with him were assembled all the chief priests and the elders and the scribes.

Mar 14:54 And Peter followed him afar off, even into the palace of the high priest: and he sat with the servants, and warmed himself at the fire.

Mar 14:55 And the chief priests and all the council sought for witness against Jesus to put him to death; and found none.

Mar 14:56 For many bare false witness against him, but their witness agreed not together.

Mar 14:57 And there arose certain, and bare false witness against him, saying;

Mar 14:58 "We heard him say, I will destroy this temple that is made with hands, and within three days I will build another made without hands." *(Dan 2:45. The church is without division. Tongues is also a unifier for the believer as the Lord caused division at the Tower of Babel (Gen 11:9) with language. He caused unification at Pentecost. Isa 28:1, Mark 16:17)*

Mar 14:59 But neither so did their witness agree together.

Mar 14:60 And the high priest stood up in the midst, and asked Jesus, saying; "Answerest thou nothing? what is it which these witness against thee?"

Mar 14:61 But he held his peace, and answered nothing. Again, the high priest asked him, and said unto him; "Art thou the Christ, the Son of the Blessed?"

Mar 14:62 And Jesus said; "I am: and ye shall see the Son of man sitting on the right hand of power, and coming in the clouds of heaven."

Mar 14:63 Then the high priest rent his clothes, and saith; "What need we any further witnesses? 64 Ye have heard the blasphemy: what think ye?" And they all condemned him to be guilty of death.

Mar 14:65 And some began to spit on him, and to cover his face, and to buffet him, and to say unto him, Prophesy: and the servants did strike him with the palms of their hands.

<u>Jesus before the council</u>

Joh 18:12 Then the band and the captain and officers of the Jews took Jesus, and bound him,

Joh 18:13 And led him away to Annas first; for he was father-in-law to Caiaphas, which was the high priest that same year.

Joh 18:14 Now Caiaphas was he, which gave counsel to the Jews, that it was expedient *(good)* that one man should die for the people.

Peter Denies Jesus and the Rooster Crows

(Roosters normally crow before dawn)

Mat 26:69 Now Peter sat without in the palace: and a damsel came unto him, saying; "Thou also wast with Jesus of Galilee."

Mat 26:70 But he denied before them all, saying; "I know not what thou sayest."

Mat 26:71 And when he was gone out into the porch, another maid saw him, and said unto them that were there; "This fellow was also with Jesus of Nazareth."

Mat 26:72 And again he denied with an oath; "I do not know the man."

Mat 26:73 And after a while came unto him, they that stood by, and said to Peter; "Surely thou also art one of them; for thy speech bewrayeth *(G4160, G1212 Delos, exposes, make manifest.)* thee."

Mat 26:74 Then began he to curse and to swear, saying; "I know not the man." And immediately the cock crew. *(Swearing for a Christian tells the world they are not with Jesus. Matt 10:32, Jam 3:10-12)*

Mat 26:75 And Peter remembered the word of Jesus, which said unto him; "Before the cock crow, thou shalt deny me thrice." And he went out, and wept bitterly.

Peter Denies Jesus and the Rooster Crows

Mar 14:66 And as Peter was beneath in the palace, there cometh one of the maids of the high priest:

Mar 14:67 And when she saw Peter warming himself, she looked upon him, and said; "And thou also wast with Jesus of Nazareth."

Mar 14:68 But he denied, saying; "I know not, neither understand I what thou sayest." And he went out into the porch; and the cock crew.

Mar 14:69 And a maid saw him again, and began to say to them that stood by; "This is one of them."

Mar 14:70 And he denied it again. And a little after, they that stood by said again to Peter; "Surely thou art one of them: for thou art a Galilaean, and thy speech agreeth thereto."

Mar 14:71 But he began to curse and to swear, saying; "I know not this man of whom ye speak."

Mar 14:72 And the second time the cock crew. And Peter called to mind the word that Jesus said unto him; "Before the cock crow twice, thou shalt deny me thrice." And when he thought thereon, he wept.

Peter Denies Jesus and the Rooster Crows

Luk 22:54 Then took they him, and led him, and brought him into the high priest's house. And Peter followed afar off.

Luk 22:55 And when they had kindled a fire in the midst of the hall, and were set down together, Peter sat down among them.

Luk 22:56 But a certain maid beheld him as he sat by the fire, and earnestly looked upon him, and said; "This man was also with him."

Luk 22:57 And he denied him, saying; "Woman, I know him not."

Luk 22:58 And after a little while another saw him, and said; "Thou art also of them." And Peter said; "Man, I am not."

Luk 22:59 And about the space of one hour after another confidently affirmed, saying; "Of a truth this fellow also was with him: for he is a Galilaean."

Luk 22:60 And Peter said; "Man, I know not what thou sayest." And immediately, while he yet spake, the cock crew.

Luk 22:61 And the Lord turned, and looked upon Peter. And Peter remembered the word of the Lord, how he had said unto him; "Before the cock crow, thou shalt deny me thrice."

Luk 22:62 And Peter went out, and wept bitterly.

Peter Denies Jesus

Joh 18:15 And Simon Peter followed Jesus, and so did another disciple: that disciple was known unto the high priest, and went in with Jesus into the palace of the high priest.

Joh 18:16 But Peter stood at the door without. Then went out that other disciple, which was known unto the high priest, and spake unto her that kept the door, and brought in Peter.

Joh 18:17 Then saith the damsel that kept the door unto Peter; "Art not thou also one of this man's disciples?" He saith; "I am not."

Joh 18:18 And the servants and officers stood there, who had made a fire of coals; for it was cold: and they warmed themselves: and Peter stood with them, and warmed himself.

(Jesus puts peter through the same experience of being cold and the fire then reverses his denial 3 times after the resurrection. Sometimes it is painful to take a splinter out for healing to begin)

Jesus Is Mocked by the Arresters

Luk 22:63 And the men that held Jesus mocked him, and smote him.

Luk 22:64 And when they had blindfolded him, they struck him on the face, and asked him, saying, "Prophesy, who is it that smote thee?"

Luk 22:65 And many other things blasphemously spake they against him.

The High Priest Questions Jesus

Luk 22:66 And as soon as it was day, the elders of the people and the chief priests and the scribes came together, and led him into their council, saying;

Luk 22:67 "Art thou the Christ? tell us." And he said unto them; "If I tell you, ye will not believe: 68 And if I also ask you, ye will not answer me, nor let me go. 69 Hereafter shall the Son of man sit on the right hand of the power of God."

Luk 22:70 Then said they all; "Art thou then the Son of God?" And he said unto them; "Ye say that I am."

Luk 22:71 And they said; "What need we any further witness? for we ourselves have heard of his own mouth."

The High Priest Questions Jesus

Joh 18:19 The high priest then asked Jesus of his disciples, and of his doctrine.

Joh 18:20 Jesus answered him; "I spoke openly to the world; I ever taught in the synagogue, and in the temple, whither the Jews always resort; and in secret have I said nothing. 21 Why askest thou me? ask them which heard me, what I have said unto them: behold, they know what I said."

Joh 18:22 And when he had thus spoken, one of the officers which stood by struck Jesus with the palm of his hand, saying; "Answerest thou the high priest so?"

Joh 18:23 Jesus answered him; "If I have spoken evil, bear witness of the evil: but if well, why smitest thou me?"

Joh 18:24 Now Annas had sent him bound unto Caiaphas the high priest.

Peter Denies Jesus Again and the Rooster Crows

Joh 18:25 And Simon Peter stood and warmed himself. They said therefore unto him; "Art not thou also one of his disciples?" He denied it, and said; "I am not."

Joh 18:26 One of the servants of the high priest, being his kinsman, whose ear Peter cut off, saith; "Did not I see thee in the garden with him?"

Joh 18:27 Peter then denied again: and immediately the cock crew.

Jesus Delivered to Pilate

Mat 27:1 When the morning was come, all the chief priests and elders of the people took counsel against Jesus to put him to death:

Mat 27:2 And when they had bound him, they led him away, and delivered him to Pontius Pilate the governor.

Meanwhile Back at the Temple

Judas Hangs Himself

Mat 27:3 Then Judas, which had betrayed him, when he saw that he was condemned, repented **(G3338. Regretted)** himself, and brought again the thirty pieces of silver to the chief priests and elders,

Mat 27:4 Saying; "I have sinned in that I have betrayed the innocent blood." And they said; "What is that to us? see thou to that." **(Heb 6:4-6, Prov 6:16-19, Isa 59:7)**

Mat 27:5 And he cast down the pieces of silver in the temple, and departed, and went and hanged himself.

Mat 27:6 And the chief priests took the silver pieces, and said; "It is not lawful for to put them into the treasury, because it is the price of blood."

Mat 27:7 And they took counsel, and bought with them the potter's field, to bury strangers in.

Mat 27:8 Wherefore that field was called, The field of blood, unto this day.

Mat 27:9 Then was fulfilled that which was spoken by Jeremy the prophet, saying; "And they took the thirty pieces of silver, the price of him that was valued, whom they of the children of Israel did value; 10 And gave them for the potter's field, as the Lord appointed me." *(Zec 11: 12,13)*

Jesus Stands Before Pontius Pilate, the Governor

Mat 27:11 And Jesus stood before the governor: and the governor asked him, saying; "Art thou the King of the Jews?" And Jesus said unto him; "Thou sayest."

Mat 27:12 And when he was accused of the chief priests and elders, he answered nothing.

Mat 27:13 Then said Pilate unto him, "Hearest thou not how many things they witness against thee?"

Mat 27:14 And he answered him to never a word; insomuch that the governor marvelled greatly.

Jesus Delivered to Pilate

Mar 15:1 And straightway in the morning the chief priests held a consultation with the elders and scribes and the whole council, and bound Jesus, and carried him away, and delivered him to Pilate.

Mar 15:2 And Pilate asked him; "Art thou the King of the Jews? And he answering said unto him; "Thou sayest it."

Mar 15:3 And the chief priests accused him of many things: but he answered nothing.

Mar 15:4 And Pilate asked him again, saying; "Answerest thou nothing? behold how many things they witness against thee."

Mar 15:5 But Jesus yet answered nothing; so that Pilate marvelled.

Jesus Delivered to Pilate

Luk 23:1 And the whole multitude of them arose, and led him unto Pilate.

Luk 23:2 And they began to accuse him, saying; "We found this fellow perverting the nation, and forbidding to give tribute to Caesar, saying that he himself is Christ a King."

Luk 23:3 And Pilate asked him, saying; "Art thou the King of the Jews?" And he answered him and said; "Thou sayest it."

Luk 23:4 Then said Pilate to the chief priests and to the people; "I find no fault in this man."

Luk 23:5 And they were the fiercer, saying; "He stirreth up the people, teaching throughout all Jewry, beginning from Galilee to this place."

Jesus Delivered to Pilate

Joh 18:28 Then led they Jesus from Caiaphas unto the hall of judgment: and it was early; and they themselves went not into the judgment hall, lest they should be defiled; but that they might eat the passover.

Joh 18:29 Pilate then went out unto them, and said; "What accusation bring ye against this man?"

Joh 18:30 They answered and said unto him; "If he were not a malefactor, we would not have delivered him up unto thee."

Joh 18:31 Then said Pilate unto them; "Take ye him, and judge him according to your law." The Jews therefore said unto him; "It is not lawful for us to put any man to death:"

Joh 18:32 That the saying of Jesus might be fulfilled, which he spake, signifying what death he should die. *(Joh 12:32)*

<u>Pilot sends Jesus over to Herod and then is returned to Pilot</u>

Luk 23:6 When Pilate heard of Galilee, he asked whether the man is a Galilaean.

Luk 23:7 And as soon as he knew that he belonged unto Herod's jurisdiction, he sent him to Herod, who himself also was at Jerusalem at that time.

Luk 23:8 And when Herod saw Jesus, he was exceeding glad: for he was desirous to see him of a long season, because he had heard many things of him; and he hoped to have seen some miracle done by him.

Luk 23:9 Then he questioned with him in many words; but he answered him nothing.

Luk 23:10 And the chief priests and scribes stood and vehemently accused him.

<u>Jesus is mocked by Soldiers</u>

Luk 23:11 And Herod with his men of war set him at nought, and mocked him, and arrayed him in a gorgeous robe, and sent him again to Pilate. *(Compare Mat 27:28 & Joh 19:2 no matter who put it on Jesus it was still put on Him by men of war.)*

Luk 23:12 And the same day Pilate and Herod were made friends together: for before they were at enmity between themselves.

Jesus possibly returned from Herod

Joh 18:33 Then Pilate entered into the judgment hall again, and called Jesus, and said unto him; "Art thou the King of the Jews?"

Joh 18:34 Jesus answered him; "Sayest thou this thing of thyself, or did others tell it thee of me?"

Joh 18:35 Pilate answered; "Am I a Jew? Thine own nation and the chief priests have delivered thee unto me: what hast thou done?"

Joh 18:36 Jesus answered, "My kingdom is not of this world: if my kingdom were of this world, then would my servants fight, that I should not be delivered to the Jews: but now is my kingdom not from hence."

Joh 18:37 Pilate therefore said unto him; "Art thou a king then?" Jesus answered; "Thou sayest that I am a king. To this end was I born, and for this cause came I into the world, that I should bear witness unto the truth. Every one that is of the truth heareth my voice."

The Crowd Chooses Barabbas

(Bar = Son. Abbas = of the father. Fulfilling the sacrifice of the scape goat; Lev 16:8) {8+8,8}

Mat 27:15 Now at that feast the governor was wont to release unto the people a prisoner, whom they would.

Mat 27:16 And they had then a notable prisoner, called Barabbas.

Mat 27:17 Therefore when they were gathered together, Pilate said unto them; "Whom will ye that I release unto you? Barabbas, or Jesus which is called Christ?"

Mat 27:18 For he knew that for envy they had delivered him.

Pilates Wife warns her husband

Mat 27:19 When he was set down on the judgment seat, his wife sent unto him, saying; "Have thou nothing to do with that just man: for I have suffered many things this day in a dream because of him."

People choose Barabas above Jesus

Mat 27:20 But the chief priests and elders persuaded the multitude that they should ask Barabbas, and destroy Jesus.

Mat 27:21 The governor answered and said unto them; "Whether of the twain will ye that I release unto you?" They said, "Barabbas."

Mat 27:22 Pilate saith unto them; "What shall I do then with Jesus which is called Christ?" They all say unto him; "Let him be crucified."

Mat 27:23 And the governor said; "Why, what evil hath he done?" But they cried out the more, saying; "Let him be crucified."

Barabbas Released

Mar 15:6 Now at that feast he released unto them one prisoner, whomsoever they desired.

Mar 15:7 And there was one named Barabbas, which lay bound with them that had made insurrection with him, who had committed murder in the insurrection.

Mar 15:8 And the multitude crying aloud began to desire him to do as he had ever done unto them.

Mar 15:9 But Pilate answered them, saying; "Will ye that I release unto you the King of the Jews?"

Mar 15:10 For he knew that the chief priests had delivered him for envy.

Mar 15:11 But the chief priests moved the people, that he should rather release Barabbas unto them.

Mar 15:12 And Pilate answered and said again unto them; "What will ye then that I shall do unto him whom ye call the King of the Jews?"

Mar 15:13 And they cried out again; "Crucify him."

Mar 15:14 Then Pilate said unto them; "Why, what evil hath he done?" And they cried out the more exceedingly; "Crucify him."

Pilot Scourges Jesus. *PS 129:3*

Luk 23:13 And Pilate, when he had called together the chief priests and the rulers and the people,

Luk 23:14 Said unto them; "Ye have brought this man unto me, as one that perverteth the people: and, behold, I, having examined him before you, have found no fault in this man touching those things whereof ye accuse him: 15 No, nor yet Herod: for I sent you to him; and, lo, nothing worthy of death is done unto him. 16 I will therefore chastise him, and release him."

Luk 23:17 (For of necessity he must release one unto them at the feast.)

Pilot Scourges Jesus.

Joh 19:1 Then Pilate therefore took Jesus, and scourged him.

Joh 19:2 And the soldiers platted a crown of thorns, and put it on his head, and they put on him a purple robe, *(Gen 3:18 Jesus took that curse as well. Purple was the colour of Royalty)*

Joh 19:3 And said; "Hail, King of the Jews!" and they smote him with their hands.

Joh 19:4 Pilate therefore went forth again, and saith unto them; "Behold, I bring him forth to you, that ye may know that I find no fault in him."

Joh 19:5 Then came Jesus forth, wearing the crown of thorns, and the purple robe. And Pilate saith unto them; "Behold the man!"

Joh 19:6 When the chief priests therefore and officers saw him, they cried out, saying; "Crucify him, crucify him." Pilate saith unto them; "Take ye him, and crucify him: for I find no fault in him."

Joh 19:7 The Jews answered him; "We have a law, and by our law he ought to die, because he made himself the Son of God."

Joh 19:8 When Pilate therefore heard that saying, he was the more afraid;

Joh 19:9 And went again into the judgment hall, and saith unto Jesus; "Whence art thou?" But Jesus gave him no answer.

Joh 19:10 Then saith Pilate unto him; "Speakest thou not unto me? knowest thou not that I have power to crucify thee, and have power to release thee?"

Joh 19:11 Jesus answered; "Thou couldest have no power at all against me, except it were given thee from above: therefore, he that delivered me unto thee hath the greater sin."

Joh 19:12 And from thenceforth Pilate sought to release him: but the Jews cried out, saying; "If thou let this man go, thou art not Caesar's friend: whosoever maketh himself a king speaketh against Caesar."

Joh 19:13 When Pilate therefore heard that saying, he brought Jesus forth, and sat down in the judgment seat in a place that is called the Pavement, but in the Hebrew *(G1447. Not Aramaic)*, Gabbatha.

Joh 19:14 And it was the preparation of the passover, and about the sixth hour (12 pm): and he saith unto the Jews; "Behold your King!"

Joh 19:15 But they cried out; "Away with him, away with him, crucify him." Pilate saith unto them, "Shall I crucify your King?" The chief priests answered, "We have no king but Caesar."

Barabbas released. *Ps 129:3.*

Mat 27:24 When Pilate saw that he could prevail nothing, but that rather a tumult was made, he took water, and washed his hands before the multitude, saying; "I am innocent of the blood of this just person: see ye to it."

Mat 27:25 Then answered all the people, and said; "His blood be on us, and on our children."

Mat 27:26 Then released he Barabbas unto them: and when he had scourged Jesus, he delivered him to be crucified.

Barabbas released

Mar 15:15 And so Pilate, willing to content the people, released Barabbas unto them, and delivered Jesus, when he had scourged him, to be crucified.

Barabbas released

Luk 23:18 And they cried out all at once, saying; "Away with this man, and release unto us Barabbas:"

Luk 23:19 (Who for a certain sedition made in the city, and for murder, was cast into prison.)

Luk 23:20 Pilate therefore, willing to release Jesus, spake again to them.

Luk 23:21 But they cried, saying; "Crucify him, crucify him."

Luk 23:22 And he said unto them the third time; "Why, what evil hath he done? I have found no cause of death in him: I will therefore chastise him, and let him go."

Luk 23:23 And they were instant with loud voices, requiring that he might be crucified. And the voices of them and of the chief priests prevailed.

Luk 23:24 And Pilate gave sentence that it should be as they required.

Luk 23:25 And he released unto them him that for sedition and murder was cast into prison, whom they had desired; but he delivered Jesus to their will.

Barabbas released

Joh 18:38 Pilate saith unto him; "What is truth?" And when he had said this, he went out again unto the Jews, and saith unto them; "I find in him no fault at all. 39 But ye have a custom, that I should release unto you one at the passover: will ye therefore that I release unto you the King of the Jews?"

Joh 18:40 Then cried they all again, saying; "Not this man, but Barabbas." Now Barabbas was a robber.

Jesus Is Mocked by the Roman Soldiers

Mat 27:27 Then the soldiers of the governor took Jesus into the common hall, and gathered unto him the whole band of soldiers.

Mat 27:28 And they stripped him, and put on him a scarlet robe.

Mat 27:29 And when they had platted a crown of thorns, they put it upon his head, and a reed in his right hand: and they bowed the knee before him, and mocked him, saying; 'Hail, King of the Jews!"

Mat 27:30 And they spit upon him, and took the reed, and smote him on the head.

Mat 27:31 And after that they had mocked him, they took the robe off from him, and put his own raiment on him, and led him away to crucify him.

Jesus Is Mocked by the Roman Soldiers

Mar 15:16 And the soldiers led him away into the hall, called Praetorium; and they call together the whole band.

Mar 15:17 And they clothed him with purple, and platted a crown of thorns, and put it about his head,

Mar 15:18 And began to salute him; "Hail, King of the Jews!"

Mar 15:19 And they smote him on the head with a reed, and did spit upon him, and bowing their knees worshipped him.

Mar 15:20 And when they had mocked him, they took off the purple from him, and put his own clothes on him, and led him out to crucify him.

Golgotha

The Crucifixion of Jesus, Simon carries the Cross.

Zec 12:10, Ps 22.

Mat 27:32 And as they came out, they found a man of Cyrene, Simon by name: him they compelled to bear his cross.

Mat 27:33 And when they were come unto a place called Golgotha, that is to say, a place of a skull,

Mat 27:34 They gave him vinegar to drink mingled with gall: and when he had tasted thereof, he would not drink.

Mat 27:35 And they crucified him, and parted his garments, casting lots: that it might be fulfilled which was spoken by the prophet; They parted my garments among them, and upon my vesture did they cast lots." *Ps 22:18*

Mat 27:36 And sitting down they watched him there;

Mat 27:37 And set up over his head his accusation written, THIS IS JESUS THE KING OF THE JEWS.

Mat 27:38 Then were there two thieves crucified with him, one on the right hand, and another on the left.

Mat 27:39 And they that passed by reviled him, wagging their heads,

Mat 27:40 And saying; "Thou that destroyest the temple, and buildest it in three days, save thyself. If thou be the Son of God, come down from the cross."

Mat 27:41 Likewise also the chief priests mocking him, with the scribes and elders, said;

Mat 27:42 "He saved others; himself he cannot save. If he be the King of Israel, let him now come down from the cross, and we will believe him. 43 He trusted in God; let him deliver him now, if he will have him: for he said, "I am the Son of God.""

Mat 27:44 The thieves also, which were crucified with him, cast the same in his teeth.

The Crucifixion of Jesus, Simon carries the Cross

Mar 15:21 And they compel one Simon a Cyrenian, who passed by, coming out of the country, the father of Alexander and Rufus, to bear his cross.

Mar 15:22 And they bring him unto the place Golgotha, which is, being interpreted, The place of a skull.

Mar 15:23 And they gave him to drink wine mingled with myrrh: but he received it not.

Mar 15:24 And when they had crucified him, they parted his garments, casting lots upon them, what every man should take.

Mar 15:25 And it was the third hour, and they crucified him.

Mar 15:26 And the superscription of his accusation was written over, THE KING OF THE JEWS.

Mar 15:27 And with him they crucify two thieves; the one on his right hand, and the other on his left.

Mar 15:28 And the scripture was fulfilled, which saith, and he was numbered with the transgressors. (Isaiah 53:12)

Mar 15:29 And they that passed by railed on him, wagging their heads, and saying; "Ah, thou that destroyest the temple, and buildest it in three days, 30 Save thyself, and come down from the cross."

Mar 15:31 Likewise also the chief priests mocking said among themselves with the scribes; "He saved others; himself he cannot save. 32 Let Christ the King of Israel descend now from the cross, that we may see and believe." And they that were crucified with him reviled him.

The Crucifixion of Jesus. Simon carries the Cross

Luk 23:26 And as they led him away, they laid hold upon one Simon, a Cyrenian, coming out of the country, and on him they laid the cross, that he might bear it after Jesus.

Luk 23:27 And there followed him a great company of people, and of women, which also bewailed and lamented him.

Luk 23:28 But Jesus turning unto them said; "Daughters of Jerusalem, weep not for me, but weep for yourselves, and for your children. 29 For, behold, the days are coming, in the which they shall say, Blessed are the barren, and the wombs that never bare, and the paps which never gave suck. 30 Then shall they begin to say to the mountains; Fall on us; and to the hills, Cover us. 31 For if they do these things in a green tree, what shall be done in the dry?"

Luk 23:32 And there were also two other, malefactors, led with him to be put to death.

Luk 23:33 And when they were come to the place, which is called Calvary, there they crucified him, and the malefactors, one on the right hand, and the other on the left.

Luk 23:34 Then said Jesus; "Father, forgive them; for they know not what they do." And they parted his raiment, and cast lots.

Luk 23:35 And the people stood beholding. And the rulers also with them derided him, saying, "He saved others; let him save himself, if he be Christ, the chosen of God."

Luk 23:36 And the soldiers also mocked him, coming to him, and offering him vinegar,

Luk 23:37 And saying, "If thou be the king of the Jews, save thyself."

Luk 23:38 And a superscription also was written over him in letters of Greek, and Latin, and Hebrew *(not Aramaic)*, THIS IS THE KING OF THE JEWS.

Luk 23:39 And one of the malefactors which were hanged railed on him, saying; "If thou be Christ, save thyself and us."

Luk 23:40 But the other answering rebuked him, saying; "Dost not thou fear God, seeing thou art in the same condemnation? 41 And we indeed justly; for we receive the due reward of our deeds: but this man hath done nothing amiss." 42 And he said unto Jesus; "Lord, remember me when thou comest into thy kingdom."

Luk 23:43 And Jesus said unto him; "Verily I say unto thee; Today shalt thou be with me in paradise." *(Luk 16:19-31)*

The Crucifixion of Jesus

Joh 19:16 Then delivered he him therefore unto them to be crucified. And they took Jesus, and led him away.

Joh 19:17 And he bearing his cross went forth into a place called the place of a skull, which is called in the Hebrew Golgotha:

Joh 19:18 Where they crucified him, and two other with him, on either side one, and Jesus in the midst.

Joh 19:19 And Pilate wrote a title, and put it on the cross. And the writing was, JESUS OF NAZARETH THE KING OF THE JEWS.

Joh 19:20 This title then read many of the Jews: for the place where Jesus was crucified was nigh to the city: and it was written in Hebrew *(Not Aramaic)*, and Greek, and Latin.

Joh 19:21 Then said the chief priests of the Jews to Pilate; "Write not, The King of the Jews; but that he said, I am King of the Jews."

Joh 19:22 Pilate answered; "What I have written I have written."

Joh 19:23 Then the soldiers, when they had crucified Jesus, took his garments, and made four parts, to every soldier a part; and also, his coat: now the coat was without seam, woven from the top throughout.

Joh 19:24 They said therefore among themselves; "Let us not rend it, but cast lots for it, whose it shall be": that the scripture might be fulfilled, which saith; "They parted my raiment among them, and for my vesture they did cast lots." These things therefore the soldiers did.

Joh 19:25 Now there stood by the cross of Jesus his mother, and his mother's sister, Mary the wife of Cleophas, and Mary Magdalene.

Joh 19:26 When Jesus therefore saw his mother, and the disciple standing by, whom he loved, he saith unto his mother; "Woman, behold thy son!"

Joh 19:27 Then saith he to the disciple; "Behold thy mother!" And from that hour that disciple took her unto his own home.

The Death of Jesus. (Psalm 22)

Mat 27:45 Now from the sixth hour there was darkness over all the land unto the ninth hour. *(12 till 3pm)*

Mat 27:46 And about the ninth hour Jesus cried with a loud voice, saying; "Eli, Eli, lama sabachthani?" that is to say; "My God, my God, why hast thou forsaken me?" *(Ps 22, of Hebrew origin not Aramaic see Strongs concordance.)*

Mat 27:47 Some of them that stood there, when they heard that, said; "This man calleth for Elias.

Mat 27:48 And straightway one of them ran, and took a sponge, and filled it with vinegar, and put it on a reed, and gave him to drink.

Mat 27:49 The rest said; "Let be, let us see whether Elias will come to save him."

Mat 27:50 Jesus, when he had cried again with a loud voice, yielded up the ghost.

Mat 27:51 And, behold, the veil of the temple was rent in twain from the top to the bottom; and the earth did quake, and the rocks rent; *(1 Kings 8:12)*

Mat 27:52 And the graves were opened; and many bodies of the saints which slept arose,

Mat 27:53 And came out of the graves after his resurrection, and went into the holy city, and appeared unto many.

Mat 27:54 Now when the centurion, and they that were with him, watching Jesus, saw the earthquake, and those things that were done, they feared greatly, saying; "Truly this was the Son of God."

Mat 27:55 And many women were there beholding afar off, which followed Jesus from Galilee, ministering unto him:

Mat 27:56 Among which was Mary Magdalene, and Mary the mother of James and Joses, and the mother of Zebedee's children.

The Death of Jesus (Psalm 22)

Mar 15:33 And when the sixth hour was come *(12 pm)*, there was darkness over the whole land until the ninth hour. *(3pm)*

Mar 15:34 And at the ninth hour Jesus cried with a loud voice, saying; "Eloi, Eloi, lama sabachthani?" *(Hebrew Chaldee not Aramaic)* which is, being interpreted; "My God, my God, why hast thou forsaken me?"

Mar 15:35 And some of them that stood by, when they heard it, said; "Behold, he calleth Elias."

Mar 15:36 And one ran and filled a sponge full of vinegar, and put it on a reed, and gave him to drink, saying, "Let alone; let us see whether Elias will come to take him down."

Mar 15:37 And Jesus cried with a loud voice, and gave up the ghost.

Mar 15:38 And the veil of the temple was rent in twain from the top to the bottom.

Mar 15:39 And when the centurion, which stood over against him, saw that he so cried out, and gave up the ghost, he said; "Truly this man was the Son of God."

Mar 15:40 There were also women looking on afar off: among whom was Mary Magdalene, and Mary the mother of James the less and of Joses, and Salome;

Mar 15:41 (Who also, when he was in Galilee, followed him, and ministered unto him;) and many other women which came up with him unto Jerusalem.

The Death of Jesus *Ps 31:5*

Luk 23:44 And it was about the sixth hour, *(12 pm)* and there was a darkness over all the earth until the ninth hour. *(3 pm)*

Luk 23:45 And the sun was darkened, and the veil of the temple was rent in the midst.

Luk 23:46 And when Jesus had cried with a loud voice, he said; "Father, into thy hands I commend my spirit:" and having said thus, he gave up the ghost. *(Proving Jesus was a man and had his own Spirit. Acts 2:22, 1 Tim 2:5, Heb 4:15)*

Luk 23:47 Now when the centurion saw what was done, he glorified God, saying; "Certainly this was a righteous man."

Luk 23:48 And all the people that came together to that sight, beholding the things which were done, smote their breasts, and returned.

Luk 23:49 And all his acquaintance, and the women that followed him from Galilee, stood afar off, beholding these things.

The Death of Jesus

Joh 19:28 After this, Jesus knowing that all things were now accomplished, that the scripture might be fulfilled, saith; "I thirst."

Joh 19:29 Now there was set a vessel full of vinegar: and they filled a sponge with vinegar, and put it upon hyssop, and put it to his mouth.

Joh 19:30 When Jesus therefore had received the vinegar, he said; "It is finished": and he bowed his head, and gave up the ghost.

Jesus' Side Is Pierced (PS 34:20, Zec 12:10)

Joh 19:31 The Jews therefore, because it was the preparation, that the bodies should not remain upon the cross on the sabbath day, (for that sabbath day was an high day,) besought Pilate that their legs might be broken, and that they might be taken away.

Joh 19:32 Then came the soldiers, and broke the legs of the first, and of the other which was crucified with him.

Joh 19:33 But when they came to Jesus, and saw that he was dead already, they brake not his legs:

Joh 19:34 But one of the soldiers with a spear pierced his side, and forthwith came there out blood and water.

Joh 19:35 And he that saw it bare record, and his record is true: and he knoweth that he saith true, that ye might believe.

Joh 19:36 For these things were done, that the scripture should be fulfilled, A bone of him shall not be broken. *(Psalm 34:20)*

Joh 19:37 And again another scripture saith; "They shall look on him whom they pierced." *(Zec 12:10)*

Jesus took all the curses upon himself, Gods wrath. Cursed is he that hangs on a tree. Deut 21:22,23. The brass serpent lifted up by Moses represented sin on the cross.

1. The crown of thorns. Represents the earths curse after Adam sinned. Gen 3:18

2. The Kingly robe represented His worldly humble position. Isah 9:6, Isah 22:21, Zec 3:4, Deut 10:17.

3. He was beaten beyond recognition for us, that we may be whole. Isa 53:5, 1 Pet 2:24. So even if Jesus was never crucified, still we would have had healing to our bodies.

4. He was pinned/nailed, with his arms open, representing the Love and call of the Father, to all who would come unto Him to be comforted, forgiven and healed, Jesus was not able to comfort himself. Joh 12:32, Num 21:9. The nails representing the work of Man, Joseph was a carpenter for a reason. Isa 22:23.

5. Jesus was hung back on the tree, to represent the Fruit of Good and Evil that was taken from the tree without permission. Ps 105:15. Jesus was good but became sin for us. God put that knowledge back where it belonged and crucified it. One of the reasons why Jesus cursed the Fig Tree as its leaves were used to hide Adams and Eves nakedness (sin). Gen 3:7, Jesus said He is the Truth, Joh 14:6.

6. The spear wound in his side with blood and water represents the curse of Eve in child birth, Gen 3:16. And the birth of the church and prophesying a new spiritual bride for the last Adam. We are born again of God, not by or for, but of. There is no pain in the second birth only righteousness, Peace and Joy in the Holy Spirit. Joh 1:13, Rom 14:17.

7. Is the rest of God. Jesus was given resurrection life and in that he shared his Victory with us. Rom 8:29, 1 Samuel 30:23-26.

Joseph Buries Jesus [Isaiah 53:9]

Mat 27:57 When the even was come, there came a rich man of Arimathaea, named Joseph, who also himself was Jesus' disciple:

Mat 27:58 He went to Pilate, and begged the body of Jesus. Then Pilate commanded the body to be delivered.

Mat 27:59 And when Joseph had taken the body, he wrapped it ***in a*** clean *(G2513)* linen cloth *(G4616)*.

"in a" has been added to make sense; should read "wrapped clean linen cloth" or "fine linen cloth". Personally, I would have put "With fine linen cloth" but who are we to question. Joh 20:7, John was an eye witness.

Mat 27:60 And laid it in his own new tomb, which he had hewn out in the rock: and he rolled a great stone to the door of the sepulchre, and departed.

Mat 27:61 And there was Mary Magdalene, and the other Mary, sitting over against the sepulchre.

Joseph Buries Jesus

Mar 15:42 And now when the even was come, because it was the preparation, that is, the day before the sabbath,

Mar 15:43 Joseph of Arimathaea, an honourable counsellor, which also waited for the kingdom of God, came, and went in boldly unto Pilate, and craved the body of Jesus.

Mar 15:44 And Pilate marvelled if he were already dead: and calling unto him the centurion, he asked him whether he had been any while dead.

Mar 15:45 And when he knew it of the centurion, he gave the body to Joseph.

Mar 15:46 And he bought fine linen, and took him down, and wrapped him in the linen, and laid him in a sepulchre which was hewn out of a rock, and rolled a stone unto the door of the sepulchre.

Mar 15:47 And Mary Magdalene and Mary the mother of Joses beheld where he was laid.

Joseph Buries Jesus

Luk 23:50 And, behold, there was a man named Joseph, a counsellor; and he was a good man, and a just:

Luk 23:51 (The same had not consented to the counsel and deed of them;) he was of Arimathaea, a city of the Jews: who also himself waited for the kingdom of God.

Luk 23:52 This man went unto Pilate, and begged the body of Jesus.

Luk 23:53 And he took it down, and wrapped it in linen, and laid it in a sepulchre that was hewn in stone, wherein never man before was laid.

Luk 23:54 And that day was the preparation, and the sabbath drew on.

Luk 23:55 And the women also, which came with him from Galilee, followed after, and beheld the sepulchre, and how his body was laid.

Luk 23:56 And they returned, and prepared spices and ointments; and rested the sabbath day according to the commandment. Friday night their sabbath started at 6 pm)

Joseph Buries Jesus

Joh 19:38 And after this Joseph of Arimathaea, being a disciple of Jesus, but secretly for fear of the Jews, besought Pilate that he might take away the body of Jesus: and Pilate gave him leave. He came therefore, and took the body of Jesus.

Joh 19:39 And there came also Nicodemus, which at the first came to Jesus by night, and brought a mixture of myrrh and aloes, about an hundred pound weight.

Joh 19:40 Then took they the body of Jesus, and wound it in linen clothes with the spices, as the manner of the Jews is to bury.

Joh 19:41 Now in the place where he was crucified there was a garden; and in the garden a new sepulchre, wherein was never man yet laid.

Joh 19:42 There laid they Jesus therefore because of the Jews' preparation day; for the sepulchre was nigh at hand.

The Saturday or Sabbath

The Guard at the Tomb on the sabbath

Mat 27:62 Now the next day, that followed the day of the preparation, the chief priests and Pharisees came together unto Pilate,

Mat 27:63 Saying; "Sir, we remember that that deceiver said while he was yet alive; "After three days I will rise again." 64 Command therefore that the sepulchre be made sure until the third day, lest his disciples come by night, and steal him away, and say unto the people; "He is risen from the dead": so, the last error shall be worse than the first."

Mat 27:65 Pilate said unto them; "Ye have a watch: go your way, make it as sure as ye can."

Mat 27:66 So they went, and made the sepulchre sure, sealing the stone, and setting a watch.

The Next Day, Sunday, after the Sabbath. Hosea 6:2

The Guards, Earthquake and Stone rolled away.

Mat 28:1 In the end of the sabbath, as it began to dawn toward the first day of the week, came Mary Magdalene and the other Mary to see the sepulchre.

Mat 28:2 And, behold, there was a great earthquake: for the angel of the Lord descended from heaven, and came and rolled back the stone from the door, and sat upon it.

Mat 28:3 His countenance was like lightning, and his raiment white as snow:

Mat 28:4 And for fear of him the keepers did shake, and became as dead men.

Stone rolled away

Joh 20:1 The first day of the week cometh Mary Magdalene early, when it was yet dark, unto the sepulchre, and seeth the stone taken away from the sepulchre.

Joh 20:2 Then she runneth, and cometh to Simon Peter, and to the other disciple, whom Jesus loved, and saith unto them; "They have taken away the Lord out of the sepulchre, and we know not where they have laid him."

Mary Sees an Angel

Mat 28:5 And the angel answered and said unto the women; "Fear not ye: for I know that ye seek Jesus, which was crucified. 6 He is not here: for he is risen, as he said. Come, see the place where the Lord lay. 7 And go quickly, and tell his disciples that he is risen from the dead; and, behold, he goeth before you into Galilee; there shall ye see him: lo, I have told you."

Mat 28:8 And they departed quickly from the sepulchre with fear and great joy; and did run to bring his disciple's word.

Mary Sees an Angel

Mar 16:1 And when the sabbath was past, Mary Magdalene, and Mary the mother of James, and Salome, had bought sweet spices, that they might come and anoint him.

Mar 16:2 And very early in the morning the first day of the week, they came unto the sepulchre at the rising of the sun.

Mar 16:3 And they said among themselves; "Who shall roll us away the stone from the door of the sepulchre?"

Mar 16:4 And when they looked, they saw that the stone was rolled away: for it was very great.

Mar 16:5 And entering into the sepulchre, they saw a young man sitting on the right side, clothed in a long white garment; and they were affrighted.

Mar 16:6 And he saith unto them; "Be not affrighted: Ye seek Jesus of Nazareth, which was crucified: he is risen; he is not here: behold the place where they laid him. 7 But go your way, tell his disciples and Peter, that he goeth before you into Galilee: there shall ye see him, as he said unto you."

Mar 16:8 And they went out quickly, and fled from the sepulchre; for they trembled and were amazed: neither said they anything to any man; for they were afraid.

Mary Sees Two Angels, reminds her of what Jesus said

Luk 24:1 Now upon the first day of the week, very early in the morning, they came unto the sepulchre, bringing the spices which they had prepared, and certain others with them.

Luk 24:2 And they found the stone rolled away from the sepulchre.

Luk 24:3 And they entered in, and found not the body of the Lord Jesus.

Luk 24:4 And it came to pass, as they were much perplexed thereabout, behold, two men stood by them in shining garments:

Luk 24:5 And as they were afraid, and bowed down their faces to the earth, they said unto them; "Why seek ye the living among the dead? 6 He is not here, but is risen: remember how he spake unto you when he was yet in Galilee, 7 Saying; "The Son of man must be delivered into the hands of sinful men, and be crucified, and the third day rise again.""

Luk 24:8 And they remembered his words,

Luk 24:9 And returned from the sepulchre, and told all these things unto the eleven, and to all the rest.

Luk 24:10 It was Mary Magdalene, and Joanna, and Mary the mother of James, and other women that were with them, which told these things unto the apostles.

Luk 24:11 And their words seemed to them as idle tales, and they believed them not.

Luk 24:12 Then arose Peter, and ran unto the sepulchre; and stooping down, he beheld the linen clothes laid by themselves, and departed, wondering in himself at that which was come to pass. *(John is not mentioned here but that doesn't mean he didn't go as well.)*

Peter and John run to the tomb

Joh 20:3 Peter therefore went forth, and that other disciple, and came to the sepulchre.

Joh 20:4 So they ran both together: and the other disciple did outrun Peter, and came first to the sepulchre.

Joh 20:5 And he stooping down, and looking in, saw the linen clothes lying; yet went he not in.

Joh 20:6 Then cometh Simon Peter following him, and went into the sepulchre, and seeth the linen clothes lie,

Joh 20:7 And the napkin, that was about his head, not lying with the linen clothes, but wrapped together in a place by itself. *(this verse refutes the validity of the Shroud or Touran)*

Joh 20:8 Then went in also that other disciple, which came first to the sepulchre, and he saw, and believed.

Joh 20:9 For as yet they knew not the scripture, that he must rise again from the dead. *(Hosea 6:2)*

Joh 20:10 Then the disciples went away again unto their own home.

Mary sees Two Angels

Joh 20:11 But Mary stood without at the sepulchre weeping: and as she wept, she stooped down, and looked into the sepulchre,

Joh 20:12 And seeth two angels in white sitting, the one at the head, and the other at the feet, where the body of Jesus had lain.

Joh 20:13 And they say unto her; "Woman, why weepest thou?" She saith unto them; "Because they have taken away my Lord, and I know not where they have laid him."

Jesus Appears to Mary Magdalene

Mar 16:9 Now when Jesus was risen early the first day of the week, he appeared first to Mary Magdalene, out of whom he had cast seven devils.

Mar 16:10 And she went and told them that had been with him, as they mourned and wept.

Mar 16:11 And they, when they had heard that he was alive, and had been seen of her, believed not.

Jesus appears to Mary Magdalene

Joh 20:14 And when she had thus said, she turned herself back, and saw Jesus standing, and knew not that it was Jesus.

Joh 20:15 Jesus saith unto her; "Woman, why weepest thou? whom seekest thou?" She, supposing him to be the gardener, saith unto him; "Sir, if thou have borne him hence, tell me where thou hast laid him, and I will take him away."

Joh 20:16 Jesus saith unto her; "Mary." She turned herself, and saith unto him; "Rabboni" *(G4462 Chaldee not Aramaic)*; which is to say, Master.

Joh 20:17 Jesus saith unto her; "Touch me not; for I am not yet ascended to my Father: but go to my brethren, and say unto them, I ascend unto my Father, and your Father; and to my God, and your God." (Hag 2:13, Lev 7:19)

Joh 20:18 Mary Magdalene came and told the disciples that she had seen the Lord, and that he had spoken these things unto her.

Jesus appears to the Disciples

Mat 28:9 And as they went to tell his disciples, behold, Jesus met them, saying; "All hail." And they came and held him by the feet, and worshipped him.

Mat 28:10 Then said Jesus unto them; "Be not afraid: go tell my brethren that they go into Galilee, and there shall they see me."

The Report of the Guard back to the Priests

Mat 28:11 Now when they were going, behold, some of the watch came into the city, and shewed unto the chief priests all the things that were done.

Mat 28:12 And when they were assembled with the elders, and had taken counsel, they gave large money unto the soldiers,

Mat 28:13 Saying; "Say ye, His disciples came by night, and stole him away while we slept. 14 And if this comes to the governor's ears, we will persuade him, and secure you."

Mat 28:15 So they took the money, and did as they were taught: and this saying is commonly reported among the Jews until this day.

Sunday afternoon, Cleophas and Simon (Not the Apostles as they went back to the 11+ people, Luke 24:33. There were also 2 Simons Mark 3:18)

On the Road to Emmaus, Jesus Appears to Two Disciples, not the apostles

Mar 16:12 After that he appeared in another form unto two of them, as they walked, and went into the country.

Mar 16:13 And they went and told it unto the residue: neither believed they them.

On the Road to Emmaus

Luk 24:13 And, behold, two of them went that same day to a village called Emmaus, which was from Jerusalem about threescore furlongs.

(7.5 miles. 8 furlongs to a mile, 5 furlongs to a kilometre)

Luk 24:14 And they talked together of all these things which had happened.

Luk 24:15 And it came to pass, that, while they communed together and reasoned, Jesus himself drew near, and went with them.

Luk 24:16 But their eyes were holden that they should not know him.

Luk 24:17 And he said unto them; "What manner of communications are these that ye have one to another, as ye walk, and are sad?"

Luk 24:18 And the one of them, whose name was Cleopas, answering said unto him; "Art thou only a stranger in Jerusalem, and hast not known the things which are come to pass there in these days?"

Luk 24:19 And he said unto them; "What things?" And they said unto him; "Concerning Jesus of Nazareth, which was a prophet mighty in deed and word before God and all the people: 20 And how the chief priests and our rulers delivered him to be condemned to death, and have crucified him. 21 But we trusted that it had been he which should have redeemed Israel: and beside all this, today is the third day since these things were done. 22 Yea, and certain women also of our company made us astonished, which were early at the sepulchre; 23 And when they found not his body, they came, saying, that they had also seen a vision of angels, which said that he was alive. 24 And certain of them which were with us went to the sepulchre, and found it even so as the women had said: but him they saw not."

Luk 24:25 Then he said unto them; "O fools, and slow of heart to believe all that the prophets have spoken: 26 Ought not Christ to have suffered these things, and to enter into his glory?"

Luk 24:27 And beginning at Moses and all the prophets, he expounded unto them in all the scriptures the things concerning himself.

Luk 24:28 And they drew nigh unto the village, whither they went: and he made as though he would have gone further.

Luk 24:29 But they constrained him, saying; "Abide with us: for it is toward evening, and the day is far spent." And he went in to tarry with them.

Luk 24:30 And it came to pass, as he sat at meat with them, he took bread, and blessed it, and brake, and gave to them.

Luk 24:31 And their eyes were opened, and they knew him; and he vanished out of their sight.

Luk 24:32 And they said one to another; "Did not our heart burn within us, while he talked with us by the way, and while he opened to us the scriptures?"

Luk 24:33 And they rose up the same hour, and returned to Jerusalem, and found the eleven gathered together, and them that were with them,

Luk 24:34 Saying; "The Lord is risen indeed, and hath appeared to Simon."

Luk 24:35 And they told what things were done in the way, and how he was known of them in breaking of bread.

Sunday night

Jesus Appears to the Disciples; giving them the authority to forgive sins

Joh 20:19 Then the same day at evening, being the first day of the week, when the doors were shut where the disciples were assembled for fear of the Jews, came Jesus and stood in the midst, and saith unto them; "Peace be unto you."

Joh 20:20 And when he had so said, he shewed unto them his hands and his side. Then were the disciples glad, when they saw the Lord.

Joh 20:21 Then said Jesus to them again; "Peace be unto you: as my Father hath sent me, even so send I you."

Joh 20:22 And when he had said this, he breathed on them, and saith unto them; "Receive ye the Holy Ghost: 23 Whose soever sins ye remit, they are remitted unto them; and whose soever sins ye retain, they are retained."

Jesus Appears to His Disciples

Mar 16:14 Afterward he appeared unto the eleven as they sat at meat, and upbraided them with their unbelief and hardness of heart, because they believed not them which had seen him after he was risen.

(Jesus did appeared a few times; but the first time Thomas was missing. John 20:24)

Jesus Appears to His Disciples. *PS 22:16*

Luk 24:36 And as they thus spake, Jesus himself stood in the midst of them, and saith unto them; "Peace be unto you."

Luk 24:37 But they were terrified and affrighted, and supposed that they had seen a spirit.

Luk 24:38 And he said unto them; "Why are ye troubled? and why do thoughts arise in your hearts? 39 Behold my hands and my feet, that it is I myself: handle me, and see; for a spirit hath not flesh and bones, as ye see me have."

Luk 24:40 And when he had thus spoken, he shewed them his hands and his feet.

Luk 24:41 And while they yet believed not for joy, and wondered, he said unto them, "Have ye here any meat?"

Luk 24:42 And they gave him a piece of a broiled fish, and of an honeycomb.

Luk 24:43 And he took it, and did eat before them.

Luk 24:44 And he said unto them; "These are the words which I spake unto you, while I was yet with you, that all things must be fulfilled, which were written in the law of Moses, and in the prophets, and in the psalms, concerning me."

Luk 24:45 Then opened he their understanding, that they might understand the scriptures,

Jesus and Thomas

(Although Mark says Jesus appeared to the 11, Mark 16:14, Mark probably wasn't there, but Jesus had appeared many times to them over a 40-day period. Mattias, was he there? Luke says he was chosen back in Jerusalem. Acts 1:26 and 120 were there also, Acts 1:15. Because it doesn't say there was no one else there it is possible more were there. John says the disciples lacked Thomas.)

Joh 20:24 But Thomas, one of the twelve, called Didymus, was not with them when Jesus came.

Joh 20:25 The other disciples therefore said unto him; "We have seen the Lord." But he said unto them; "Except I shall see in his hands the print of the nails, and put my finger into the print of the nails, and thrust my hand into his side, I will not believe."

Eight Days Later

Joh 20:26 And after eight days again his disciples were within, and Thomas with them: then came Jesus, the doors being shut, and stood in the midst, and said; "Peace be unto you."

Joh 20:27 Then saith he to Thomas; "Reach hither thy finger, and behold my hands; and reach hither thy hand, and thrust it into my side: and be not faithless, but believing."

Joh 20:28 And Thomas answered and said unto him; "My Lord and my God."

Joh 20:29 Jesus saith unto him; "Thomas, because thou hast seen me, thou hast believed: blessed are they that have not seen, and yet have believed."

The Purpose of This Book

Joh 20:30 And many other signs truly did Jesus in the presence of his disciples, which are not written in this book:

Joh 20:31 But these are written, that ye might believe that Jesus is the Christ, the Son of God; and that believing ye might have life through his name.

Sea of Galilee

Jesus Appears to Seven Disciples a Third time

Joh 21:1 After these things Jesus shewed himself again to the disciples at the sea of Tiberias; and on this wise shewed he himself.

Joh 21:2 There were together Simon Peter, and Thomas called Didymus, and Nathanael of Cana in Galilee, and the sons of Zebedee *(James and John)*, and two other of his disciples.

Joh 21:3 Simon Peter saith unto them; "I go a fishing." They say unto him; "We also go with thee." They went forth, and entered into a ship immediately; and that night they caught nothing.

Joh 21:4 But when the morning was now come, Jesus stood on the shore: but the disciples knew not that it was Jesus.

Joh 21:5 Then Jesus saith unto them; "Children, have ye any meat?" They answered him; "No."

Joh 21:6 And he said unto them; "Cast the net on the right side of the ship, and ye shall find." They cast therefore, and now they were not able to draw it for the multitude of fishes.

Joh 21:7 Therefore that disciple whom Jesus loved saith unto Peter; "It is the Lord." Now when Simon Peter heard that it was the Lord, he girt his fisher's coat unto him, (for he was naked,) and did cast himself into the sea.

Joh 21:8 And the other disciples came in a little ship; (for they were not far from land, but as it were two hundred cubits,) dragging the net with fishes.

Joh 21:9 As soon then as they were come to land, they saw a fire of coals there, and fish laid thereon, and bread.

Joh 21:10 Jesus saith unto them; "Bring of the fish which ye have now caught."

Joh 21:11 Simon Peter went up, and drew the net to land full of great fishes, an hundred and fifty and three: and for all there were so many, yet was not the net broken.

Joh 21:12 Jesus saith unto them; "Come and dine." And none of the disciples durst ask him; Who art thou? knowing that it was the Lord.

Joh 21:13 Jesus then cometh, and taketh bread, and giveth them, and fish likewise.

Joh 21:14 This is now the third time that Jesus shewed himself to his disciples, after that he was risen from the dead.

<u>Jesus confirms Peter 3 times</u> *Ps 78:52, Ps 95:7*

Reversal of the denials, same setting with the smell of fire and being cold

Joh 21:15 So when they had dined, Jesus saith to Simon Peter; "Simon, son of Jonas, lovest (Agape) thou me more than these?" He saith unto him; "Yea, Lord; thou knowest that I love (Phileo) thee." He saith unto him; "Feed my lambs."

Joh 21:16 He saith to him again the second time; "Simon, son of Jonas, lovest (Agape) thou me?" He saith unto him; "Yea, Lord; thou knowest that I love (Phileo) thee." He saith unto him; "Feed my sheep."

Joh 21:17 He saith unto him the third time; "Simon, son of Jonas, lovest (Phileo) thou me?" Peter was grieved because he said unto him the third time; "Lovest (Phileo) thou me?" And he said unto him; "Lord, thou knowest all things; thou knowest that I love (Phileo) thee." Jesus saith unto him; "Feed my sheep." (1 Corrin 16:22, Tit 3:4)

Joh 21:18 "Verily, verily, I say unto thee; When thou wast young, thou girdedst thyself, and walkedst whither thou wouldest: but when thou shalt be old, thou shalt stretch forth thy hands, and another shall gird thee, and carry thee whither thou wouldest not."

Joh 21:19 This spake he, signifying by what death he should glorify God. And when he had spoken this, he saith unto him; "Follow me."

<u>Jesus Tells Peter not to look at others, but to follow Him.</u>

Joh 21:20 Then Peter, turning about, seeth the disciple whom Jesus loved following; which also leaned on his breast at supper, and said; "Lord, which is he that betrayeth thee? *(John)*

Joh 21:21 Peter seeing him saith to Jesus; "Lord, and what shall this man do?"

Joh 21:22 Jesus saith unto him; "If I will that he tarry till I come, what is that to thee? follow thou me."

Joh 21:23 Then went this saying abroad among the brethren, that that disciple should not die: yet Jesus said not unto him; "He shall not die; but, If I will that he tarry till I come, what is that to thee?"

Joh 21:24 This is the disciple which testifieth of these things, and wrote these things: and we know that his testimony is true.

Joh 21:25 And there are also many other things which Jesus did, the which, if they should be written every one, I suppose that even the world itself could not contain the books that should be written. Amen.

The end of the gospel of John.

<u>Galilee</u>

<u>The Great Commission given in Galilee</u>

Mat 28:16 Then the eleven disciples went away into Galilee, into a mountain where Jesus had appointed them.

Mat 28:17 And when they saw him, they worshipped him: but some doubted.

Mat 28:18 And Jesus came and spake unto them, saying; "All power is given unto me in heaven and in earth. 19 Go ye therefore, and teach all nations, baptizing them in the name of the Father, and of the Son, and of the Holy Ghost: 20 Teaching them to observe all things whatsoever I have commanded you: and, lo, I am with you alway, even unto the end of the world. Amen."

<u>*The end of the gospel of Matthew.*</u>

<u>The Great Commission given in Galilee</u>

Mar 16:15 And he said unto them; "Go ye into all the world, and preach the gospel to every creature. 16 He that believeth and is baptized shall be saved; but he that believeth not shall be damned. 17 And these signs shall follow them that believe; In my name shall they cast out devils; they shall speak with new tongues; *(Zep 3:9, Isa 28:11. An important fact is; God confused with language, Gen 11:9, but has restored with tongues.)* 18 They shall take up serpents; and if they drink any deadly thing, it shall not hurt them; they shall lay hands on the sick, and they shall recover."

<u>Returning to Jerusalem to wait for Power</u>

<u>Go back to Jerusalem and Wait for Power.</u> *Acts 1:8*

Luk 24:46 And said unto them; "Thus it is written, and thus it behoved Christ to suffer, and to rise from the dead the third day: 47 And that repentance and remission of sins should be preached in his name among all nations, beginning at Jerusalem. 48 And ye are witnesses of these things. 49 And, behold, I send the promise of my Father upon you: but tarry ye in the city of Jerusalem, until ye be endued with power from on high."

<u>Jesus Ascends,</u> *Ps 110:1*

Mar 16:19 So then after the Lord had spoken unto them, he was received up into heaven, and sat on the right hand of God.

Mar 16:20 And they went forth, and preached everywhere, the Lord working with them, and confirming the word with signs following. Amen.

The end of the gospel of Mark.

Jesus ascends.

Luk 24:50 And he led them out as far as to Bethany, and he lifted up his hands, and blessed them.

Luk 24:51 And it came to pass, while he blessed them, he was parted from them, and carried up into heaven.

Luk 24:52 And they worshipped him, and returned to Jerusalem with great joy:

Luk 24:53 And were continually in the temple, praising and blessing God. Amen.

The end of the gospel of Luke.

The Promise of the Holy Spirit

Act 1:1 The former treatise have I made, O Theophilus, of all that Jesus began both to do and teach,

Act 1:2 Until the day in which he was taken up, after that he through the Holy Ghost had given commandments unto the apostles whom he had chosen:

Act 1:3 To whom also he shewed himself alive after his passion by many infallible proofs, being seen of them forty days, and speaking of the things pertaining to the kingdom of God:

Act 1:4 And, being assembled together with *them,* commanded them that they should not depart from Jerusalem, but wait for the promise of the Father, which, *saith he;* "Ye have heard of me. 5 For John truly baptized with water; but ye shall be baptized with the Holy Ghost not many days hence."

The Ascension Reiterated.

Act 1:6 When they therefore were come together, they asked of him, saying; "Lord, wilt thou at this time restore again the kingdom to Israel?"

Act 1:7 And he said unto them; "It is not for you to know the times or the seasons, *(Rev 6:10,11)* which the Father hath put in his own power. 8 *(Ps*

68:18) But ye shall receive power, after that the Holy Ghost is come upon you: and ye shall be witnesses unto me both in Jerusalem, and in all Judaea, and in Samaria, and unto the uttermost part of the earth."

Act 1:9 And when he had spoken these things, while they beheld, he was taken up; and a cloud received him out of their sight.

Act 1:10 And while they looked stedfastly toward heaven as he went up, behold, two men stood by them in white apparel;

Act 1:11 Which also said; "Ye men of Galilee, why stand ye gazing up into heaven? this same Jesus, which is taken up from you into heaven, shall so come in like manner as ye have seen him go into heaven."

<u>Back in the upper room in Jerusalem</u>

<u>Matthias Chosen by prayer and Lot casting for the 12th Apostle</u>

(Paul was chosen by God)

Act 1:12 Then returned they unto Jerusalem from the mount called Olivet, which is from Jerusalem a sabbath day's journey.

Act 1:13 And when they were come in, they went up into an upper room, where abode both Peter, and James, and John, and Andrew, Philip, and Thomas, Bartholomew, and Matthew, James *the son* of Alphaeus, and Simon Zelotes, and Judas *the brother* of James.

Act 1:14 These all continued with one accord in prayer and supplication, with the women, and Mary the mother of Jesus, and with his brethren.

Act 1:15 And in those days Peter stood up in the midst of the disciples, and said; (the number of names together were about an hundred and twenty,)

Act 1:16 "Men *and* brethren, this scripture must needs have been fulfilled, which the Holy Ghost by the mouth of David spake before concerning Judas, **(Ps 41:9, Ps 55.)** which was guide to them that took Jesus. 17 For he was numbered with us, and had obtained part of this ministry. 18 Now this man purchased a field with the reward of iniquity; and falling headlong, he burst asunder in the midst, and all his bowels gushed out. 19 And it was known unto all the dwellers at Jerusalem; insomuch as that field is called in their proper tongue, Aceldama" (Chaldee/Hebrew G184), that is to say; "The field of blood."

Acts 1:20 "For it is written in the book of Psalms, (Ps 69:25) Let his habitation be desolate, and let no man dwell therein: and his bishoprick let another take. 21 Wherefore of these men which have companied with us all the time that the Lord Jesus went in and out among us, 22 Beginning from the baptism of John, unto that same day that he was taken up from us, must one be ordained to be a witness with us of his resurrection."

Act 1:23 And they appointed two, Joseph called Barsabas, who was surnamed Justus, and Matthias.

Act 1:24 And they prayed, and said; "Thou, Lord, which knowest the hearts of all *men,* shew whether of these two thou hast chosen, 25 That he may take part of this ministry and apostleship, from which Judas by transgression fell, that he might go to his own place."

Act 1:26 And they gave forth their lots; and the lot fell upon Matthias; and he was numbered with the eleven apostles.

Stephen's short account of the Bible.

Act 7:1 Then said the high priest, Are these things so?

Act 7:2 And he said, Men, brethren, and fathers, hearken; The God of glory appeared unto our father Abraham, when he was in Mesopotamia, before he dwelt in Charran,

Act 7:3 And said unto him, Get thee out of thy country, and from thy kindred, and come into the land which I shall shew thee.

Act 7:4 Then came he out of the land of the Chaldean's, and dwelt in Charran: and from thence, when his father was dead, he removed him into this land, wherein ye now dwell.

Act 7:5 And he gave him none inheritance in it, no, not *so much as* to set his foot on: yet he promised that he would give it to him for a possession, and to his seed after him, when *as yet* he had no child.

Act 7:6 And God spake on this wise, That his seed should sojourn in a strange land; and that they should bring them into bondage, and entreat *them* evil four hundred years.

Act 7:7 And the nation to whom they shall be in bondage will I judge, said God: and after that shall they come forth, and serve me in this place.

Act 7:8 And he gave him the covenant of circumcision: and so *Abraham* begat Isaac, and circumcised him the eighth day; and Isaac *begat* Jacob; and Jacob *begat* the twelve patriarchs.

Act 7:9 And the patriarchs, moved with envy, sold Joseph into Egypt: but God was with him,

Act 7:10 And delivered him out of all his afflictions, and gave him favour and wisdom in the sight of Pharaoh king of Egypt; and he made him governor over Egypt and all his house.

Act 7:11 Now there came a dearth over all the land of Egypt and Chanaan, and great affliction: and our fathers found no sustenance.

Act 7:12 But when Jacob heard that there was corn in Egypt, he sent out our fathers first.

Act 7:13 And at the second *time* Joseph was made known to his brethren; and Joseph's kindred was made known unto Pharaoh.

Act 7:14 Then sent Joseph, and called his father Jacob to *him,* and all his kindred, threescore and fifteen souls.

Act 7:15 So Jacob went down into Egypt, and died, he, and our fathers,

Act 7:16 And were carried over into Sychem, and laid in the sepulchre that Abraham bought for a sum of money of the sons of Emmor *the father* of Sychem.

Act 7:17 But when the time of the promise drew nigh, which God had sworn to Abraham, the people grew and multiplied in Egypt,

Act 7:18 Till another king arose, which knew not Joseph.

Act 7:19 The same dealt subtilly with our kindred, and evil entreated our fathers, so that they cast out their young children, to the end they might not live.

Act 7:20 In which time Moses was born, and was exceeding fair, and nourished up in his father's house three months:

Act 7:21 And when he was cast out, Pharaoh's daughter took him up, and nourished him for her own son.

Act 7:22 And Moses was learned in all the wisdom of the Egyptians, and was mighty in words and in deeds.

Act 7:23 And when he was full forty years old, it came into his heart to visit his brethren the children of Israel.

Act 7:24 And seeing one *of them* suffer wrong, he defended *him,* and avenged him that was oppressed, and smote the Egyptian:

Act 7:25 For he supposed his brethren would have understood how that God by his hand would deliver them: but they understood not.

Act 7:26 And the next day he shewed himself unto them as they strove, and would have set them at one again, saying, Sirs, ye are brethren; why do ye wrong one to another?

Act 7:27 But he that did his neighbour wrong thrust him away, saying, Who made thee a ruler and a judge over us?

Act 7:28 Wilt thou kill me, as thou diddest the Egyptian yesterday?

Act 7:29 Then fled Moses at this saying, and was a stranger in the land of Madian, where he begat two sons.

Act 7:30 And when forty years were expired, there appeared to him in the wilderness of mount Sina an angel of the Lord in a flame of fire in a bush.

Act 7:31 When Moses saw *it,* he wondered at the sight: and as he drew near to behold *it,* the voice of the Lord came unto him,

Act 7:32 *Saying,* I *am* the God of thy fathers, the God of Abraham, and the God of Isaac, and the God of Jacob. Then Moses trembled, and durst not behold.

Act 7:33 Then said the Lord to him, Put off thy shoes from thy feet: for the place where thou standest is holy ground.

Act 7:34 I have seen, I have seen the affliction of my people which is in Egypt, and I have heard their groaning, and am come down to deliver them. And now come, I will send thee into Egypt.

Act 7:35 This Moses whom they refused, saying, Who made thee a ruler and a judge? the same did God send *to be* a ruler and a deliverer by the hand of the angel which appeared to him in the bush.

Act 7:36 He brought them out, after that he had shewed wonders and signs in the land of Egypt, and in the Red sea, and in the wilderness forty years.

Act 7:37 This is that Moses, which said unto the children of Israel, A prophet shall the Lord your God raise up unto you of your brethren, like unto me; him shall ye hear.

Act 7:38 This is he, that was in the church in the wilderness with the angel which spake to him in the mount Sina, and *with* our fathers: who received the lively oracles to give unto us:

Act 7:39 To whom our fathers would not obey, but thrust *him* from them, and in their hearts turned back again into Egypt,

Act 7:40 Saying unto Aaron, Make us gods to go before us: for *as for* this Moses, which brought us out of the land of Egypt, we wot not what is become of him.

Act 7:41 And they made a calf in those days, and offered sacrifice unto the idol, and rejoiced in the works of their own hands.

Act 7:42 Then God turned, and gave them up to worship the host of heaven; as it is written in the book of the prophets, O ye house of Israel, have ye offered to me slain beasts and sacrifices *by the space of* forty years in the wilderness?

Act 7:43 Yea, ye took up the tabernacle of Moloch, and the star of your god Remphan, figures which ye made to worship them: and I will carry you away beyond Babylon.

Act 7:44 Our fathers had the tabernacle of witness in the wilderness, as he had appointed, speaking unto Moses, that he should make it according to the fashion that he had seen.

Act 7:45 Which also our fathers that came after brought in with Jesus into the possession of the Gentiles, whom God drave out before the face of our fathers, unto the days of David;

Act 7:46 Who found favour before God, and desired to find a tabernacle for the God of Jacob.

Act 7:47 But Solomon built him an house.

Act 7:48 Howbeit the most High dwelleth not in temples made with hands; as saith the prophet,

Act 7:49 Heaven *is* my throne, and earth *is* my footstool: what house will ye build me? saith the Lord: or what *is* the place of my rest?

Act 7:50 Hath not my hand made all these things?

Act 7:51 Ye stiffnecked and uncircumcised in heart and ears, ye do always resist the Holy Ghost: as your fathers *did,* so *do* ye.

Act 7:52 Which of the prophets have not your fathers persecuted? and they have slain them which shewed before of the coming of the Just One; of whom ye have been now the betrayers and murderers:

Act 7:53 Who have received the law by the disposition of angels, and have not kept *it.*

Stephen Martyred

Act 7:54 When they heard these things, they were cut to the heart, and they gnashed on him with *their* teeth.

Act 7:55 But he, being full of the Holy Ghost, looked up stedfastly into heaven, and saw the glory of God, and Jesus standing on the right hand of God,

Act 7:56 And said, Behold, I see the heavens opened, and the Son of man standing on the right hand of God.

Act 7:57 Then they cried out with a loud voice, and stopped their ears, and ran upon him with one accord,

Act 7:58 And cast *him* out of the city, and stoned *him:* and the witnesses laid down their clothes at a young man's feet, whose name was Saul.

Act 7:59 And they stoned Stephen, calling upon *God,* and saying, Lord Jesus, receive my spirit.

Act 7:60 And he kneeled down, and cried with a loud voice, Lord, lay not this sin to their charge. And when he had said this, he fell asleep.

The Beginning of the Church

The Resurrection of Jesus

1Co 15:1 Moreover, brethren, I declare unto you the gospel which I preached unto you, which also ye have received, and wherein ye stand;

1Co 15:2 By which also ye are saved, if ye keep in memory what I preached unto you, unless ye have believed in vain.

1Co 15:3 For I delivered unto you first of all that which I also received, how that Christ died for our sins according to the scriptures;

1Co 15:4 And that he was buried, and that he rose again the third day according to the scriptures:

1Co 15:5 And that he was seen of Cephas, then of the twelve:

1Co 15:6 After that, he was seen of above five hundred brethren at once; of whom the greater part remain unto this present, but some are fallen asleep.

1Co 15:7 After that, he was seen of James; then of all the apostles.

1Co 15:8 And last of all he was seen of me also, as of one born out of due time.

1Co 15:9 For I am the least of the apostles, that am not meet (worthy) to be called an apostle, because I persecuted the church of God.

1Co 15:10 But by the grace of God I am what I am: and his grace which *was bestowed* upon me was not in vain; but I laboured more abundantly than they all: yet not I, but the grace of God which was with me.

Appendix
Numbers and their values
These are only a few, do some research
into Gematria and other things.

1 . = God, unity.

Deu 6:4 Hear, O Israel: The LORD our God is one LORD: John 10:30, Acts 2:22.

Mar 12:29 And Jesus answered him; "The first of all the commandments is, Hear, O Israel; The Lord our God is one Lord:"

2 . = Witnesses

Deu 19:15 One witness shall not rise up against a man for any iniquity, or for any sin, in any sin that he sinneth: at the mouth of two witnesses, or at the mouth of three witnesses, shall the matter be established.

Mark 6:7 (NKJV) 7 "And He called the twelve to Himself, and began to send them out two by two, and gave them power over unclean spirits." "Christ sent forth his disciples to preach the gospel not singly, but by twos, that they might labour unitedly in spreading the truth.

Act 1:8 But ye shall receive power, after that the Holy Ghost is come upon you: and ye shall be witnesses unto me both in Jerusalem, and in all Judaea, and in Samaria, and unto the uttermost part of the earth.

3 . = Wholeness/Godhead.

Deu 14:28 At the end of three years thou shalt bring forth all the tithe of thine increase the same year, and shalt lay it up within thy gates:

Ecc 4:12 And if one prevails against him, two shall withstand him; and a threefold cord is not quickly broken.

Hos 6:2 After two days will he revive us: in the third day he will raise us up, and we shall live in his sight.

1Jn 5:7 For there are three that bear record in heaven, the Father, the Word, and the Holy Ghost: and these three are one.

1Jn 5:8 And there are three that bear witness in earth, the Spirit, and the water, and the blood: and these three agree in one.

2Ki 20:8 And Hezekiah said unto Isaiah; "What shall be the sign that the LORD will heal me, and that I shall go up into the house of the LORD the third day?" (Jesus entered Heaven on the third day)

Est 5:1 Now it came to pass on the third day, that Esther put on her royal apparel, and stood in the inner court of the king's house, over against the king's house: and the king sat upon his royal throne in the royal house, over against the gate of the house. (Jesus went without food for 3 days and then came into the presence of the King, God the Father. John 20:17, 1John 5:7,8.)

4 . = Creation.

North, South East and West; 4 seasons, 4 elements, 4 weeks per lunar month. Did you know if you are married, take note which moon phase you wife mensurates, and you will never be caught out.

Gen 1:14 And God said; "Let there be lights in the firmament of the heaven to divide the day from the night; and let them be for signs, and for seasons, and for days, and years: 15 And let them be for lights in the firmament of the heaven to give light upon the earth:" and it was so. 16 And God made two great lights; the greater light to rule the day, and the lesser light to rule the night: he made the stars also. 17 And God set them in the firmament of the heaven to give light upon the earth, 18 And to rule over the day and over the night, and to divide the light from the darkness: and God saw that it was good. 19 And the evening and the morning were the fourth day.

5 . = Represents the Holy Spirit of God. God's Grace and Favor.

Five senses, God created the fish and birds on the Fifth day (Animals that float on breath or wind; (Ruach H7307 Job 27:3, Pnoe G4157 both mean wind). Fivefold ministry. And five offerings sacrificed to God, burnt, sin, trespass, grain and Peace offerings.

Mar 1:10 And straightway coming up out of the water, he saw the heavens opened, and the Spirit like a dove descending upon him: (see the connection, floating on wind?)

Eph 4:11 And he gave some, apostles; and some, prophets; and some, evangelists; and some, pastors and teachers;

6 . = Man was created on the 6th day; Jesus was crucified on the 6th day. The Flesh and Time is represented by the veil in the temple and the veil was torn apart on the 6th day, Gods presence was exposed.

Gen 1:31 And God saw everything that he had made, and, behold, it was very good. And the evening and the morning were the sixth day.

Heb 10:20 By a new and living way, which he hath consecrated for us, through the veil, that is to say, his flesh; 1 Peter 1:20, (Ps 78:2, time, Mat 13:35.)

7 . = Completeness of God. There is a common number of 7 running through the bible in the Hebrew letters. God rested on the 7th day; Jesus rested on the 7th day in the grave.

8 . = Resurrection; new beginnings Jesus Rose on the 8th day. Circumcism was on the 8th day. They worshipped on the 8th day; or can also be the first day of the week.

Php 3:5 Circumcised the eighth day, of the stock of Israel, of the tribe of Benjamin, an Hebrew of the Hebrews; as touching the law, a Pharisee;

Luk 1:59 And it came to pass, that on the eighth day they came to circumcise the child; and they called him Zacharias, after the name of his father.

Mat 28:1 In the end of the sabbath, as it began to dawn toward the first day of the week, came Mary Magdalene and the other Mary to see the sepulchre.

Act 20:7 And upon the first day of the week, when the disciples came together to break bread, Paul preached unto them, ready to depart on the morrow; and continued his speech until midnight.

9 . = Fruit bearing. The Gifts of the Holy Spirit (can also represent judgement)

1Co 12:7 But the manifestation of the Spirit is given to every man to profit withal.

1Co 12:8 For to one is given by the Spirit the word of wisdom; to another the word of knowledge by the same Spirit;

1Co 12:9 To another faith by the same Spirit; to another the gifts of healing by the same Spirit;

1Co 12:10 To another the working of miracles; to another prophecy; to another discerning of spirits; to another diverse kinds of tongues; to another the interpretation of tongues:

10 . = The meaning of 10 is one of testimony, law, responsibility and the completeness of order.

10 Commandments, Exo 20. The number 10, in the Bible, is used 242 times. The designation "10th" is used 79 times. Ten can be also viewed as complete.

10 Virgins. Ten talents Matt 25.

10 pieces of silver; Luke 15:8

10 servants, 10 pounds; Luke 19:13.

11 . = Can represent disorder as there are 11 disciples and comes between 12 and 10. Acts 1:26 see #12.

12 . = Represents government.

12 disciples, Matt 10:1, 12 tribes of Israel, twelve gates in new Jerusalem, Rev 21:21. There are six Passovers mentioned in the Old Testament and six in the New Testament for a total of 12. And the tree of Life has 12 fruits on it, Rev 22.2

7 Feasts	Date
Passover	April 12, 2025 (observed evening of April 11)
Feast of Unleavened Bread	April 13-19, 2025
Pentecost	June 1, 2025
Feast of Trumpets	September 23, 2025
Day of Atonement	October 2, 2025
Feast of Tabernacles	October 7-13, 2025
The Eighth Day	October 14, 2025

Hebrew Religious Calendar

Modern	Old Testament	Gregorian
Nisan	Abib	Mar/Apr
Iyyar	Ziv	Apr/May
Sivan	Sivan	May/June
Tammuz	Tammuz	June/July
Ab or Av	Ab	July/Aug
Elul	Elul	Aug/Sept
Tishri	Thanim	Sept/Oct
Marheshvan or Cheshvan	Bul	Oct/Nov
Kislev	Chislev	Nov/Dec
Tebet or Tevet	Tebeth	Dec/Jan
Shevat	Shebat	Jan/Feb
Adar	Adar	Feb/Mar

From my understanding the month of Adar is repeated. All months start with the first sighting of the new moon slither in the Jewish tradition and the Shofar is blown, Ps 81:3. The moon does a full cycle each month of 28 days, Four weeks. Times that by 13 months (according to the Bible when the Hebrews were about to have their first Passover.) equals 364 days in a year and their first month is Spring time in the northern hemisphere. Something to meditate on. It is Strange that Oct is Eight, Nov is nine, Dec is Ten. So, maybe our year really did start the beginning of March, in springtime, just a thought. Note that the days of 7, Sunday to Saturday don't change and line up with the new moons and sabbaths. I also find it amazing that the menstrual cycle of women is the same as the moons cycle, it is like all creation is blended in and somehow connected.

Basic Rules on Bible interpretation

Just to lay a foundation of Scripture interpretation these are just some basic rules to follow to stay within the guard rails.

1. Bible interprets Bible. If a scripture contradicts another scripture, then the Doctrine is wrong. Yes, no scripture is of private interpretation. 2Pet 1:20, 2Tim 3:16. I.E. Thorn in the flesh. Num 33:55, 2Cor 12:7. The people that wrote the word, lived, thought, dreamed and spoke the Word. The Mind of Christ is the Word.

2. Laws of First mention. The first use of a word in Hebrew is how it is to be used in the New Testament and meant to be used that way for a reason. Gods' ways are higher than our ways. Isa 55:8. Words like oil and salt can be used as representations. Remember also, there is an earthy meaning and a spiritual meaning to all that Jesus taught and spoke.

3. The law of progression. Things mentioned under moses law and changed by the prophets. IE generational curses, from Deut 23:2 to Exo 34:7 to Jer 31:29 and Eze 18:2 it had to be changed for Jesus to be able to join Josephs heritage and worship in the Temple, even obedient strangers were counted as family, Lev 19:34; Sabbaths (worship days), new moons, tithes, Col 2:16, Rom 6:14, Heb 7:5. The believing Gentiles only had to keep 4 things under Grace. Acts 15:29.

4. Keep in Context, read in context, consider the cultural background. God doesn't change, so don't try and fit our cultural rules to the church of Jesus Christ, or dress sense. I.E. 1Cor 14:34, women keep silent in church. If you have been to India the church is male one side and female the other, same would be for any church at the time of Paul. Women walked behind their husbands. Culturally the thing to do, if the women start yelling across the church what would be the result and if they all started talking at the same time? Yes chaos. Another is Tattoos; Rev 19:16 Jesus has a name on His thigh. 1. Who rides a horse in shorts to battle?? No one, so how were they dressed with a long robe and long pants under. We are told to abstain from tattoos in Lev 19:28. Applying the law of progression #3 we go to Acts 21:25. Tattoos draw blood and are a symbol of covenants

the Japanese Yakuza for example, so it wasn't just drinking blood but the shedding of any blood. Remember the body is the temple of Whom? God, so don't graffiti it. We are bought with a price my friend. I say, tattoos hide the emotional bruises. Let them be a testimony of our old lives.

5. The Character of God. Who God is. God will not go against His word nor his promises. He will not lie nor have to say sorry. James 1:17. 2Cor 1:20. God only does Good. Ps 145:9, Jer 29:11. Deut 7:9 even to a thousand Generations. And if a generation is 20 years, then that is 20,000 years, maybe it means he has always has been faithful? God has to keep His word. The earth is His, Ps 24:3, and has told us to occupy until He returns. Luk 19:13. The Lord uses people to do His will in earth whether they are good or bad. Zech 4:6, Hag 1:14. You can be an instrument of honour or dishonour, what are you praying into your life? 2Tim2:20,21.

6. The Heart of God. What God wants. God is Love and correction. Ps 145:9, Joh 3:16. 2 Pet 3:9. He will let you reap what you sow though, Gal 6:7. God wants none to perish. He promised never to leave you nor forsake you, because Jesus was forsaken, we won't have to experience that feeling, nor ever will. Even when we weren't saved Jesus was still there for us, His mercy Endures forever. Joel 2:13. Jesus said we must become like little children not in behaviour but understanding and acceptance of the truth; What Jesus said is what He means, whether parable or other like being born again, we must listen to the Spirit, there are no deep and hidden meanings that we can't comprehend as the Gospels spell everything out for us to be able to act upon. Scripture can be built upon but must agree and be built on the revelation of Jesus. 1Cor 14:29-30, even All prophesy must be based on the Word.

Gods' presence will never depart unless we turn from Him first and ignore all the warnings He gives. Deut 31:6. Heb 13:5. The Lord will not do something to endanger any person or thing, it's the devil that comes to steal, kill and destroy, John 10:10.

If the doctrine breaks any of those rules, then the doctrine is wrong. <u>Remember being humble is being teachable</u>, Stubbornness is idolatry. Jobs friends thought they were right and blamed Job, looking for fault. If it can't be backed up with scripture then it's not scriptural. Don't think I didn't have to learn these lessons; I have been corrected many times and yes it cost me a lot of pride and now I have been given this opportunity to be entrusted with Gods word. If every word in the bible was Gods word the why does the scripture says; "the Letter kills but the Spirit gives life," rightly divide.

Dividing the word correctly also is gathering all the prophesies and putting them in order of fulfilment. Searching the scriptures like the Bereans. 2thess 2:3 says "you are deceived if you believe that the day of the Lord will happen before the son of perdition is revealed and sits in the Temple of God," which isn't even built yet. Wouldn't it be amazing if the last temple is built in three days? Watch for the number three to be connected to the temple. Did you know the first resurrection has the martyrs in it from the great tribulation who didn't worship the beast? Rev 20:4-6. Rule #1. Bible interprets Bible.

Rev 6:9-11 talks about the first martyrs and gives a key to when the first resurrection will happen in Rev 20. Do a study on the day of the Lord, the great and terrible day of the Lord. My bible says AT the Last trump and the dead in Christ shall rise first. The last trump is in Revelation and Mat 13 and 24, Jesus explains when the angels are sent out. Many accompanying scriptures have been provided to confirm what the apostles knew.

There is a great problem when even Jesus own words are not received or believed by Christians. Do a "for and against list" and remember Rule #1. If the verses contradict each other, then the doctrine is wrong. Don't make up stuff to fit the narrative, as some say; "I Heard. They said". But What does the Bible say?

About the Author.

John Martin has been in ministry since early 2018 in a Para-ministry, Fishers of Men Brisbane Australia. Serving the Lord, the community and the homeless, as a live in-house leader in a Christian based Drug Rehab for men of all ages, Fishers of Men. Brisbane, Qld. Australia.

In 1997 he became the one of the first bus drivers for Fisher of Men as they started out, bringing in the homeless for a Sunday meal and service, laying a foundation for the Love of Christ to the lowest people. John had his personal problems but knew God was greater. John grew up a Baptist, He had completed bible college night courses and was grounded in the Word and many other self-help courses throughout his life. It wasn't until the Lord showed up in the low parts of his life that things changed for the better, where that head knowledge became experiential; sometimes our life reflects where we should be serving, surrender is always a good philosophy, but without submitting to the Lord first we aren`t able to resist the devil especially seeking and having the gifts of the Holy Spirit.

fishersofmen.org.au

If you would like to give to a good cause, give in secret and the Lord will honour you publicly.

The pathway to Johns calling all started in the year 2000, he was called in a prayer time of desperation, he heard Gods Voice, clear and loud, He said; "If you overcome, I will grant you to sit with me", no more and no less. It all became clearer after he surrendered to the Lord from a desperate and hungry heart, as he has many times before and after. We go line by line, precept upon precept, glory to glory, but we have to be willing to be made willing and pray that into our lives, staying on track. When the word of the Lord came to him it started directing his steps, laying the foundation of faith for the ministry the Lord would have for him, confirming his position, identity and path. The Lord will do the same for you too, providing and lovingly guiding.

A personal note from the Author

When a Prophesy comes, a rebuke sometimes comes with it, through a rebuke we can get understanding. The Lord cares about us and our situations, He also knows what we will do in the future, so if you have any unfulfilled prophesies then maybe you have strayed from the track God set out. Repent and get back on track and confirmations will come. All of my books have been confirmed with a prophesy so far, that's how I know it is the Lords will that allows me to write for Him to edify his body. I started out as a shop assistant at 16 and ended up serving Jesus at 58. I look at Smith Wigglesworth, he started at 65. What can the Lord do if you are fully surrendered to Him? It is just a matter of when.

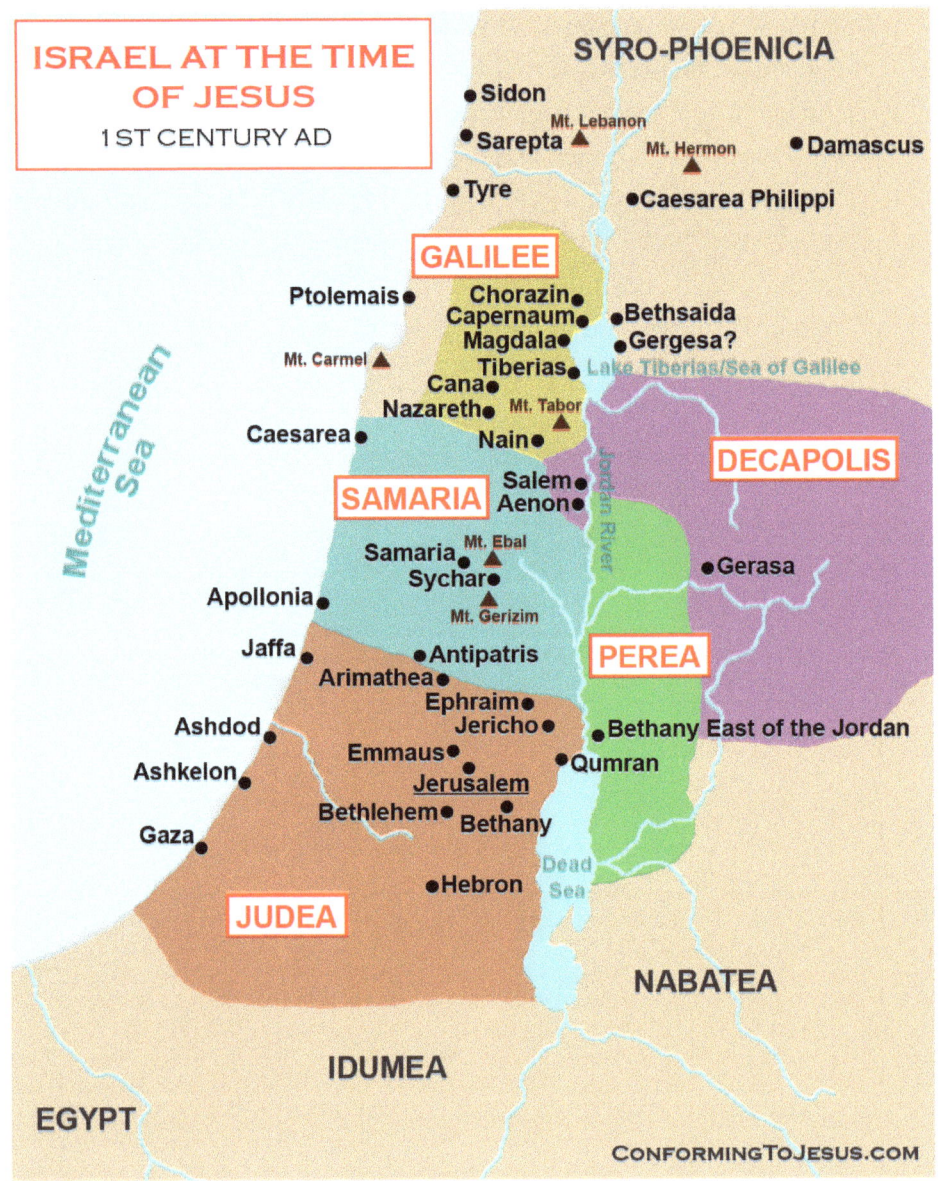

Maps are licenced.

www.ingramcontent.com/pod-product-compliance
Lightning Source LLC
Chambersburg PA
CBHW061725070526
44583CB00024B/3007